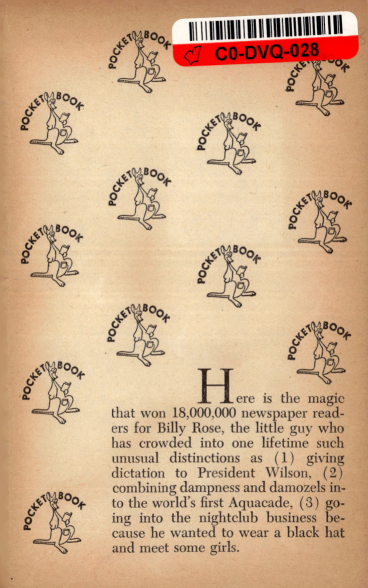

Here is the magic that won 18,000,000 newspaper readers for Billy Rose, the little guy who has crowded into one lifetime such unusual distinctions as (1) giving dictation to President Wilson, (2) combining dampness and damozels into the world's first Aquacade, (3) going into the nightclub business because he wanted to wear a black hat and meet some girls.

Wine, Women and Words

BY BILLY ROSE ❁ ❁

POCKET BOOKS, INC.

NEW YORK, N.Y.

The Printing History of

Wine, Women and Words

Simon & Schuster editions published October, 1948
1st printing ....September, 1948
2nd printing ....November, 1948

Reader's Digest condensation published September, 1948

Danish edition (Eiler Wangel, Copenhagen) published December, 1948

POCKET BOOK edition published February, 1950
1st printing ....January, 1950

Trade-mark Registered in U. S. Patent Office, and in foreign countries including Great Britain and Canada.

POCKET BOOK editions are published only by POCKET BOOKS, INC., POCKET BOOKS [G.B.] LTD., and POCKET BOOKS of CANADA, LTD.

L

Printed in the U. S. A.

COPYRIGHT 1946, 1947, 1948, BY GLENMORE PRODUCTIONS, INC.

This POCKET BOOK edition is published by arrangement with Simon and Schuster, Inc.

To
B. M. B., of course

CONTENTS

Wine, Women and Words

Look, Ma, I'm Writing

❧ ❧

WHAT I DON'T know would fill a book. And, dear reader, it's going to.

If *Wine, Women and Words* sells more than two copies, it's a cinch I'll be asked how a fellow whose literary background is bounded on the north by Nick Carter and on the south by *Captain Billy's Whiz Bang* ever managed to break into print. Let me give it to you fast.

I own a cabaret which features the usual fifty girls in forty-nine costumes. One day it occurred to me I might sell more whiskey if I could get more zing into

1

my advertisements. Next morning the following ad appeared in the New York papers:

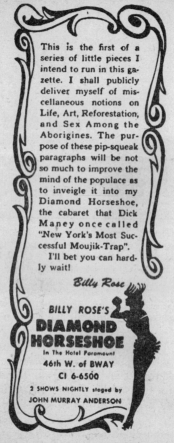

This is the first of a series of little pieces I intend to run in this gazette. I shall publicly deliver myself of miscellaneous notions on Life, Art, Reforestation, and Sex Among the Aborigines. The purpose of these pip-squeak paragraphs will be not so much to improve the mind of the populace as to inveigle it into my Diamond Horseshoe, the cabaret that Dick Maney once called "New York's Most Successful Moujik-Trap".

I'll bet you can hardly wait!

Billy Rose

BILLY ROSE'S
**DIAMOND
HORSESHOE**
In The Hotel Paramount
46th W. of BWAY
CI 6-6500
2 SHOWS NIGHTLY staged by
JOHN MURRAY ANDERSON

Well, no writer ever got published any faster. And as long as I paid the space rates, there were no rejection slips.

A hundred ads later, John Wheeler of the Bell Syndicate dropped in to see me. "I think I can sell your chunks of chit-chat to a lot of newspapers," he told me. "Sign here."

A month later, people who had never noticed me before thought nothing of walking all the way across a room just to insult me. But I didn't care. Seeing my stuff in print was like having my back scratched. And when the New York *Herald Tribune* took on the column, Rita Hayworth was doing the scratching.

The next thing that happened to me was Max Schuster. One afternoon I bumped into this publisher in one of those restaurants where everybody looks like Clifton Webb. "How would you like to write a book?" he said.

"Not on your printing press," I answered. "I can't see myself on a bookshelf between Rabelais and Shakespeare." Max went into his soft-shoe dance, and a few minutes later I was signing a contract with one of those fountain pens which write under a dry Martini.

When I got home, I said to my wife, "In the future, please call me Somerset."

"What are you going to call your book?" asked Eleanor.

"Don't know yet," I said. "Something catchy and commercial."

"I've got it," said my missus. "Call it *Forever Amber*. And a good title for the opening chapter might be, 'How I Learned to Read at the Age of Thirty-Five.'"

"Wise guy," I snapped. "I'll bet it'll sell plenty."

"I'm certain it will," said Eleanor. "Especially if they give away a station wagon with every copy."

This is my first book and it includes a lot of stuff from my columns. To give it tone and class, it's being brought out in a limited edition—limited to people with twenty-five cents.

A Funny Thing Happened on the Way to the Theatre

❧ ❧

I WAS BORN the night President McKinley was shot, and a lot of fellows around Broadway will tell you they shot the wrong man.

The coming-out party took place on a kitchen table in a tenement on the lower East Side. When my mother first saw me, she prophesied, "Some day he'll be President." My father looked at me and said, "He's all right, I guess, but what we really needed was an icebox."

My Pop was what you might call a non-persuasive salesman. When fringe was the fashion, his sample-case would only contain passementerie. When people were crying for passementerie, he would only handle fringe. Consequently, money was a sometime thing around our house, and for years we changed residence every few months. It was cheaper to move than pay rent.

When I went to the High School of Commerce in 1915, the family sock was still empty. It was imperative that I learn something I could merchandise quickly, and so I concentrated on shorthand and typewriting. By working like an Igorot, I got to be something of a shorthand expert, and in 1917 I left school, went to Washington and got myself a job as stenographer with the War Industries Board. There I met its chairman, Bernard M. Baruch. He took a shine to me. I've been seeing him for thirty years, and he's still the Mr. Big in my life.

I was several hundred dollars ahead when the war

ended, and for reasons I can't remember, I decided to take a trip around the world. But my money lasted only as far as New Orleans. On the way back to New York, the boat I was on rammed and sank a freighter in a fog off Cape Hatteras. One of the survivors we picked up was a pretty girl named Edna Harris. When I handed her one of the five life-preservers I was wearing, it started a beautiful friendship. Before we docked, I made a date to see her in New York.

The first night I took her out, we walked up Broadway. Though I was crowding twenty at the time, I had never been on the Big Street at night. But Edna knew her way around. She steered me to Wolpin's, one of those underground delicatessens where celebrities gathered to eat the life-giving pastrami and quaff great beakers of celery tonic.

"That's Fred Fischer," she said, pointing to a man with an outsized head. "He wrote 'Dardanella.' And that's Walter Donaldson, the writer of 'Mammy.'"

"What kind of money do they make?" I asked.

"No telling," said Edna. "Couple of thousand a week, maybe."

"How long has this been going on?" I said to myself.

From then on, I did most of my eating at Wolpin's, and after a while got to know most of the songwriters. In those days I was a simple-hearted little bloke. My ambitions were to make a million dollars and marry Mary Pickford. I believed what everybody believed in 1922—that U. S. Steel would hit 500, that nice girls didn't kiss the first time you took them out, and that Heaven was not for Democrats.

One night at Wolpin's I asked Harry Ruby, the composer, "Has anybody ever thought of rhyming 'June' with 'macaroon'?"

The entire delicatessen applauded and Harry shook

my hand. A waiter handed me a pencil and a clean menu and said, "Mr. Rose, you're in business."

Six cups of coffee later, I dotted the last "i" on my first masterpiece.

> *Does the Spearmint lose its flavor on the bedpost*
> *   overnight?*
> *If you paste it on the left side will you find it on the*
> *   right?*
> *When you chew it in the morning will it be too hard*
> *   to bite?*
> *Does the Spearmint lose its flavor on the bedpost*
> *   overnight?*

It was published by Watterson, Berlin and Snyder, and the early ten-watt radio transmitters smallpoxed the air with it. I got an appointment with a Wrigley executive and told him I thought I was entitled to some money for my efforts on behalf of his product. He booted me out of his office without so much as a pack of gum for my trouble.

But I got my revenge. The time bomb I lit in 1922 exploded in 1939 with the Pepsi-Cola jingle. The rest, God help us, is history.

I wrote the first singing commercial.

There, I've said it! And I'm glad. For years I've been walking around with this secret, fraternizing with people who are kind to small animals and bathe every day. Now I've come clean.

Chop me up in little pieces and feed me to the lions. You won't hear a peep out of me.

Besides the Spearmint classic, I was responsible for "You Tell Her I Stutter," and "You Gotta See Mama Every Night." These songs made quite a bit of money, and the following year I invested some of this loot in the nightclub business—principally, I think, because I wanted to wear a black hat and meet some girls. My first waterhole was hidden over a garage on 56th Street near Sixth Avenue. The iron-stomached citizens who survived the Noble Experiment may remember it as the Backstage Club—the place where Helen Morgan first climbed up on a piano to avoid the tables which were advancing upon her across the dance floor.

The Backstage Club represented an outlay of $4,000. It amortized itself the opening night.

A few months later I opened a second trap on Fifth Avenue—I wanted to meet a better class of girls. It was called the Fifth Avenue Club, and it exhaled so much fake swank that on opening night my French head-waiter suggested I stay out of sight in the office. The show was written by a couple of kids fresh out of Columbia—Rodgers and Hart. I felt I had really arrived socially. My new neighbors included Samuel Untermyer, the Union League Club, and John D. Rockefeller, Sr.

Eyebrows shot up all over the neighborhood the night we opened. John D. was at the age when he needed his sleep something fierce, and when my bug-eyed musicians erupted with "Somebody Stole My Gal" at four in the morning, he hollered copper at the top of his ancient lungs. A dozen of New York's Finest roared up on motorcycles, but when they found I wasn't selling whiskey, they compromised on making me mute half my trumpets.

To keep the club exclusive, I slapped on a $5 cover charge. Well, that did it. Pretty soon it was so exclusive the waiters were playing penny casino with each other. In a couple of months I was feeling through the pockets of old suits for lunch money.

One night I got an idea. I would sell my club to a blonde who was running a speakeasy in Greenwich

Village. Her boy friend was one of our leading bathtub chemists.

I went down to the Village to see her. "Queenie," I said, "this speak is no showcase for a woman of your talents. You belong on Fifth Avenue."

"You can say that again, dearie," said Queenie, "but what would I do up there? I can't sing and my gentleman friend made me give up hoofin'."

"All great women of the world have had salons," I said airily. "Du Barry, Pompadour, Marie Antoinette. Princes and statesmen flocked around just to hear these women talk."

I moved in for the kill. "Get your boy friend to buy my club for you. Advertise yourself as 'Mistress of Conversation.' Wear a stylish gown—something transparent and expensive. And when the customers arrive, talk to them—just talk to them. It'll be tremendous!"

Queenie bought the dream, and next morning the bathtub chemist bought my sick little nightclub. He ran big ads, billing her as "Mistress of Conversation." But the place folded in a few weeks.

Poor Queenie! Though she was willing to talk to anybody, nobody wanted to talk to *her*.

After the Fifth Avenue Club, I went back to songwriting. You may remember one of the ditties I wrote around that time—"Barney Google with the Goo-Goo-Googly Eyes." Deems Taylor said it was probably the worst song in the history of the music business—but Deems always was a jealous fellow.

In 1926 I wrote a vaudeville act for Fanny Brice. During its out-of-town tryouts, I found that Fanny and I liked the same jokes and disliked the same people. In 1928 I persuaded the great comedienne to become Mrs. Rose. The day she did, I automatically became known as Mr. Brice. You see, in those days, Fanny's house was a hangout for the Whitneys and Wanamakers, and outside of Irving Berlin, a pop songwriter was considered small spuds.

One night C. B. Dillingham attended one of Fanny's at-homes. I noticed that everybody made a fuss over the producer. A few nights later a similar fuss was made over Ziegfeld. "If you want your name back," I said to myself, "you'll have to become a producer."

And so, in 1931 I made my bow on Broadway with a musical revue called *Sweet and Low*. Though I had worked on it for a year and put every penny I had in it, it wasn't much of a show. An angry critic dismissed it with the line, "The Rose that does not smell so sweet."

The day after it closed a press agent named Ned Alvord came into my office. He was sporting a seersucker cutaway, a derby hat and a turned-around collar like a minister. In a train-whistle voice he announced I could get my dough back if I had the guts to juice up the show, take it to the hinterlands, and sell it like Barnum used to sell his circus. He gave off sparks and I caught fire.

I went out and hocked my ASCAP royalties, revamped *Sweet and Low*, and changed the title to *Crazy Quilt*. And I'll never forget how Ned advertised this pale little revue—"A Saturnalia of Wanton Rhythm"—"Voluptuous Houris"—"Dashing Demoiselles"—every sentence ending with "Since the Dawn of Time!"

When I pointed out that we were carrying only a few curtains and eighteen bandy-legged chorus girls, Ned fog-horned, "Take the money and run for the train." And for a screamingly successful year that's just what we did!

It was Ned who taught me that the short cut to the customer's poke is by way of the roadside fence—that "bill it like a circus" sells more tickets than "to be or not to be."

My first lesson in paper-and-paste came when I commissioned a lad with a lavender tie to design a twenty-four-sheet for our traveling show. He delivered a layout in delicate blues and pinks. I showed it to Alvord. "It stinks, sir," he said.

"But it's pretty," I protested.

"Then hang it in your bedroom," he snapped. "It's a foggy night in Kansas and our poster is on an outhouse. I want to see it, sir!"

We settled on something in black and yellow—you couldn't look at it without smoked glasses. And the only switch I've made in twenty years was when I ordered the posters for *Carmen Jones*. Instead of yellow and black, I changed the color scheme to black and yellow.

Shortly after *Crazy Quilt* closed, I produced a play called *The Great Magoo* by Ben Hecht and Gene Fowler. It lasted a week. The following year, I opened a theatre restaurant called the Casino de Paree. It was bankrolled by a group of gentlemen whose pictures have appeared in some of our finest post offices.

A few months later, I ripped the insides out of Arthur Hammerstein's pretty theatre on 53rd and Broadway and opened another cabaret called The Billy Rose Music Hall. Its feature number was a potpourri of oldtime vaudevillians—fire-eaters, acrobats and Swiss bell-ringers—who did an abbreviated version of their turns. This was my first meeting with the pretty lady called "Nostalgia" and we've been big buddies ever since.

The electric sign on this music hall was a seven-day wonder on Broadway. It was eighteen stories high and the mazdas spelled out just two words—"BILLY ROSE." The first night it was burning, I went outside to admire it. As I stood on the corner, I heard someone ask, "Billy Rose? Who dat?"

"That's Fanny Brice's husband," someone answered.

I finally took care of this Mr. Brice situation a few

months later when I gave birth to a theatrical dream-child called *Jumbo*. No year in my life has been wackier than the one devoted to producing this musical circus at the New York Hippodrome. The author, director, and player credits read like a Burke's Peerage of the theatre —Hecht and MacArthur, Rodgers and Hart, John Murray Anderson, George Abbott, Jimmy Durante, Paul Whiteman and his orchestra.

This county-sized candy box was largely financed by Jock Whitney and his sister, Joan, a couple of amiable tots whose Pop had left them $175,000,000. As production costs mounted, the standard gag around Broadway was, "This show will make Rose or break Whitney."

Carried away by the notion of marrying a circus to a musical comedy, we showed no more respect for the law of gravity than do the characters in a Silly Symphony. The opening number was climaxed by shooting an adagio dancer out of a cannon into the arms of her partner fifty feet away. Dohoes, an educated white horse from Copenhagen, did everything but play first base. In one sequence a troupe of daredevils indulged in fingertip balancing over an open cage of lions.

But *Jumbo* was too big for its cash registers. Though it received superb notices and played to over a million customers, it lost money. A few years ago the Whitneys got some of it back when Metro bought the movie rights. I don't know when the studio is going to get around to making this picture, but before it does, I would suggest that it send the director to New York and instruct him to stand still some night near the parking space at 43rd Street and Sixth Avenue where the old Hippodrome stood. If he listens closely, he'll still hear them yocking it up at what drama critics agree was the biggest laugh in the history of show business. It came near the end of the first act when a sheriff caught Jimmy Durante trying to steal an elephant.

"Where are ya going with that elephant?" yelled the copper.

"What elephant?" asked Jimmy.

Finding the elephant for the title role in *Jumbo* was quite a chore. A fellow who had sold me some monkeys said I might be able to rent one from Mr. Charles W. Beall in Oceanside, Long Island.

According to the monkey man, this Mr. Beall was quite a fellow. From Monday to Friday, he was vice-president of the Chase National Bank; Saturdays and Sundays he devoted to training wild animals.

The following Saturday I drove out to Oceanside. The monkey man hadn't overstated the case. On his beautiful ten-acre estate, Mr. Beall, a fine figure of a tycoon, maintained one of the most complete private zoos in America. In addition to lions, tigers, leopards, and black panthers, his cages contained at least one each of the animals on exhibit at the Bronx Zoo.

At the house, a butler told me Mr. Beall was working out with the animals in a cage back of the garage. I walked around and watched the amateur Clyde Beatty. He handled the whip and chair like a pro, and the big cats were slinking around as though they had guilt complexes.

"What can I do for you, young man?" he said when the beasts were all up on their inverted tubs.

"Want to sell, lease or rent an elephant?" I called through the bars.

Mr. Beall clicked the cage door open. "Come in," he said. "They won't hurt you."

You can judge how badly I needed an elephant when I tell you I walked into that cage.

"Afraid I can't do anything for you," said the banker after I had explained my problem. "I'm down to six elephants, and I like to have at least that many around. They relax me."

After lunch he showed me around his place. I didn't see any women on the estate and I got the impression he was a bachelor.

On my way back to town, I got to wondering about his private life. What sort of women, for instance, would appeal to a millionaire who hobnobbed with lions and panthers?

A few years later, the tabloids told me. It appeared that Mr. Beall had hired a vaudeville performer named Nana Bates as secretary. He had seen this lady do a tiger dance in a local theatre and had been impressed by her qualifications.

According to the tabloids, Mr. Beall had gotten along fine with his secretary until he sent her to Hollywood on business. During her absence, he had made the mistake of hiring another actress-stenographer. When the Tiger Woman returned unexpectedly and found her pretty successor on the porch, she reached for a hatpin.

The two shorthand experts indulged in some fancy scratching and floor-rolling. A neighbor phoned the Oceanside police. The old financier was caught in the middle—something which hadn't happened to him either on Wall Street or in the lions' cage.

Most of the later rounds were staged in court, where the judge finally told the banker to make up his mind which secretary he wanted. Mr. Beall chose the Tiger Woman.

While these legal shenanigans were going on, I happened to be driving through Oceanside. I found Mr. Beall sitting on a stool in the lions' cage. The big cats were on their tubs, unusually quiet. The amateur trainer's face was all scratched up and there were bits of court plaster on his neck and hands.

"Did a cat take a poke at you?" I asked

The financier nodded. "Yes," he said. "One of the two-legged ones."

"What's the idea of sitting out here?" I said.

Mr. Beall got up, walked over to one of the lions and scratched it behind the ears. "Frankly," he sighed, "this is the only place on the estate where I feel perfectly safe."

On the strength of the *Jumbo* press notices, Amon Carter and the other city fathers of Fort Worth asked me to stage the Texas Centennial Exposition of 1936-37. Dallas, thirty-two miles away, was preparing a $25,000,000 industrial fair, and "Little Old Cowtown" wanted a show that would steal the spotlight from its rival.

Carter told me the job had to be done in a hundred days and asked what I wanted for my services. Taking a deep breath, I said, "A hundred thousand dollars." The city fathers conferred for all of three minutes and agreed. And if I may be pardoned a brag, I think I earned my fee the next day when I coined the slogan, "Dallas for Education, Fort Worth for Entertainment."

I arrived in Fort Worth with a small boy's notions of the Wild West. As a kid, I had read Zane Grey with a flashlight under the blankets after my old man had chased me off to bed. In the nickelodeons I had whooped "Look out!" when the bad guy snuck up behind William S. Hart.

Naturally, when I planned the shows for the Exposition, I included one with cowboys and Indians. I labeled it "The Last Frontier," and you'll get some idea of the dimensions of this hootnanny when I tell you we used a quarter of a million dollars' worth of livestock in it.

I started out by hiring the cowboy stars who had won important prize money at every rodeo from Pendleton to Madison Square Garden. These lads were wonderful at riding, roping, and bulldogging the wild steer. But they were not so good when it came to Deadeye Dick stuff with a pistol.

The cowboys could draw quick and shoot straight, provided the target was man-sized and close-up. But when I wanted somebody to pop a clay pipe out of a girl's mouth at fifty feet, I had to import the national pistol champion, a slicker from Brooklyn who had studied marksmanship in a Coney Island shooting gallery. The cowboys oohed and aahed when they saw this kind of shooting, and my kid dreams got their first kick in the chaps.

But that was nothing compared with what the Indians did to my illusions. One day I called Carter and told him I needed some redskins for a big war-dance number. "How many?" he said, as if I had asked for desk blotters.

"Oh, a hundred and fifty," I said.

A couple of weeks later, a gent walked into the air-conditioned blockhouse in which I was officing. "I got your Indians," he said. "Where shall I put them?" I went outside and looked. There they were, blankets, feathers, papooses and goats. It looked like an explosion in a paint factory.

"They're all yours," said the agent. "Sign here."

"Have your people down at the Last Frontier arena at five this afternoon," I told the boss Indian. "I want to see them dance."

When I got to the arena a couple of braves were half-heartedly knuckling tomtoms. The Indians had already been dancing for half an hour, but their movements had as much abandon as those of a man standing in a moving bus.

"Tell 'em to cut loose," I said to the agent.

"They've cut," he replied. "Takes 'em a little time to warm up. They ought to git goin' good along about midnight. By tomorrow afternoon they should be jumpin'."

The Last Frontier opened with a parade of covered wagons instead of a war-dance. . . .

I would have written off the whole Wild West legend as Gene Autry publicity except for one incident. One night there was a riot on the Midway. Somebody claimed he'd been cheated and the first thing I knew a hundred people were swinging at each other.

I phoned for the Rangers. A few minutes later one of them showed up. He walked into where they were fighting. Word wild-fired through the melee that a Ranger was there, and the brawl was over in a minute.

As I watched him walk away, it was with the same eyes that used to read Zane Grey under the blanket.

One number in The Last Frontier was built around a song called "Memories of Buffalo Bill." I thought it would be a nice touch to close this scene with a herd of buffalo coming down the hills and exiting stage right to eight bars of music.

I phoned Carter. "Three dozen buffalo?" said Amon. "Will do!"

My good right arm in staging the Exposition was John Murray Anderson, the soft-spoken Englishman who has fashioned a score of musical successes on Broadway and Piccadilly. The night before the Exposition opened, I was scooting around on a motorcycle, putting Big Genius touches to this and that.

I dragged Murray away from the platoons of girls he was directing at the Casa Mañana cabaret and took him in my sidecar to the dress rehearsal of The Last Frontier. Anderson had no zest for this Wild West show, but he went to work setting the light-cues in his best Nelson Monument manner.

Around four in the morning, we got to the Buffalo Bill sequence. I went over the number with Murray. It started with half a dozen cowboys around a campfire on one of the prop hills. To the plunking of a guitar, one of them would sing about his memories of Cody's famous Wild West show. As he finished the first chorus, the thirty-six buffalo would enter and come down the hills while the orchestra went heavy on the fiddles. Behind the smelly monsters would come a man on horseback, togged out like the Buffalo Bill of the posters.

I told Murray I wanted a soulful shade of blue to light my herd of buffalo. There are many blues a director can choose from, ranging from the sky-blue of gelatin No. 29 to the purplish-blue of gelatin No. 37. At his seat in the grandstand, Anderson picked up a portable phone and called the stage-manager behind the hills two blocks away. "Turn on the 29 blues," he said.

A moment later the giant sun-arcs flooded the field. Then Murray said in a bored voice, "Now the buffalo, please."

Zowie! They stormed out of the chutes and charged down the hills hellbent for the Gulf of Mexico. When they were halfway down my man-made cliffs, Murray raised a well-manicured hand as if he were addressing a line of Shubert chorus boys.

"Hold it please," he said. "Change that gelatin to a 31."

The hit of the Exposition was the Casa Mañana cabaret, featuring Sally Rand. Her fan-is-quicker-than-the-eye routine went over big with the art-conscious customers that summer.

One night, Governor Dave Sholtz of Florida was in the house. I stopped by his table to ask if he'd mind being introduced from the stage before the show. Sholtz said he'd be honored.

As I started to walk away he asked if Miss Sally Rand were around. Said he had met her some years back when she played the Citrus Circuit in his state. I told him Sally was in her dressing room and offered to take him backstage.

When the Governor and I entered Sally's room, she was flat on the floor, wrapped in something pink, her chin propped up on her hands. And she was reading the Bible!

Scoffers will please leave quietly. Sally is always reading something or other. That summer it was the Bible, straight through from Genesis to Revelation.

After Sally and the Governor had swapped hellos, he picked up the Good Book and said, "Let me read you a short passage which has always been a source of comfort to me." He turned to the Book of Psalms and began reading quietly.

It was almost show time. I heard Whiteman's orchestra tuning up and slipped out of the dressing room. A few minutes later I was at the center microphone on the big stage. As I introduced the first couple of celebrities, I kept looking off-stage towards Sally's room.

Someone in Sholtz's party hollered, "Introduce the Governor of Florida!"

"I'm sorry," I lied. "The Governor's talking long-distance to Tallahassee."

I wasn't going to stand there with my bare face hanging out and tell four thousand people that the Governor of Florida couldn't appear because he was reading the Bible in Sally Rand's dressing room!

The first year of the Exposition, we played to over a million customers. My problem in 1937 was to gimmick up the Midway so attendance wouldn't fall off as much as it usually does the second year of a fair.

What to do? Hire more girls to please the male customers? Hardly. I was already using more girls than there are in Rhode Island. Well, then, how about hiring some gents to please the lady customers? Moved, seconded, and carried. But what gents?

Hollywood actors? Too expensive. College boys? Not bad, but liable to break up the furniture. Noblemen—dukes, counts, barons? Ah, an interesting notion! No one is more snobbish than the wife of a good Democrat. Idea lends itself to ballyhoo—"Polka with a Prince! Buddy up to a Baron! Cuddle with a Count! Hurry! Hurry! Hurry!"

I called my press agent in New York. "Dick," I said to Maney, "I want to hire a couple of thousand pounds of peerage as dancing partners."

"Okay," said Maney. "There's a noblemen's association which meets once a month at the St. Moritz Hotel. I think it's affiliated with the CIO."

"Tell them the job pays seventy-five a week," I said, "and they can keep all the tips and oil heiresses they get. And hire me a baroness to introduce the noblemen to the gals who want to dance."

Next day Maney ran an ad which began, "Noblemen Wanted," and ended, "Sons of the Dauphin will receive short shrift."

Dick called me that evening. Several hundred had applied and he had selected a dozen whose blood was not only blue but deep purple.

"How about my baroness?" I asked.

"I got you one in first-class condition," said Maney, "except for the charley-horse she got curtsying at the Court of St. James."

A week later I was down at the station to see the blue-bloods come in. And what a darling set of people they were. Charming, witty, and civilized. They treated the whole thing as a daffy adventure.

Seeing as how they put on no fake airs, Fort Worth took to them like a kid to cotton candy. The tattered titles were entertained in the best homes, and not once was a six-shooter emptied around their heels. And as dancing partners at Casa Mañana, they were in great demand. Whenever a lady felt like tangoing with a title, the baroness would introduce a nobleman. It was all very formal, and both Europe and Cowtown did themselves proud.

One day an assistant bounced into my office. "There's a prince outside to see you," he announced.

"We have no princes on our payroll," I said. "Maney couldn't dig up anything better than a duke."

"Ah, but there will be a prince on your payroll," chirped a little man in the doorway. It was my old friend, Mike Romanoff, the prince of hokus-bogus. To-day, Mike owns the swankiest eatery in Hollywood, but in 1937 when he showed up in Fort Worth, all he had was an old jalopy, 17 cents, and a teacup of gas.

"I hear you're paying seventy-five and supplying free monocle polish," said the ragbag royalist. "You haven't a prince on the lot. I'm your prince."

Naturally I engaged him. Mike is a classy little gent, and I figured he'd be good copy for the newspaper boys. After dinner, I escorted him to Casa Mañana. The prince had put an extra-high polish on his eyepiece and was all set to begin dancing for his doughnuts.

But when I got to the box where the noblemen sat between dance assignments, I sensed trouble. The baroness said, "This is a strike. None of us will set foot on the dance floor until that impostor is fired."

"You're asking for a closed shop," I said. "Every red-blooded American is entitled to a chance to become a prince."

"Sorry," said one of the dukes politely. "We have reached a point where we have nothing to lose but our titles. The commoner must go."

At first I thought they were kidding. When I realized they weren't, I bowed and said, "It shall be as you wish."

Next morning I staked Mike to a little cash and a lot of gasoline, and he headed for Hollywood.

Why did I give in so easily to the noblemen? Well, maybe it was because I was afraid one of them might get up on a chair and holler, "Bluebloods of the world, unite!"

In addition to my chores in Forth Worth in '37, I had agreed to stage a spectacle for the Great Lakes Exposition in Cleveland. I got to Cleveland about three months before the fair was due to open, and Lincoln G. Dickey, its manager, showed me around the grounds.

As we walked along the boarded-up Midway, I noticed a crowd on one of the Lake Erie piers. Dickey and I walked over to see what was going on. There were two girls in the lake, swimming in time to a phonograph record of "The Blue Danube Waltz."

As I watched them, I began to multiply, and the more I multiplied, the more excited I became. "If a water ballet looks that good with two girls," I said to Dickey, "imagine what it would be like with two hundred. If it's okay with you and your committee, I'd like to produce a water show for your fair."

"What would you call it?"

Across the Midway there was a penny arcade. "Watercade," I said, "or, if you want to get fancy, Aquacade."

Next spring we put the show together, using Lake Erie for a stage and Canada for a backdrop. The big production numbers were to be staged on a block-long platform fastened to a couple of motor barges. Before and after the water sequences, this floating stage would be shuttled back and forth.

When I found I needed some vaudeville acts to break up the swimming sequences, an agent brought around a trained seal. He told me the mackerel-eater could juggle, do a hootchy-kootchy in a grass skirt and, for a finish, play "Yankee Doodle" on toy trumpets. I hired him.

Came the night of dress rehearsal. Platoons of stage hands. Two tugboat crews. Sixty of Petrillo's boys. Regiments of swimmers, actors and chorus boys. Costume fitters running around with mouthfuls of pins. Rehearsal costs, a thousand bucks an hour.

I got to the trained-seal act around four that morning. I figured it would take about five minutes to set the lights and music cues. The trainer threw the seal a rubber ball. It bounced off the beast's snoot and he knocked it into Lake Erie with his flipper.

"Butternose is a little nervous," said the trainer. "The lights have him confused."

"Skip the ball trick," I megaphoned down from the grandstand. "Go into the hootchy-kootchy dance."

The grass skirt was brought out. Before the trainer could tie it on, the seal started eating it.

I climbed down from the grandstand and went into a huddle with the trainer. "It's the fish in the lake," he said. "They're distracting my artist."

Over the communicating system I told the tugboat captains to bring in the stage. Bells rang, propellers churned, the floating platform eased up to the shore and locked.

The trainer brought out the brass horns. Something like a thousand employees quieted down to listen. Butternose looked worried. He sniffed at one horn, blew a blast on another, then jumped back three feet at the sound which came out.

All mixed up, he picked up the horn-stand and tried to balance it on his schnoz. The apparatus crashed down on his flippers. The seal yorked, snorked, and waddled off the stage.

By this time a rising sun was playing peekaboo with

my arc lights. "Next number," I shouted. "Places, everybody, for the Girls of All Nations finale."

What was the matter with Butternose? Simple. Vaudeville was dead and the seal had been out of work so long he'd forgotten his act.

During the Aquacade rehearsals, I fell in love with its star, Eleanor Holm. When I was sure it wasn't just one of those things, I flew out to Hollywood and told Fanny about it. Fanny took it in stride and said, "If you love her, there's nothing to discuss. Good luck, kid!"

In November the Fort Worth and Cleveland fairs folded. I went back to New York and moved into a hotel with twenty-four-hour switchboard service. Object: to give Grover Whalen, head of the New York World's Fair, a chance to get in touch with *me*. I figured I was a cinch to hear from him for several reasons: (a) the successful shivaree I had produced at Fort Worth; (b) my merger of dampness and damsels at the Cleveland Aquacade; (c) the six pages *Life* had devoted to saying I was almost as good as my press agents made me out to be; and (d) the size-12 fedora I was wearing that season. I couldn't see how anybody in his right mind would try to run a midway without me.

And then came hit on the head No. 1. The papers announced that a gent named John Krimsky had been put in charge of entertainment. "Krimsky?" I screeched. "What did he ever do?"

A few days later came hit on the head No. 2. A press agent named Maurice Mermee was appointed director of concessions. "Rose," I said to myself, "maybe they can't run a World's Fair without you, but it sure looks as if they're going to try."

I decided to swallow my ego, and phoned Messrs. Krimsky and Mermee for an appointment. After letting me polish their waiting-room furniture for a while, the great men finally received me in a room full of graphs and charts. They were painfully polite, but unfortunately most of the space on the Midway had been allotted.

"Allotted to what?" I snarled. "Peep shows, shooting galleries, babies in bottles? What makes you think these *ausgespielt* wonders will bring Peoria to New York?"

The Messrs. K. and M. smiled patronizingly and pointed to the graphs and charts which proved the Fair was going to play to 75,000,000 customers.

That night I wore out a lot of carpet. "If you want a piece of the pie," I said to myself, "you'd better get to the head baker himself—Grover Whalen. And if he won't let you in to see him, you've got to figure out a plot to make him come to see you."

By morning I had such a plot, and it was as complicated as a Rube Goldberg invention. It involved writing and producing a musical comedy and finding a theatre-restaurant big enough to house it.

The following week I rented the French Casino—formerly the Earl Carroll Theatre. I concocted an extravaganza with an Exposition background, titled "Let's Play Fair," and its hero was—you guessed it!—Grover Whalen. Then I engaged the elegant Oscar Shaw to portray the elegant Grover. The scenery and costumes for this pretty package came to a not-so-cool $75,000.

An hour after the papers announcing the show hit the street, Mr. Whalen was on the phone. "I understand you're going to do a show ridiculing me," he said.

"I'd suggest you come and see for yourself," I purred. "I'll save a down-front table for you on opening night."

I was betting no man could stay away from a show in which he was the leading character. It was a cinch bet. On opening night, Mr. Whalen arrived half an hour before curtain time. My maître d' did everything but sweep the aisle with palms, and well-coached waiters formed a bucket line to insure an adequate supply of Pol Roger '26.

Before Oscar Shaw came onstage, you could have toasted bread on Grover's good-looking face. But a moment later, he was all smiles. The actor was wearing striped pants and a morning coat which had set me back 200 simoleons. He walked, talked, and sang gracefully, wisely, and knowingly.

When the show was over, Mr. World's Fair invited me to join him.

"How'd you like it?" I asked.

"Delighted," said Mr. Whalen. "It's a fine show, and we could use something like it out at the Fair. Drop into my office tomorrow morning and we'll talk about it."

Next day the Messrs. Krimsky and Mermee didn't know what hit them. With Grover's help, I tied up the 10,000-seat Marine Amphitheatre at the entrance to the Midway. And in fairness to Grover, let me say that the Aquacade paid more rent the next couple of seasons than the rest of the Midway put together.

The day we clocked our 5,000,000th customer, I dropped in at the Administration Building and told Grover about the hoax. He laughed.

"It was a lucky thing for the Fair you selected Oscar Shaw to play me," he said. "If I'd seen myself as Jimmy Durante, I don't think there would have been an Aquacade."

A month after the water show opened, flash bulbs were popping in my face and delirious caption writers were dubbing me "Public Showman No. 1." High over the New York State Amphitheatre, a block-long neon sign ballyhooed my name in letters of fire. And money?

Why, old-time gold prospectors were fighting for the chance to pan out my bath water!

One afternoon an assistant came panting into my office. "Boss, boss!" he puffed. "A guy at the other end of the Midway is swiping your name. He sells canaries. Calls his place 'Billy Rose's Pet Shop.'"

To me that was like putting the snatch on the Holy Grail. "I'll run him out of the Fair!" I bellowed.

Next afternoon, at the head of a committee of lawyers, managers and Fair officials, I marched up to the pet shop.

"Live Souvenirs," read a sign over the door. Above it, in bigger letters, there it was—"Billy Rose's Pet Shop."

Breathing fire, I stomped in. My board of strategy squeezed in after me. The shop was empty, except for a little man feeding goldfish.

"Where do you get off using my name on this sparrow loft?" I said. "Rip down those signs or I'll have you and your two-bit menagerie put in jail!"

The pet-shop owner never stopped feeding the goldfish. "Don't holler," he said. "It scares the canaries. Perhaps you'd like to see my birth certificate. It happens my name really is Billy Rose—after an uncle on my mother's side, in case you're interested. If I didn't believe in live and let live, I'd make you take those signs off the Aquacade, *Mr. William S. Rosenberg!*"

For a long moment, nothing could be heard in that shop but the twittering from the cages. One of my lawyers hid a smile behind his briefcase.

"Run along," I told my committee. "I'll settle with this gentleman myself."

I settled with him by buying several of his canaries and taking them back to my Aquacade office, where they got a lot of attention that summer.

Eleanor knows the story. To this day, whenever I let

the swelling in my scrapbook go to my head, she chirps, "Tweet-tweet, tweet-tweet."

One evening, while I was trying to figure out a way to seat customers on the rafters of the Aquacade, the phone rang. "This is Eggleston," said the caller. "Captain Eggleston of Sheepshead Bay. How would you like to buy a whale?"

"With or without tartar sauce?" I asked.

"My whale," said the Captain, "is forty feet long, and although somewhat dead, it's in good condition. I'm asking five hundred dollars for it."

"You're kidding," I said. "Where'd you get a whale?"

Eggleston assured me he wasn't kidding. He had been fishing in his boat, the *Nirvana III*, and had sighted the whale floating belly-up off Sandy Hook. He had sunk the *Nirvana's* anchor in the carcass and towed it back to Sheepshead Bay.

I told the Captain I'd think it over. Well, the more I thought it over that night, the more I liked the idea. I could see the stuffed monster outside the main entrance to the Aquacade. I could hear my barkers spieling about "Pulchritude and Poundage," "The Behemoth of the Briny," and "Rose's Babes and Neptune's Blubber."

Early next morning I drove out to Sheepshead Bay. Sure enough, there was a dead whale tied up to the small pier from which the Captain operated his fishing-excursion boat. A crowd was gawking and a cop was doing his best to keep the kids from hacking souvenirs out of Big-and-Wet's hide.

"There she is," said the Captain. "All yours for six hundred dollars."

"You said five hundred."

"I know," said the Captain, "but the whale is a lot bigger today."

The cop, whose name was McNiddle, confirmed this. The dead whale was absorbing air and water and getting bigger by the hour. I told Eggleston I didn't relish having the price jacked up. The Captain said it was a bargain at $600—I might even find ambergris.

Next morning, most of the metropolitan papers carried pictures of the whale. For reasons that escape me, a seagull with a broken wing or a steer loose on Tenth Avenue brings out the Walter Pater in every copyreader's dusty soul. I decided to pay the $600 and drove back to Sheepshead Bay. By this time, the crowd around the pier had assumed Roxy Theatre proportions.

"The whale's much bigger today," said Eggleston. "It'll cost you a thousand dollars. That's still less than two cents a pound."

"This is a holdup," I said, and started to walk away. The Captain let me walk.

That afternoon it drizzled at the Fair and the Aquacade fell off to capacity. I put ten one-hundred-dollar bills in my pocket and headed back for the Bay. The crowd was now World Series size.

"Fifteen hundred," was the Captain's greeting.

I noticed Officer McNiddle talking to an earnest little man. They both looked worried.

"What's the trouble?" I asked.

"This fellow claims to know about whales," said the cop. "He says if it keeps sucking up air and water much longer, it's liable to explode."

Well, I read the rest of the story in the morning papers. Officer McNiddle saw his duty and did it. He got a sledge hammer and drove a hole in the monster's ever-expanding abdomen. And with results that Laurel and Hardy would have loved.

Nearby schools closed for the day. The Coast Guard had to rush oxygen tanks to the scene. And according to the columnists, there wasn't a shore dinner served at Sheepshead Bay for the next forty-eight hours.

Eggleston phoned me that night and offered me the whale for fifty bucks. "No spik Ingleesh," I told him.

In November of 1939, my divorce came through and Eleanor and I got married. We decided to winter in Florida and figured on leaving a few days before Thanksgiving. But on Thanksgiving Eve I was at the Diamond Horseshoe—the cabaret I had opened in 1938. And I was there for a very good reason.

On November 22nd, an old lady walked into my office and told me she had overheard two hard-faced characters in a pawnshop plotting to stick up my night-club at midnight on Thanksgiving.

I took a careful look at the old girl. At first I thought it might be a practical joke. Then I noticed her hands—the hands of a woman who had worked all her life—and I reached for the phone. Soon a couple of detectives came padding over from the 47th Street station house.

Late that night the detectives phoned to say they hadn't been able to turn up anyone who fitted the woman's description of the two bandits. The woman herself seemed okay. She was cashier in a downtown restaurant. Her husband ran an elevator. According to neighbors in their walk-up tenement, they were quiet, respectable folk.

Next day, when I talked again to the old lady in my office, I got an idea. "Would you recognize these men if you saw them?" I asked her.

"I think so," she replied.

"Fine," I said in my best Baker Street manner. "You come to the club on Thanksgiving Eve. Bring your husband along. We'll put you at a table near the door, and when these mugs come in, you can signal the police."

Thanksgiving Eve, my club was jammed to the steam

pipes. But for the first time in my life this gave me no pleasure. Half a dozen detectives had been shoehorned into tuxedoes and were masquerading as assistants to the headwaiter. That night, many a peace-loving gent was bewildered when he was patted on the hip and under the arm as he was ushered to his table.

The old lady and her celluloid-collared husband were established at a table near the door. They seemed remarkably calm for a pair of oldsters about to be involved in a shooting party.

I sent a waiter over with the supper menu. The woman looked it over and ordered—caviar canapé, cold vichysoisse, breast of guinea hen under glass, chef's salad suprême, cherries jubilee, and a couple of bottles of Mumm's Extra Dry '28. It was one-thirty when the old folks topped off their supper with Napoleon brandy in the big snifter glasses. My own supper consisted of two sets of fingernails.

Two o'clock came—but no stickup men. The old gal patted her lips with a napkin, tipped the waiter a dollar, and came over to where I was standing behind a big detective.

"You can arrest me now," she said.

"Arrest you?" I said. "I don't understand."

"It's very simple," she said. "Pop and I were married twenty-five years ago tonight. We wanted to celebrate our silver wedding anniversary in style—but we couldn't afford to. Then I thought of this plot. It's been a wonderful evening, and I don't care what you do with me now."

Well, at five o'clock that morning, six detectives, an old married couple, and a smallish saloonkeeper were still putting away champagne as fast as it could be iced. The musicians had forgotten Mr. Petrillo's overtime rules and were playing chorus after chorus of "Let Me

Call You Sweetheart" and "Down By the Old Mill Stream."

I'm not famous around Broadway for picking up checks, but any time a gentle grafter can dream up a plot as sweet as this one, the party's on me.

Eleanor and I left for Florida a couple of days later, and it was late March before I had my fill of sun and serenity. When I got back to New York, I held a series of conferences with myself and decided to retire. For the next few months I puttered around the 57th Street art galleries, looking a lot and buying a little. Then I put in several months catching up on my reading. It was all very pleasant, but after a while I got the feeling that vegetables were growing up the side of my leg.

In 1943, Oscar Hammerstein handed me the script of *Carmen Jones,* which Max Gordon and the Theatre Guild had turned down because they didn't think it was commercial. I read it and phoned the janitor to clean up my office. I didn't know whether *Carmen Jones* was commercial—but I did know I liked it.

A few months later, it opened to cheers in Philadelphia. But instead of coming directly to New York, we had to move on to Boston because there wasn't a theatre available on Broadway.

"This won't happen to me again," I told Eleanor. "I'm going to buy me a theatre the first chance I get."

The following April, I learned that the Ziegfeld Theatre was for sale. After a bit of financial shadow boxing with the movie company which had been using it as a neighborhood house, I bought it.

The first thing I did was engage Dorothy Hammerstein, Oscar's talented wife, to fancy up Ziggy's deserted offices. She turned the seventh floor of the theatre into a charming apartment where I live and work every summer, Monday through Friday, while Eleanor is up in the country.

I share this apartment, of course, with a host of other tenants whose names don't appear on the lease—the sprightly shades of Marilyn Miller, Will Rogers, Helen Morgan, Jack Donahue and many of the Glorified Girls.

One recent midnight I let myself into the apartment —I was expecting a call from the Coast. As I was about to sit down at my desk, which stands exactly where the Great Glorifier's used to stand, I could have sworn I heard Ziegfeld's voice say, "Are you kidding?"

To this generation, Ziegfeld is William Powell with talcum at the temples—but to anyone who knew Broadway in the Twenties, Flo was the splendiferous genie out of the Arabian Nights. He spent money like the Government—and worried as little about how much he owed. The newsboy outside my theatre tells me Ziggy died owing him $1,800 for papers—and that was in the days when papers sold for a penny.

As I run down the list of shows on Broadway these nights, I can't help wishing Ziegfeld were still around. And David Belasco, Morris Gest, Charlie Dillingham, Sam H. Harris, George M. Cohan, and the rest of the tinsel-and-thunder boys.

By some footlight magic, the wonder of their own lives used to spill over onto the stage. Their shows didn't succeed or fail—they exploded over the clouds or went down like the *Titanic*.

The current crop of producers may be smart and competent, but no psychiatrist would give them a second glance. The Inverness cape and beaver collar have been replaced by banker's gray and the worried look. And their shows show it. You could lose any of today's extravaganzas in a corner of *Ben Hur* or *The Miracle*.

What piece of madness can any of today's impresarios look back on which compares with the story of Ziegfeld and the petticoats? In one of his shows, the girls wore Irish lace petticoats that cost $600 apiece. The audience never got to see these hand-tatted underthings—they were hidden under huge bouffant skirts.

When one of Ziggy's backers beefed about spending that kind of money for something the audience never saw, Flo smiled and said, "My girls know they're wearing Irish lace, and it does something to the way they walk. . . ."

I have a similar beef about the current crop of ditties. I don't think there's been a knock-'em-down, kick-'em-in-the-subconscious song written in years. "Over There," "Smiles," "Till We Meet Again," "Sorry I Made You Cry"—I've seen crowds get drunk with the sound of them—stop dancing and sing together, laugh together, cry together.

These days, Tin Pan Alley writes for the dance band rather than the give-it-everything song salesmen. Most of the ballads are styled for little boys and girls with trick adenoids who whisper into microphones.

As for barrel house, bebop and boogie-woogie, I've never known or cared what they were getting at. To me a riff is an Arab tribesman, and tomtom is the piper's son. I once let an agent fast-talk me into hiring the late Bunny Berigan. This trumpeter's platter of "I Can't Get Started with You" is Beethoven's Fifth to the hep-cats. I listened to his men play for a few minutes, thought they were hanging a cow, and canned them that night. When an orchestra buries the tune, I'm for burying the orchestra. . . .

I'm not impressed with today's crop of movie heroes either. I recently saw an old Doug Fairbanks flicker at the Museum of Modern Art. This was really the daring young man on the flying trapeze! When Doug got up

out of a chair, it was big-top acrobatics. When he
walked, it was pure ballet.

Do you remember Fairbanks in *The Mark of Zorro*,
hand-over-handing up a twenty-foot wall? Do you remember him in *The Black Pirate*, when he dived from
the topmast of a ship, jabbed a knife into the sail, and
rode the blade all the way down to the deck through
ripping canvas? I invite Tyrone Power to try it.

And speaking of heroes, we could use a few of them
in the legitimate theatre. I mean those romantic roosters
who used to bring the ladies in from Montclair and
Larchmont on matinee days. The gals around here could
sure use a couple of one-chin, original-teeth-and-hair
actors. We have plenty of talented lads, but no Barry-
mores; plenty of actors who can make the girls applaud,
but none who can make them whistle.

Once in a great while, a bucko like Gregory Peck
does turn up on Broadway. But he doesn't stay long. A
movie scout hits him over the head with a sockful of
gold and mails him out to Paramount. I can't think of
a single pair of pants around the theatre today that
draws silk stockings to the ticket window.

Matter of fact, there are only two young fellows coming up that I would rate with the great stars I saw years
ago. These fledglings haven't been around much, but
from the little I've seen of them, I'm willing to go out on
a limb and predict a great future for them.

One is a juvenile named Al Jolson. The other is a
whippersnapper named Maurice Chevalier.

They may not have the surefootedness and experience of a Danny Kaye or a Danny Thomas, but what
they lack in authority and wisdom, they more than
make up for in spirit and bounce.

Take this boy Jolson. I'll never forget the night I saw
him in *Bombo*. When he got going, you could attach a
wire to him and he'd light up the city of Pittsburgh.

Halfway through the second act, he stepped to the footlights and said, "Do you want the rest of this plot, or would you rather have me sing a few songs?" The cast went home, and Jolson took his coat off. At one o'clock in the morning, Al literally had to beg the audience to leave.

Another night comes back to me—an all-star benefit at the Metropolitan Opera House. Caruso had just sung "Ridi Pagliaccio." Right after the tenor's ovation, little Al strutted out—white gloves and black face—grinned at the audience and cracked, "You ain't heard nothin' yet"! When he finished singing "Rockabye Your Baby with a Dixie Melody," it wasn't applause—it was a sixteen-inch gun going off in a bedroom. . . .

The other boy wonder, Chevalier, is even younger than Jolson.

In November, 1945, I caught the Big Boy of the Boulevards at the ABC, a shoebox of a theatre in Montmartre. It was numbing cold in Paris that night. I sat there in the unheated theatre, a fuzzy muffler up to my eyes.

But when Maurice strutted out on the stage wearing a straw skimmer, the temperature shot up thirty degrees. This was the gay young man of Paree—and there is no other.

He took the audience on a two-hour tour of a picture postcard world, where gentlemen wear flowers in their buttonholes and gendarmes kiss the nursemaids in the park. Of course, he missed out on a lot of surefire laughs —seltzer in the face, water in the pants, and "the funny thing that happened to him on the way to the theatre." But remembering his youth, I forgave him. And when he encored with "Valentina," I decided Maurice was the nicest thing France had invented since champagne.

Except for Jolson and Chevalier, I can't get very

excited about the new arrivals in the entertainment business. They amuse me, but they don't hit me where I live.

I guess I'm getting old. . . .

Holm, Sweet Holm

I REMEMBER the exact minute I fell in love with Eleanor Holm. It was 8:56 on the opening night of the Cleveland Aquacade in 1937.

The first of these big water shows had taken a lot out of me. Into sixty minutes of running time, I was trying to cram spectacle, water and comedy—and make it all come out like a slick Broadway revue. I knew that what it needed was precision—split-second timing —no stage waits.

Opening night the show began at 8:40. Everything clicked. No missed cues. Spot and floodlights flickered on and off. Fountains, water curtains, barge stages— everything was right on the nose.

I sat high up in the stands with a stop-watch. The great Gertrude Ederle—exactly 46 seconds. Eighteen water clowns—90 seconds on the dot. Johnny Weismuller and Stubby Kreuger—4 minutes and 20 seconds.

At the end of the first quarter-hour, the show wasn't ten seconds off schedule. Then, at 8:55, the lights blacked out. Over the loudspeaks a voice boomed, "Ladies and gentlemen, the back-stroke champion of the world, Miss Eleanor Holm!"

The fiddles began going like crazy as America's favorite mermaid walked out, wearing a cape of silver and sequins. She moved gracefully to stage center. Casually, she shrugged off the silver mantle and stood there in a one-piece bathing suit.

Then Eleanor put on her bathing cap. She put it on like a woman alone in front of a mirror. She played with it as if she were trying on a gay, beautiful hat.

I fidgeted. The star was chewing up valuable seconds. A dozen times at rehearsals I had told her to speed up this business with the cap. Nothing interesting about a girl putting a piece of rubber on her head, I had insisted. Yet here on opening night, in front of twenty thousand eyes, she was doing it *her* way, fussing, pushing around stray wisps of hair.

Then I sensed a tenseness in the audience. It seemed more fascinated by this natural and intimate bit of business than by all my manufactured hoopla.

Finally, the lady was satisfied with how she looked. As she stepped to the edge of the pool, ten thousand people began to breathe again. And when she hit the water, there was a round of applause that darn near knocked out the electric lights. The audience was applauding the loveliest stage wait it had ever seen. And so was I.

I looked at my stop-watch. It was 8:56.

When I went backstage after the show, Eleanor apologized. "Gee, Billy," she said, "I'm sorry I forgot and slowed things up with my bathing cap."

"Keep doing it your way," I told her. "By the way, champ, how about letting me take you out for a bite of supper?"

The romance which followed was compounded of the usual ingredients—fried shrimp, Chanel No. 5, big telephone bills, and an old Russ Columbo record of "I'll See You in My Dreams." We had only one tiff, and that was about how much chlorine to use in a swimming pool.

The inevitable fade-out took place two years later in Judge Pecora's chambers in New York. Right after the wedding, we moved into a little house on Beekman Place, a fancy dead-end on the East River. Up until that time, I had never bought furniture except for my nightclubs—tables $6, chairs $18 a dozen.

Eleanor steered me into a Madison Avenue shop which was so classy it didn't even have a name on the window. I told the clerk I wanted to see some chairs. He brought out one that looked like a prop from *The Student Prince.* The gilt was peeling off, and a self-respecting termite would have sneered at it.

"Seven hundred dollars," he announced.

"It isn't even new," I said.

"It's a genuine Louis the Fourteenth," he purred.

"It's too small," I purred back. "Show me a Louis the Sixteenth."

As we left, Eleanor said, "We'd better postpone our shopping until you get hep to Hepplewhite."

So I did what I always do when I'm confused—I went to the Public Library. I started reading up on antiques, the furniture that is worth more than it is worth. I learned that much of what is sold as old is merely in its second-childhood.

I read about the furniture fakers and how they turn Grand Rapids into old Gyppendale; that Duveen had once asked a million dollars for a sofa and six chairs because they had belonged to Madame Pompadour; that a silver dish is worth more if George the Third slobbered in it.

I decided to forget about antiques and have a look at modern furniture.

But again I was in trouble. Every room they showed

me looked like a bathroom. There was one modern living room done in stainless steel, glass tubing and burlap. The lighting was supposed to be indirect, but to me it looked undecided. When I sat in one of the foam-rubber chairs, I felt like saying, "Have the hostess bring me a cardboard container. The air's awfully bumpy today."

Eleanor and I decided we'd better have another look at the antiques. We traipsed around for weeks before we bought anything. Finally my eyes got into focus, and I realized a lot of the old stuff was pretty—that some furniture, like Bing Crosby, improves with age.

We started buying, a piece here, a piece there. It gave us something to talk about at dinner parties, a chance to show off for people who knew almost as little as we did. What started out as affectation has grown into affection, and today we're genuinely fond of the old junk. . . .

In addition to antique furniture, Eleanor bamboozled me into getting some old silver. And then some old porcelain. Finally, without quite knowing how it happened, I found myself at the Parke-Bernet Galleries bidding on a Frans Hals and buying it.

Well, it was like throwing a rock into a beehive. Next day practically every phony art dealer in New York invited me to have a cup of tea with him. And what a charming set of chiselers they were. With their own hot little hands they brought me paintings and swore on their mothers' milk they were Titians, Holbeins, Raphaels, Da Vincis. And I'll never forget the hurt look on their sensitive faces when I suggested having their masterpieces X-rayed.

My special sweetheart among the swindlers was an old lady, right out of the Eden Musee. She came to my office one day—Whistler's Mother in black lace gloves

—clutching a painting which, she explained, had been in her family for generations. Timidly she told me she was hard-pressed, and that a kindly old loan company had agreed to lend her $25,000 if I would guarantee the note. As security, she would let me hold her greatest treasure—a portrait by Rembrandt.

With a lump in my throat, I examined the painting. It was easily worth $8 in a rising market.

What a sweet scheme! Had I endorsed her note for a year, she could have moved her bag and bustle into the Waldorf and lived like Queen Victoria for 364 days. And until the note fell due, I couldn't have uttered a legal peep, even if I had learned the second day that she had painted the Rembrandt herself.

She was such a nice old lady, and I felt like a heel when I told her I was sorry, but my money was tied up in old joke books.

It took me almost two years to fix up the house the way Eleanor wanted it, but when it was finished, I had to admit it was quite a house. Of course, at the start, I was worried about living in a place where room service wasn't at the other end of the phone, but I got over it in a hurry. I don't know what the connection is between swimming and running a house, but my mermaid does one as well as the other. We've had three cooks in ten years, and each one could have matched skillets with the great Escoffier himself. And with everyone screaming about the help problem, it's never been a problem with us. Eleanor's custom of opening a case of my best champagne in the kitchen on New Year's Eve may have something to do with it.

The first year, my frau almost broke me buying brooms and vacuum cleaners. Quietly but firmly she made me understand that (a) cigarette butts don't go with Aubusson rugs, (b) aspidistras aren't ashtrays, (c) jugglers don't belong under Waterford chandeliers, and (d) one doesn't audition pigeon acts in a paneled living room.

To this day, cleanliness rates with her right up there with godliness, and I'm sure there are jiggles on the seismograph at Fordham University whenever spring cleaning time comes around.

Last April the banging of doors and the whir of the vacuum signaled the opening of the annual offensive. With a kerchief wrapped around her head, my wife looked like the lady on the Old Dutch Cleanser can.

I was working at my desk when she charged into my room. The morning papers were scattered every whichway beside the bed. Eleanor gathered up the rumpled pages.

"A sick flounder wouldn't let itself be wrapped in one of these," she said.

I was too battlewise to be drawn into the old argument about mussing the papers. Months before, when Eleanor complained about not being able to find the funnies, I had informed her I stood ready to increase her allowance a nickel a day for an extra set.

The Sapolio kid looked down at the toy junk yard on my desk. "You'll have to do something about that," she said. "It has mice."

"A man's desk is his castle," I announced in my best Republican voice.

"It might be interesting to clean the castle up," said my helpmeet. "Maybe you'll find Orson Welles at the bottom."

I couldn't see anything wrong with my desk. The papers on the left, under the ashtray, were important letters requiring immediate attention. The papers in the middle, under the magazines I hadn't read yet, were letters I should have answered a month back. The papers on the right, under the box of gumdrops, were letters too old to bother answering.

Suddenly I heard a yelp of anguish. I looked over at the open closet and saw the back bow of Eleanor's apron vibrating. She was tossing out scrapbooks, bundles of letters, photo albums, and a rare book on hypnotism.

"Go easy on that stuff," I hollered. "I need everything in there." From the top of the heap, I picked up a magazine. It was the June, 1934, issue of *Amazing Stories*.

"Look what you want to throw out," I said to my wife. "'The Goose Men of Mars!' I intend to read this first chance I get."

"Into the flames, Junior," said my missus firmly.

"And look at this," I said. "An autographed picture of Gypsy Rose Lee."

"Out!"

I picked up a bundle of letters. "Well, maybe you're right about this old junk," I said. "Why should I keep the letters you wrote me when I first knew you in Cleveland?"

There was a nice moment of silence. Eleanor took the letters out of my hand. She half-read a couple, then handed them back. "You mean you've kept these since 1937?"

I nodded.

"You win," she smiled, and walked out of the room.

As I crammed the junk back into the closet, I heard the vacuum start up in another part of the house.

Eleanor's fastidiousness doesn't stop at her home. It goes even further when it concerns her own person. In her bathroom are enough oils, unguents, creams, lotions, pigments, perfumes, pads, and brushes to stock a small drugstore. And I'll be darned if I know why.

My girl was born pretty. Why should it take her an hour to put on her make-up?

Recently I had a pair down front for the opening of a musical. "Let's get to the theatre on time for a change," I said.

"All right," said Eleanor. "What are you standing there for? You know I always have to wait for *you*."

I swan-dived into the tub, hacked wildly at my beard, shifted coins and keys from Pants A to Pants B, leaped into my tux like a fireman, and in exactly twelve minutes presented myself for inspection.

Eleanor had placidly planted herself before the triple mirror of her dressing table. In addition to the usual assortment of goop, there were one or two gadgets which looked like hold-overs from the Inquisition.

"Darling," I said, "what's this drugstore for?"

"Go away," she explained.

I stomped off and found the evening paper. I read the editorials, the ads, and did as much as I could of the crossword puzzle. It got to be 8:20.

"Look," I said, "it took Da Vinci four years to paint the *Mona Lisa*. Do you think you could shave a few seconds off his record?"

"Don't talk to me now," said Eleanor. "I'm putting on my lips."

At 8:40 the little woman came out of her bedroom. She posed for an instant on the threshold. She looked wonderful—*but she looked wonderful before she started!*

Our drive to the theatre was like a Mack Sennett chase. We stumbled to our seats over umbrellas, coats, and feet. As we settled down to enjoy the play, the lights came up and the first act was over.

"I'll see you in the lobby," said Eleanor. "I'm going down to the powder room to freshen up a bit."

This make-up ritual is only one of many things I can't understand about Eleanor. I'm equally in the dark about her little-girl trick of making me jealous.

The other day as I was shaving, she came into the bathroom and perched on the edge of the tub—she once saw Helen Hayes do it in *Victoria Regina* when the Prince Consort was lathering up.

"I'll be working late tonight," I said.

"That's all right," said Eleanor. "I'm having dinner with Paul Gilbert."

"Who else will be in the party?"

"Just the two of us," said my wife. "We're dining at The Stork."

I put down my razor and took a deep breath. "I'd rather you didn't go out with that nanny goat," I said. "If the columnists see you with him, tomorrow morning eight hundred papers will print that we have Reno in the beano."

"I thought you said you didn't want me to be lonely when you were working," said Eleanor.

"I don't mind your going out," I said, "but why must it be with the president of the wolf pack? How'd you happen to make a date with him anyway?"

"He telephoned and asked me."

Just then the doorbell rang. "If you go out with Paul Gilbert tonight," I said, "I'll . . . I'll . . . I'll . . ."

"Why, darling," said Eleanor as she went to answer the bell, "what big veins you have!"

Skyrockets went off in my head. With my face still dripping soap, I picked up the telephone and got Gilbert on the wire.

"This is Billy Rose," I snarled. "I see you're auditioning for a shroud. What size do you take?"

"Hello, Rose," said Gilbert. "Isn't it a bit early in the morning for practical jokes?"

"Never mind the chit-chat," I said. "What's the idea of asking my wife for a date?"

"Gently," said the menace-about town. "I have no date with your wife—though it's an enchanting idea. I've never even met the lady."

I sensed he was telling the truth. "I'm sorry," I said. "I've got my wires crossed."

"Take a bromo or something," said Gilbert. "You'll feel better."

I went looking for Eleanor. "Why'd you tell me that fib about Paul Gilbert?" I demanded. "I just made an ass of myself on the phone."

"What did you say to him?" asked my child bride, her eyes shining. "I want to hear every word."

"Why did you tell me you had a date with him?" I persisted.

Eleanor smiled and put her arms around me. "There was no date, silly," she said. "I just wanted to see if you still cared."

Having made a go of her own marriage, Eleanor can't understand why everybody else doesn't get married. And being a girl who suits the deed to the thought, she's always arranging dinner parties at which Jane may hook Joe. For years it's been a stock joke around the house that she has a map hanging on her bedroom wall with colored pins showing the location of the town's eligible bachelors.

One day last December I came down to breakfast and found Eleanor having a heart-to-heart with her chum Dolores. They were discussing a New Man that Dolores had met the night before at El Morocco. And to hear her tell it, he was Gary Cooperish in build, Ronald Colmanish in mustache, and RFC-ish in bankroll. The paragon's name was George Huelsenbeck.

"You're not thinking of marrying a man for his money?" I said.

"Certainly not," Dolores deadpanned, "but I want my next husband to have a good disposition, and if he's poor, he'll be worried and irritable."

"You've only met George once," I said. "How can you talk about marrying him?"

Eleanor piped up, "It's not as if he were a stranger. A girl we know was engaged to him for almost a year."

With the scrambled eggs, I got the story of the previous evening. Friends had introduced Dolores to George, and they had danced. Dolores told George a little lie about planning to spend the Christmas holidays at Acapulco, Mexico. George said it was Kismet—by coincidence he was spending the holidays in Acapulco too.

Eleanor reacted to this story like the Master of the Hounds when "Tally-ho!" rings out in the morning air. "We must be all set for him when he gets to Acapulco," she said briskly.

"What do you mean, *we* must be all set?" I asked.

"I'm going with her," said Eleanor. "If Dolores went down there alone, people would say she was husband-hunting. Hand me that pad. I want to list the summer things I'll have to buy."

I sat there brooding. Suddenly I was facing a wifeless Christmas. "Billy no like-um," I said to myself.

When Dolores left, I decided to use the Approach Financial and commenced maneuvers.

"I think you're doing a fine thing," I told Eleanor, "but it's going to cost you a packet of dough—plane fare, hotel, clothes, sun-tan oil—over a thousand dollars would be my guess."

Eleanor looked up. I had hit a two-bagger, but I wasn't home yet. I took a long lead off second.

"I'll make a deal with you, Baby," I went on. "Forget

Acapulco and I'll buy you the wristwatch with the red stones we saw in Cartier's window yesterday. That way you'll be ahead a wristwatch, plus the thousand you would have spent on the trip."

I was rounding third now. "Besides," I said, "it won't seem like Christmas without you."

Eleanor gave my offer deep consideration for all of three seconds. "I wouldn't want to spoil your Christmas," she said. "Don't forget to pick up the watch on your way to the office."

That night as we were finishing dinner, the doorbell rang. It was Dolores again, crying mad. "The heel!" she exploded. "The heartless heel!"

"What happened?" asked Eleanor.

"I just found out that George is married!" said Dolores. "And what's worse, he's in love with his wife!"

"Don't let it throw you, darling," said Eleanor. "Jimmy Stewart is coming to town next month and—"

"We're going to be late for the theatre," I cut in. "What time is it getting to be?"

"Ten after eight," said Eleanor, consulting the Watch with the Red Stones.

If I ever run into George Huelsenbeck, I'm going to spit right in his eye.

Besides running a matrimonial agency for her single pals, Eleanor operates a court of human relations for the married ones. Whenever the marriage of one of her girl friends is in danger of becoming unstuck, my little Portia steps in with a bucket of glue. And over the years, her services to the lovelorn have cost the Reno hotels many a buck.

Eleanor's favorite strategy is what she calls "the kid-'em-out-of-it treatment." At first, I refused to help her with these emotional therapeutics, but I reconsidered the first cold night when the extra quilt was missing.

Her most recent use of the "treatment" was on behalf of a couple we're particularly fond of, named Danny and Cora. One night when it was raining hard enough to put Noah back in business, the doorbell rang. I let in Cora and a bucket of rain.

Her eyes looked as if she had been fighting a forest fire. She buried her head in Elly's lap. "Danny and I are through," she blubbered.

My wife let Cora cry herself out. Then we got the story. Danny had been out three nights in a row, making big man talk with the boys at Toots Shor's. When he started out for the fourth night, Cora accused him of not wanting to be with her any more. Well, one word led to a hundred others. She had decided to see her lawyer in the morning and then leave for Reno.

Eleanor and I gave each other the "let's go" look. My frau kicked off. "If you're going to get divorced," she said, "we'll have to line up another husband for you."

Cora looked startled and began to say something, but I took her out of play. "There's always Johnny Rice," I said. "He ought to make a faithful husband—he's always preferred married women."

"I know another man who would go for Cora," said Eleanor. "Harry Brandon."

"I don't think Cora could stand him after Danny," I said. "Harry is an old-fashioned fellow—one Old-Fashioned after another."

Cora had stopped crying now and was listening. "Don't worry about getting another husband," I told her. "There are lots of lonely, middle-aged men around."

"Stand up," said Eleanor to Cora. "Let's look at you. Hmm, a little overweight, but I know a place where they'll pound it off in a couple of weeks. And it won't cost you over five hundred dollars."

"It should be fun being back in circulation," I chimed in. "Of course, you'll have to listen to the same old routines, but it's worth it to get rid of a bum like Danny."

Eleanor picked up the ball and ran for the goal line. "While you're in Reno," she said, "I'll try to find you an apartment with a phone. A single girl is as good as dead without one."

"I think you're doing the smart thing," I said. "Danny makes a good living and everybody likes him, but a girl needs something more substantial."

Eleanor made the touchdown. "Don't start feeling sorry for Danny," she said. "I know a couple of girls who have always been crazy about him. One of them will grab him off, and you won't have him on your conscience."

A quick look at Cora's eyes told me it was all over. I went into the next room and called Danny at Toots Shor's. A few minutes later his car drove up. Cora was on the curb waiting for him. From the window Eleanor and I watched them clinch.

"It's been a long day," said the missus. "Put out the lights, Mr. Anthony, and let's turn in."

"I don't feel sleepy," I said, "I think I'll go down to Toots Shor's for a while."

"All right," said Eleanor. "But I'm going with you."

When we got to Toots's we found Danny and Cora celebrating their reunion. We all tied on a bit of a brannigan, and it was almost morning when we got back to the house. Getting out of the car, I forgot to give Eleanor a hand. "Sorry," I said.

"Don't give it a thought, Kurt Weill," said my spouse.

"Are you going to start that again?" I said as I fumbled for the keys.

"Only when you rate it, Kurt," said Eleanor.

Let me explain. Whenever my missus wants to put the zing in, she calls me Kurt Weill. If one of her friends shows up wearing a silver-blue mink, Eleanor hits me with, "Do you think I'll ever have one like it, Kurt Weill?" If I forget to light her cigarette or hold her coat for her, she sideswipes me with, "You fumbled that one, Kurt."

This has been going on since we attended the opening night of a bum little musical called *The Firebrand of Florence* back in 1945. Kurt Weill composed the music for this show.

One of the big parts in *The Firebrand* was that of a sexy duchess, and it needed someone with the full-blown charms of Irene Bordoni or Vivienne Segal. Kurt handed the role to his wife Lenya. And this bit of casting puzzled a lot of people on Broadway—Lenya is a competent actress, but hardly a big, sexy duchess.

On opening night, Kurt's wife made her first appearance about fifteen minutes after the curtain went up. She was gay and expert, but definitely wrong for the role. When Lenya finished her first song, Eleanor nudged me. "Would you do that for me?" she whispered.

"Would I do what?" I asked.

"Would you let me play the duchess if this were your show?"

"Sssh!" I said. "There's a performance going on."

"Don't shush me," said Eleanor. "You're not fit to shine Kurt Weill's shoes."

A man sitting behind us tapped me on the back. "Very interesting dialogue," he said, "but I don't see your names on the program. Would you mind saving it for intermission?"

In Act Two, Lenya was still gay and expert—but still not the sexy duchess.

As we drove home, Eleanor said, "Admit it. You'd never do for me what Kurt did for Lenya."

"I don't think Kurt realized his wife wasn't right for the part," I said. "Love is sometimes blind, you know."

"*You* would have seen," said Eleanor.

"All right," I admitted. "I would have seen. A show is more important to me than the people in it."

"That's the difference between you and a gentleman like Kurt Weill," said my wife. "If I hadn't looked good at the first rehearsal of the Aquacade, you'd have phoned the Coast for Esther Williams."

I was so busy trying to think of an answer that I forgot to help Eleanor out of the car. "Sorry," I said.

"Don't give it a thought, Kurt Weill," said Eleanor as she brushed past me into the house.

And it's been that way ever since.

Of course, I don't worry about these pinpricks. They're what the French call "pour le sport" and help keep the matrimonial cement from coming loose.

Besides, I'm not Eleanor's only pincushion. Some of her happiest evenings are those she spends with her friends putting other girls on the pan. But don't get me wrong. My wife and her pals aren't peeved at their targets. As a rule, they bear them no more malice than the skeet shooter does the clay pigeon.

One night I was reading the papers while Eleanor was talking to her two big chum-buddies, Virginia Reynolds and Wes Bernie.

"Jane is a lovely girl," I heard Eleanor say. "But that *dress!* All her taste is in her mouth."

"Her face had more character before she got her nose bobbed," said Wes.

"I hear she has a new Pomeranian," said Ginny. "A Pomeranian with pants."

"No wonder," said Wes. "Her husband is very cruel to her. He made her go on a diet."

"I don't blame him," said Eleanor. "Did you see her at the Turkish bath? Down to here!"

And so on until the room was littered with arms, legs and little-girl chops.

After a few minutes of this cat-nipping, I broke in, "I thought you girls liked Jane."

"Of course we like her," said Eleanor. "This is just constructive criticism. Besides, what do you think she's saying about us right this minute?"

Last summer an actress spent a week-end with us up in the country. We were sitting around the playroom after dinner when she got a New York call. As the actress left the room she threw a look of despair over her shoulder. The girls smiled reassuringly, but the instant she was out of the room, the anvil chorus began.

"Lovely girl," said Ginny. "You have to admire a person who won't let anything stand in the way of her success."

"Did you notice her at dinner?" said Eleanor. "She eats like after a fever."

"How old do you suppose she really is?" asked Wes.

"She says she's thirty-two," said Ginny. "In other words she admits to forty."

"Sssh," said Eleanor. "Here she comes."

As the actress entered, sweet smiles lit up the sweet faces of the three sweet girls.

"I hope you weren't too hard on me while I was gone," she said.

"Of course not, silly!" said Eleanor. "Who called?"

"That was Ilka," said the actress. "Lovely girl. She's having trouble with her chauffeur. He objects to her husband."

As the kitty-cats went into their four-part harmony, I ducked into the library, picked up a good gory thriller and relaxed.

If the last few pages read as if I'm putting the whammy on my wife, then I've written them badly. Eleanor comes very close to being what pulp writers call "The one girl in a million." As you know, her prettiness is not exactly a secret. Some years ago *Life* ran half a dozen pages of her pictures and wrote her up as one of the all-time photogenic greats. She rides, swims and plays tennis with confidence and style. She laughs easily, cries easily, and is as feminine as a piece of black lingerie. And having been a world champion, she isn't in awe of anybody. There are only two kinds of people in her book—nice people and mean people. There are no important people.

As an old sharpshooter, I know how rare a specimen this title girl is. My cockeyed kingdom is built around her, and without her it would be for sale cheap. After ten years of seeing her with her hair up in curlers, I'm more stuck on her than ever.

Last February, Eleanor went to Florida to spend a couple of weeks with Wes Bernie. The night before she left, we walked up Broadway. It was snowing a little—red, green or yellow, depending on what neon sign was in the background.

"Looks as if somebody crumpled up a rainbow and is tossing handfuls down on Times Square," I said.

"Save those birdcalls for your column," my frau said gaily.

We stepped into a penny arcade. As I was about to buy a candy apple on a stick, Eleanor sing-songed, "Mustn't touch—nine million calories." We compromised on a souvenir turtle.

Then I picked up a rifle at the shooting gallery and knocked over fifteen ducks with fifteen shots. Eleanor pretended to be impressed and lettered out a medal for me on the nickel stamping machine.

While I squeezed the handles of the Strength-Tester,

she dropped a penny in the Gypsy Lady fortune machine. A little card popped out. It read, "You are going to take a long trip."

Eleanor, with a ticket to Miami in her pocketbook, turned to me and smiled, "And you don't believe in fortune tellers!"

A week later I walked up Broadway alone. There was a dirty mist on the windows of the orange-juice joints. The hodge-podge of electric signs reminded me of G. K. Chesterton, who looked at Times Square and said, "A magnificent sight—for a man who can't read."

I watched the stock characters shuffling past in the slush. There was the old lady selling papers, with a muffler tied around her head, and the little girls who should have been home in bed, giggling at the bum jokes of little boys who should have been home in bed. Broadway without Eleanor reminded me of the scene in *Fury* when Spencer Tracy gets hungry for the sound of voices, runs into a noisy bar, and finds nothing but a radio blaring and an old Negro sweeping up.

As I walked, I found myself humming a song I had written almost twenty years ago:

> *Me and my shadow,*
> *Strolling down the avenue.*

I stepped into the penny arcade where I had bought Eleanor the souvenir turtle and noticed for the first time that the paint was peeling off the machines. When I dropped a coin in the mechanical baseball game I found it out of order. At a handcrank movie, I took a peek at Ten Nights in a Turkish Bath. I walked away on the second night.

As I was leaving the arcade, I passed the Gypsy Lady machine. I dropped a cent in, looked at the little card which popped out and threw it away. And I threw away the second and third cards. The fourth was the one I wanted. "You are going to take a long trip," it read.

"You can say that again, Gypsy Lady," I said as I stepped into a phone booth to call the airline.

"Any reservations open on the midnight plane to Miami?" I inquired.

"How many, please?" asked the clerk.

"One," I said, "unless you charge extra for shadows."

Next morning at ten o'clock, Eleanor was rubbing suntan oil on my back.

"How'd you manage to get away?" she asked.

"That's a secret between me and a Gypsy lady," I said.

"I think I know the dame you're talking about," said my missus. "She lives at Broadway and 52nd."

As we walked to the beach, Eleanor asked me if I remembered a swimmer named Red Morton.

I scratched my brain for a second. "Come again," I said.

"He won third place in the 1928 Olympics," said Eleanor. "I think you told me you once loaned him twenty dollars."

"Oh, that one," I said. "What about him?"

"Nothing," said Eleanor, "except I met him yesterday at the tennis courts."

"Did he look as if he had the twenty on him?" I asked.

"I wouldn't know," said my wife, "but the gal he was with had a chunk of ice on her wrist worth twenty thousand. She's the widow of a Canadian lumberman. It takes four hours to fly over her forests."

"How did Morton meet up with her?"

"He gave her some swimming lessons a couple of years ago and she's still taking them," said Eleanor. "I'm playing tennis with her tomorrow. Want to watch?"

At the courts next morning, Red gave me the big hello and introduced Mrs. Myra Coleman. Myra looked like a gal who had spent a lot of time and money on herself. Her sport coat and tennis togs had real style. Mrs. Coleman didn't. And when she told Red to open a can of balls, her voice had that boss-lady ring.

The girls got on the court and hit a few practice shots. Myra's tennis was like Myra—unspectacular but tough. Eleanor won the serve, and they started to play. Red and I squatted on a sideline bench.

"How's your marriage with the Champ?" he asked me. There was something nice about the way he said "Champ"—the respect of the runner-up who knows how good the champ has to be.

"We're getting along fine," I told him.

Just then Mrs. Coleman put away an overhead smash. Red applauded, and the widow smiled at him like a bondholder clipping an interest coupon.

I sensed this was not just another game to Myra. Maybe it was because she was playing Eleanor Holm, a world champion in the business her pretty boy used to be in. Maybe Morton had told her too many times what a fine gal Eleanor was. Anyhow, Myra was playing to win.

And she was playing dirty. She kept foot-faulting on her serves. She gave herself several close sideline decisions. A couple of times she cheated at the net by leaning over.

Eleanor never beefed. The first time it happened, she gave Mrs. Coleman a funny look. When it happened again, my little champion started playing over her head.

Half an hour later, it was 7—6, Eleanor's favor, and set point coming up. Mrs. Coleman was serving. She zipped over a hard one. Eleanor barely managed to get it back. Myra moved in to murder it. She was too anxious. The ball flicked the clay a good six inches past the white line on our side.

"Too bad," said Eleanor, and started walking off the court.

"It was in," insisted Mrs. Coleman.

"I thought it was out," said Eleanor quietly.

Mrs. Coleman turned to Morton. "You saw it," she said. "Was it in or out?"

I started to say something, then shut my mouth. I knew how much was riding on the gigolo's answer. The fellow who had won a third in the Olympics looked at the girl whose hundred-yard backstroke record is still on the books.

"It was out," he said. "Out by a mile."

I knew I'd never collect my twenty bucks. But I didn't much care.

It was April before we got back from Florida, and outside of breakfast and dinner, I didn't see much of Eleanor that month. Besides being busy with her spring cleaning, she was busy shopping for her spring outfit.

Night after night, she and Virginia Reynolds got together and studied the department store ads as SHAEF must have studied the maps of the Normandy coast. Day after day they traipsed from shop to shop like questing beagles. I estimated that the girls were wearing out thirty dollars' worth of shoe leather for every ten-dollar purchase they made, but of course I kept these statistics to myself.

A few days after Easter, however, Eleanor told me something which, in good conscience, I couldn't keep to myself. I'm very fond of Virginia's husband and I felt duty bound to let him know what was going on. And so I wrote him the following letter:

Dear Quent,

I think you're in trouble—serious trouble. And I'll tell you why.

A few weeks ago I was browsing around one of those antique shops which specialize in Larceny and Old Lace. In a tray of whatchamacallits, I came across a brass mermaid which I thought might look good on one of Eleanor's handbags.

When I gave it to her, Eleanor said, "It's just what I've always wanted. What is it?"

"It's a whatchamacallit," I said.

"It's about time you called off your buyer's strike," said my wife. "Now all I need is a handbag to put it on."

"But you have a handbag," I said. "Several of them."

"None of them is right for it," said Eleanor firmly.

The following evening when we went to the movies, Eleanor was toting one of her old pocketbooks. I asked how come. "My new hat won't be ready for a few days," she said.

I thought I understood. "You mean you ordered a hat to match the handbag which you bought to match the mermaid," I said.

"Not exactly," said Eleanor. "The hat is to match the new suit. My other suit clashed with the new shoes."

"Let's begin at the beginning," I said. "I bought you a whatchamacallit. . . ."

"So I bought a bag to put it on," said Eleanor. "Naturally, I had to get shoes to go with the bag. You always match handbags with shoes."

"*I* do?" I inquired. "You know, I hate to think what would happen to me if you ever decided *I* clashed with your ensemble."

I gave my wife a little lecture on economy. When I told her how much theatre business was off, Eleanor was impressed. The upshot of our talk was that I promised not to take so many taxis.

Next evening when I got home, Eleanor flashed her No. 1 smile. For dessert we had chocolate profiterole. "Let's stay home tonight," she said. "We'll light a fire and listen to the radio."

"What are you after now?" I asked.

Eleanor grinned. "A little fur around my neck to match the new suit. I just want to show the girls how generous my husband is."

Easter morning, Eleanor dolled up like the girl in Irving Berlin's *Easter Parade*. Her handbag matched her shoes. Shoes matched gloves. Gloves matched hat. Hat matched blouse. Blouse matched suit. Suit matched her fur piece—and the fur piece matched what it costs to police Bowling Green, Kentucky.

But as we strolled up Fifth Avenue, I got the feeling that something was missing. "What happened to the brass whatchamacallit on your handbag?" I asked her.

"Oh, that," she said. "I had to take it off. It clashed with these earrings."

I suppose, my dear Quent, you're wondering why I bore you with this melancholy recital. Well, today I asked Eleanor for the brass mermaid—thought it might make an interesting paper-weight for my desk. Eleanor told me she had given the whatchamacallit to your wife, Ginny.

That's all, brother!

Billy Rose.

Bathroom Soliloquies

❀ ❀

Shaving

Every morning I darn near cut my throat when I perform the boring, irritating, infuriating, maddening ritual of shaving. There's nothing I dread more than having to spend that quarter hour face to face with my face.

I pick up the razor each day determined not to inflict any new wounds. The wide open spaces of my cheeks are a cinch—it's the delicate work around the chin and upper lip where I get into trouble. Sometimes I forget the deadly weapon in my hand and daydream a bit. But I am soon jerked back to reality by the sight of my own blood welling out of a gash in the jowl. . . .

There are about fifty million guys in this country who devote fifteen minutes a day to shaving—ninety-one man-hours a year each. This comes to something like a half billion working days a year, which could be used for sleeping or improving the mind.

Why don't the scientific boys forget nuclear energy for a while and go to work on whiskers?

Belittling

I wish the maid wouldn't put the razor blades on the top shelf of the medicine chest. . . . For a little gink like me, they might as well be on top of Mt. Everest. . . .

It's not much fun being five-three in a five-nine world.

Why doesn't my press agent lay off those tired phrases—The Bantam Barnum, The Gremlin of 54th Street, The Shorty with the Fringe on Top. And why doesn't Eleanor stop telling people I wear a bow-tie because I trip on the other kind?

Bet the reason Stalin is mad at us is because we keep sending six-foot ambassadors. He can't fool another Tiny Tim about why he won't be photographed standing next to anybody. . . .

Alexander the Great, Caesar, Napoleon—bet the real reason these peewees wanted to conquer the world was to make sure no one would stand in front of them when a parade went by.

Griping

I used to run a hundred yards in eleven seconds, but like the American dollar, my feet ain't what they used to be. I wish Nature had taken a couple of extra seconds and figured out a better gadget for us to get around on. Like wheels, for instance. . . .

Nature might also have done a better job on our eyes. Nowadays, unless I wear glasses, I can't read the fine type in a contract, and as the comics are always telling us, the fine type is there to take away what the big type gives. To make matters worse, when I lose my glasses I can't even look for them until I find them. . . .

Another place where I got short-changed by evolution is the teeth. I still have most of my choppers, but the last time I went to the dentist he told me to swear off caramels. He might as well have told me to give up kissing. . . .

No, I can't go along with the anthropologists who think Man is the last stone on the evolutionary pyramid.

Seals swim faster, eagles see farther, chickens get born easier, turtles live longer, roses smell better, and an alley cat is more graceful.

And judging from the headlines in the newspapers these days, I'm not even sure that we think better.

Resolving

I suppose they know what they're doing, but I sometimes wonder why the cigarette companies spend so much money advertising. They don't have to put bands on the radio and pretty girls on billboards to sell *me*. They've got me—lungs, throat and nasal passages. . . .

Mark Twain once said, "To stop smoking is the easiest thing in the world. I've done it hundreds of times." Well, him and me both. . . .

I burn something like sixty cigarettes a day—and that ain't hay, although they begin to taste like it around midnight. When I've chewed up the pack in my pocket, I mooch them from friends, steal them out of Eleanor's pocketbook, and if I weren't afraid someone might step on my thumb, I'd sometimes be tempted to even more desperate measures.

The first thing I do in the morning, even before I've inspected the plumbing, is to light up and make like a dragon. And I don't care what the brand is as long as I can set fire to it and gulp it down. . . .

Last year I stopped smoking for four whole days. On the first day I screeched at the phone operator and sent her home in hysterics. Item: A box of chocolates and a raise.

The second day I bawled out Eleanor for changing the blotter on my desk. Item: One of those black beaded handbags.

The third day a cop suggested I move my car from a

fireplug. I made a little speech about Cossacks. Item: Four hours in court and a $25 fine.

The fourth day, I was ready to pack and walk out on myself. A depressing thing had happened—my mind had become crystal clear. . . .

As a kid, I had a trick memory, what the lit'ry fellows describe as "total recall." But for years my mind had been pleasantly obscured by the haze of cigarette smoke. Suddenly all the rubbish in my think-tank floated to the surface—numbers of telephones long since disconnected, verbatim recollections of train-ride small-talk, mental images of whole pages of Frank Merriwell and the Liberty Boys of '76.

I got panicky. I saw myself spending the rest of my life in an attic full of moldy newspapers. . . .

That night Eleanor said, "Stop sticking pins in yourself," and handed me a cigarette. I lit up, made smoke like an Indian sending signals, and swore off swearing off. . . .

I don't want anyone to think I'm blowing the whistle on the cigarette business. I, too, get my crackers and caviar by peddling quick looks at Never-Never Land. I want it thoroughly understood that I'm not saying tobacco is habit-forming.

All I know is—I've got the habit.

Believing

I wish people wouldn't tell me the truth about certain things. I wish the engineers would keep their slide rules out of the bits of fairyland left in this bolixed-up world. . . .

The other day the Cunard-White Star Line admitted that one of the three funnels on the *Queen Mary* is a phony. Who asked them? I've always believed the number of smokestacks was a measure of the power of the ship. Now, a marine architect says the biggest ship needs only a dinky little pipe. A pox on him. To me a stackless ocean liner is like a Hungarian without a lawyer. . . .

I've been raised to believe that if I find a cockroach in a bottle of Coca-Cola, I can collect a million dollars from the company. For years, this has been my ace in the hole. Why rob me of it? . . .

I believe that if somebody hands an elephant a peanut shell full of pepper, Jumbo will pick him out of a crowd twenty years later and kill him. When I saw this ridiculed in a pocket know-it-all magazine, I canceled my subscription. . . .

I recently stopped talking to an aviator friend who told me he didn't get dizzy on top of the Empire State Building. I don't trust such a man. . . .

I'm convinced that in the early days of the West, there were doctors who could perform delicate operations while blind drunk. Touch this one, and I'll never step into a movie theatre again. . . .

And I love to think that if I were to move several hundred miles away and leave my dog behind, two weeks later faithful old Rover would be scratching at the new kitchen door. Deny this, and if Rover doesn't bite you, I will.

Revamping

I'd like to sneak into the Hall of Fame some night and chop up most of the statues. A little bug keeps whispering in my ear that too many of our historical hotshots were in the business of hurting people. You can't make me believe that Hiram Maxim, inventor of the machine gun, rates a thousand pounds of bronze. . . .

I wish I had enough dough to build an opposition Hall of Fame. We sure could use one, and in it I'd reserve the first niche for the obscure Italian who invented ice cream. The history books can have General Sherman —I'll take vanilla.

I'd reserve the second niche for the benefactor who invented the chair. And niche number three for the inspired plumber who gave us hot and cold running water.

My fourth candidate would be the only man who ever did anything that actually helped the common cold— the inventor of the handkerchief.

Next on my list would be the humanitarian who gave us bedroom slippers. His should be a full-length statue— people would want to lay flowers at his feet because of what he did for theirs.

And of course I'd put up a statue to the gent who invented the animated cartoon. His was the greatest contribution to world gaiety since popcorn. . . .

In my Hall of Fame there would also be busts of the immortals who produced toothpicks, buttonholes, doorknobs, mosquito netting, the tangerine, the nectarine, and the seedless grape. And baby spotlights over the statues of the artists who gave us the red fire engines and white houses with green shutters.

Even though I don't know their names, I'd put up plaques to honor the shepherd who first blew into a reed and made music, and the Neanderthaler who hit on the happy idea of bringing flowers into a cave.

And finally, at the top of a marble staircase, I would erect a solid gold statue in memory of the most impetuous man in the history of the world. I mean the audacious fellow who, dim centuries ago, said, "Nuts to the single life. I'm going to get married."

Reporting

Newspaper editors sometimes give me a pain where I sit.

Recently a floozie was found naked and dead in her apartment on 51st Street. The papers referred to her as an "actress." In my book, that was pretty corny journalism.

When an editor is too scared of the libel laws to name a lady's real profession, he usually plays it safe and labels her an "actress." This feeds the stale legend that show people are naughtier than ordinary people. Well, it ain't so.

The sock-and-buskin kids may have their wacky moments—praise Allah!—but they're no police problem. They belong to unions, go to church, take their kids to the zoo Sunday afternoons, and squawk about their mothers-in-law. They average about the same percentage of thinkers, drinkers, and stinkers as other folks.

This business of labeling every floozie an actress is as old-timey as depicting every newspaperman with a battered hat and a pair of hollow legs. It's partly a hangover from the days of Oliver Cromwell, when merely being of the theatre was reason for arrest, and partly the desire of editors to glamourize gritty stories and sell out the edition.

But it all adds up to bad reporting, not unlike that of certain right-wing papers which call every liberal a "Red," and certain left-wing papers which call every conservative a "Fascist!"

Saluting

For my dough, the most important people in the world are doctors. . . .

If you cut yourself, if something starts biting at your insides, if your kid breaks out in spots, whom do you holler for? Your Congressman? The president of your bank? The Secretary of War? Not on your tintype. You send for the man with the little black satchel. . . .

I sometimes think it wouldn't make very much difference to this world if it took most of its inventors, politicians, and generals, and ground them up for hamburger. Inventors have given us a lot of cute toys to play with—steam heat, electric lights, radio, and the telephone. But inventors are also responsible for the airplane, the submarine, and the atomic gadget which has the world standing on one foot. . . .

I feel pretty much the same about politicians. After being in charge for five thousand years, they've still got us up the well-known creek. Every twenty years or so, one of them makes the same speech: "As of yesterday, my country is at war with your country. . . ."

And as for generals, I never could get very excited about any of them. Patton was a picturesque fellow and a fine strategist, but let's face it: Was he as important as Pasteur, who put the hex on germs, or Fleming, who put the finishing touches to penicillin? Not in my book. . . .

When I was a kid, I had scarlet fever, and they tacked up a sign on my house and nobody could come near me. But a small gent with a black bag walked right in. I can still see the tiny red veins on his nose and smell the iodoform and tobacco on his suit.

I remember asking my mother, "Can't doctors catch scarlet fever?" She said they couldn't—but she was fibbing. The list of doctors who were killed by the bugs they were chasing would stretch from here to Valhalla. . . .

During the last century, doctors have added something like thirty years to the average life expectancy.

I can't speak for the fellow next door, but I wouldn't swap one spring of that extra thirty for a chunk of gold as big as Radio City. . . .

Of course the great standouts of medical science don't need any ballyhoo from me. But the doctor who rides around in that 1937 Chevvy could use a little applause. In a civilization that rates a guy by how big a check he can write, the doctor knocks his brains out for less than we pay a bricklayer or a plumber. Sun or slush, he's on tap if you're in trouble. Twenty-four hours a day he stands ready to stop what's hurting you.

To me that's as important as anybody can get.

Giving

I've been going into my poke to buy gifts since I first saw the statues in a museum and discovered the thing called Woman. . . . According to my wife, there are forty-three days on the calendar when a real gentleman sends around a package with a ribbon on it. When I forget one of these occasions, Eleanor is too nice a girl to complain. She says nothing—for a whole week! . . .

I can understand about Christmas, Easter, and Valentine's Day, but why does she rate a present on Teddy Roosevelt's birthday? . . .

When Eleanor pouts, there's only one remedy— a present. And not just any present. The guy who gives his wife a lampshade or a bathroom scale is apt to find himself spending Saturday night curled up with Dr. Eliot's Five-Foot Shelf. The gent who gets the large-size hug is the one who buys her something she can put on and run to see how it looks in the mirror. . . .

Of course, if a guy is trying to melt down a gal who carries a jeweler's eye-piece in her handbag, he's in trouble. Either he gets himself a machine that prints money, or he gets a new wife. But if you're hitched to a nice, normal girl, you don't need a stack of blue chips—though I've never heard that it hurt any. The important thing is to buy her something that's the best of its kind. . . .

If I could only afford to spend five dollars for Baby's birthday, instead of buying a bargain handbag or a cheesy piece of costume jewelry, I'd blow it all on something that was pure madness—like a single cake of soap. For five bucks I could get a hunk scented by Schiaparelli, and every time Eleanor used it, she'd feel like the Duchess of Windsor.

Brooding

A bat is flying around my house, and I don't know what to do about it. There's a row of push buttons on the left side of my desk and a quartet of telephones on the right. What buttons do I press? Whom do I call? Where does it say, "Bat Remover . . ."?

I have to do something quick—I promised Eleanor I'd take care of it. As she stomped out of the office this morning she said "Okay, Daniel Boone, you wear the pants in this family. Make me know it. . . ."

She came in from the country in a tizzy. She and Ginny Reynolds were having dinner last night when a couple of bats flew into the room. Thirty seconds later, the kids were swinging brooms, Eleanor in a shower cap, Ginny with a pillowcase wrapped around her head. Real zoologists these gals—they know if a bat gets in your hair, you carry it to the grave. But after ten minutes of batting practice, the score was: bats, 0; lamps, 2; vases, 1.

Exhausted, the big game hunters went to bed, first hanging a quilt over the fireplace. In the morning, they came upon one of the black witch-things behind a mirror, hanging upside down and dreaming its batty dreams. Now get this, Frank Buck—they got the vacuum cleaner, switched on the motor, and sucked it into the bag!

Whooping like drunken Comanches, they carried it outside, let the bat out of the bag and fell upon it with brooms.

"It got away," said Eleanor, "but I think it will wait to be invited before it visits us again. The other bat is still flying around. You sleep in the master bedroom. Well, prove you're the master. . . ."

What do I do now? If my bathtub won't drain, I phone for the plumber. If I get arrested, I holler for my lawyer. Eye doctors, tree surgeons, tax experts, psycho-analysts—a hundred trouble-shooters are at the other end of my telephone. But a little piece of the primitive has flown in through the window, and I might as well be naked in a cave. . . .

This is the mighty United States, Anno Domini 1948. We have jet planes, radar, nuclear energy, and the FBI. But here I sit, modern man after fifty centuries of progress. A bat is flying around my house, and I'll be darned if I know what to do about it.

Planning

Relax, Rose, and cut out the nonsense about the well-ordered life. There are things called the breaks, and your two-penny plans for the future won't stand up against them. . . .

Remember that afternoon in 1917 in Newburgh, New York? You were out walking and the wind blew a piece of newspaper your way. One of the ads read, "Stenographers Wanted—War Industries Board, Washington, D. C."

You went down there next day and got a job. And there you got to know Mr. Baruch. Well, suppose the wind had blown that piece of paper in another direction? . . .

And how about that day in 1936 in Hollywood when you went out to the Metro lot to see a friend? As you walked by the executive building, Rufus Le Maire happened to look out of his office window and hollered for you to come up.

"My friend Amon Carter," he said, "asked me to find someone to stage the Fort Worth Centennial Exposition. I hadn't thought of you, but maybe you're the man for the job."

Next morning you were in Texas. One of the shows you produced there gave you the idea for the Aquacade. And when you did the water show in Cleveland, you met Eleanor Holm. And it was the Aquacade at the New York World's Fair which made it possible for you to buy a theatre and a few other knick-knacks. What if Mr. Le Maire had looked up at the ceiling instead of out of the window?

Disintegrating

According to the Bureau of Vital Statistics, I am forty-eight years of age.

That's plain silly. Somewhere along the line somebody must have picked twenty years out of my pocket. . . .

It was only a couple of years ago that I was saving the colored pictures they gave away with Sweet Caporal cigarettes. It was only a few months ago that I sat on a hard bench in a lot up in the Bronx and saw a movie of Mary Pickford in pigtails. It was only last week that

I sat in the bleachers and watched Christy Mathewson pitch for the Giants.

But my birth certificate says I'm old enough to be my own father. I demand a recount! . . .

On the tennis court, if my wife hits the ball where I ain't, instead of legging over and knocking the cover off it, I holler, "Good shot!" That doesn't mean my heart is getting tired—it's just getting tender. . . .

Suppose I do cry at the movies? That doesn't prove I'm getting old—it only means Bette Davis is getting to be a better actress. . . .

I recently threw a cemetery salesman out of my office when he asked if I'd be interested in a family plot. I told him there had been a plot in our family for years, and that was to get my sister Miriam married. . . .

On the level, do I look forty-eight to you? Don't spare my feelings. I want you to be completely frank. . . .

Thanks, pal. I didn't think so. . . .

By the way, what ever happened to Sessue Haya-kawa?

Bequeathing

For years my lawyers have been at me to draw up a last will and testament. But I've kept putting it off—sort of figured I'd be in there scratching until Gabe blew that high note.

Well, I'd better quit stalling. The other day I got caught in a traffic jam and a Boy Scout offered to help me across the street. What's more, last Saturday Eleanor belted my ears off on the tennis court, 6–0 instead of the usual 6–1.

How am I going to divvy up the loot? Well, I guess the right and proper is to leave most of it to my missus, and the rest to kinfolk and pet charities. . . . But wait a minute! It wouldn't look good if I slighted my personal piggy-bank—show business. I must leave it something. But what? . . .

I've got it. After the manner of the famous will which left the fields to small boys and the stars to lovers, I'll tack on the following codicils:

Last Will and Testament

TO LEGITIMATE THEATRES:—I leave cooling systems that don't go out when the audience comes in, and some fruit for those fresh fruit drinks.

TO AUDIENCES:—A theatre architect who knows the difference between a lobby and a telephone booth.

TO NEW HAVEN, BOSTON AND PHILADELPHIA:—A show that has first been tried out in New York.

TO STAGE UNIONS:—Time-and-a-half for all the time on every stagehand's hands.

TO TICKET-SCALPERS:—A 100 percent surplus profits tax.

TO PIT MUSICIANS:—The *Racing Form* disguised as sheet music.

TO THEATRICAL AGENTS:—An agent who will take 10 percent of their 10 percent.

TO YOUNG ACTORS AND ACTRESSES:—A law compelling producers to pick up unfamiliar scripts and audition for *them*.

TO UNDERSTUDIES:—The plagues of Egypt, to wish upon the leads an hour before curtain time.

TO SHAKESPEAREAN ACTORS:—A giant echo-chamber where they may always hear themselves chanting the Bard's iambic pentameter.

TO SHOWGIRLS:—A line of dialogue and a set of theatrical offices without divans.

TO CHORUS GIRLS:—The report of the American Wildlife Society on the preservation of the mink.

TO OSCAR HAMMERSTEIN 2ND AND RICHARD RODGERS:— Two of those fountain pens that write forever.

TO YOUNG LYRICISTS AND COMPOSERS:—The wastebaskets of Larry Hart and Jerome Kern.

TO GEORGE S. KAUFMAN:— Moss Hart's address.

TO MOSS HART:—George S. Kaufman's address.

TO GEORGE JEAN NATHAN:—William Saroyan.

TO WILLIAM SAROYAN:—William Saroyan.

TO JIMMY DURANTE:—The prayer that he never has the feeling that he wants to go and always has the feeling that he wants to stay because nobody will be with us when he's far away.

TO THE MARX BROTHERS:—Another day at the races and another night at the opera.

TO MAURICE CHEVALIER:—Fifty years' solid booking for his sinus condition.

TO BILL ROBINSON:—The hope that he never hears taps except from his own shoes.

TO AL JOLSON, ED WYNN, FANNY BRICE, BEATRICE LILLIE, FRED ALLEN, BOBBY CLARK AND WILLIE HOWARD:— Three shots of that Russian serum which makes you live a hundred and fifty years.

TO MIDTOWN RESTAURANTS:—A coffee cup that bites waiters' thumbs.

TO ORANGE JUICE STANDS:—A million customers but not on Times Square.

TO NIGHTCLUB PROPRIETORS:—Smoked glasses to keep them from going snowblind looking at white table-cloths.

TO DIALECT COMEDIANS:—A bad taste in the mouth to match the one they leave in mine.

TO CROONERS:—A season in summer stock to teach them that hands weren't made just to see if it's raining.

TO GYPSY ROSE LEE:—A G-string to replace her typewriter ribbon.

TO FEMALE IMPERSONATORS:—Testosterone.

TO 52ND STREET:—Whiskey bottles that light up and play "Ol' Man River" whenever water hits their insides.

TO WRITERS OF SINGING COMMERCIALS:—A radio.

TO QUIZ SHOWS:—A $64 question: Is the whole thing worth $64?

TO H. V. KALTENBORN:—Two minutes of silence—every two minutes.

TO NEWSREEL THEATRES:—A ten-year ban on shots of ski jumps.

TO FRENCH AND ITALIAN FILM PRODUCERS:—Bigger and better shoestrings.

TO KATHARINE HEPBURN:—More Main Line, less Party line.

TO LANA TURNER:—A jar of rubber cement for the third finger of her left hand.

TO WALTER HUSTON:—More sons.

TO JOHN HUSTON:—More fathers.

TO GRETA GARBO:—My private phone number.

TO THE CIRCUS:—Less passion and more pachyderms.

TO THE COLUMNISTS:—A *sotto voce* which has been in my family for God knows how long.

TO FUTURE WORLD FAIRS:—One of Eleanor's old bathing suits.

The Rod and Gun Club

EVERY NOW AND THEN the papers print a piece about what a great place Broadway was back in the Twenties.

Don't believe an adjective of it. Broadway during Prohibition was as glamorous as a thumb in the eye, and those of us who were mixed up in it are lucky to still be in one piece.

Before you hear it from Westbrook Pegler, let me get it into the record that I once operated a speakeasy. The Backstage Club referred to in a previous chapter sold liquor when selling liquor was illegal. Many of its customers wore .38's on their keyrings.

I was a pretty naïve kid in 1922 when I plunked down a deposit for a piece of space over a 56th Street garage. My principal contact with tough guys up to that time had been in newspapers and movies. Occasionally one of the more celebrated hoodlums had been pointed out to me in some nightclub or restaurant, but I had never met any of them socially, and had no desire to.

A few days after the Backstage Club opened, it was raided. But by the time the cops got past the iron door, we had smashed the few bottles of liquor we kept on ice in the kitchen sink. The next night there was another raid, and again we wound up with a sinkful of broken glass.

The following afternoon a gent in a gray fedora and a barbershop sunburn dropped in to see me. "I think you can use a partner," he said. "I'd like to buy twenty-five percent of the joint." He threw a packet of hundred-dollar bills on the table.

"Not so fast," I said. "Who said anything about wanting a partner?"

"Think it over," said the sunburned gent, picking up his money. "I'll be around tomorrow."

"Who is that guy?" I asked the headwaiter.

"That's Arnold Rothstein's bodyguard," he told me. "Everybody likes him, especially the cops. If he were your partner, you wouldn't have to smash your liquor every night."

That night the cops came calling for the third time.

When Gray Fedora showed up next day, I told him he had a deal. "Meet me at my lawyers," I said, "and we'll draw up the papers."

"We don't need any lawyers," said my new **partner.** "We both know how to add."

As he counted out the sum we agreed on, he flipped the bills away from him as if they were contaminated. And I guess they were. But from then on, we were never bothered by cops except when the man on the beat came up for a shot and a sandwich.

During the six months of the club's life, it wasn't unusual for one of the tommygun tycoons to walk in and announce he was going to buy a thousand dollars' worth of champagne. He would put a G-note on the table, set an empty glass on it, and keep sending wine around the room until the thousand was used up.

Knowing in their hearts they were nothing but nothings, these bums were always trying to prove they were something. And outside of the notches on their sawed-off shotguns, the only way they could prove it in those days was by throwing their money around. The night the Silver Slipper opened, they spent $60,000 at one sitting—more than it cost to build the place.

These trigger-happy slobs were vainer than any woman I ever met. As soon as one of them assault-and-battered his way into a bankroll, he would preen himself like a king's mistress. In addition to buying $200 suits in dozen lots, he would have his initials embroidered on shirts, pajamas, hankies and underpants. Togged out in his new duds, the gangster was no longer satisfied to pitch pennies in a garage or talk shop in the vat room at the brewery. All dressed up, he needed a place to glow. And the only place where he was welcome was Broadway.

I feel like rushing for the rail whenever I think of the fuss we used to make over these pistol peacocks.

Their entrance into a café was something like the Victory March of Rhadamès in *Aïda*.

When they invested in nightclubs, it wasn't only profits they were after. A gangster who owned a piece of a famous nightclub was a special fellow. He could get you a down-front table and introduce you to a pretty girl. When the Capone boys from Chicago or the Purple Mob from Detroit came to New York, he could entertain them in his own salon. Instead of being merely a hijacker, he was a host.

And it was the same kind of daffy reasoning which prompted these toughies to back shows and stock them with the Silly Sallies who played checkers with them on wintry nights. I remember one producer who had to plead with them not to put George Jean Nathan in a sack because they didn't like his review of a show they had financed.

Because they were making money so quickly, some of these pointy-heads decided they were smart businessmen. One combination took over a brewery in Brooklyn and manufactured a brand of Chipso Water called Queen's Beer. When Repeal came along, they began worrying about competition from the big pre-Volstead breweries like Ruppert's and Anheuser-Busch. And the plan they worked out to stand off this competition was a beaut.

They took every nickel they could borrow or steal—especially the latter—and began buying beer boxes. They filled block after block of warehouses with these empty crates. But to their amazement, the legitimate brewers kept right on doing business.

The combination went bankrupt, and for years its stockholders would break your arm if you mentioned wood. Poor little hoodlums—they thought they could corner the market on trees!

Another interesting angle to the vanity of these punks was their yen to be identified with their murders. It wasn't enough to leave a man face down in a ditch or build him into the West Side Highway—a little recognition was necessary. This led to some of the more imaginative killers signing their homicides much as an artist signs a painting.

An icepick between the eyes of the corpse was the identification mark of Little Ziggy of Brooklyn. The thin wire around the neck meant that Murder, Inc., was entitled to a bow. The cement overcoat was the by-line of the Jersey contingent. Some of the boys kept scrapbooks and I've heard them gripe about editors who dismissed their performances with a few lines on page two.

Of course, most of the members of the rub-out ring were a nickel phone call away from the loony bin. I once met Jack "Legs" Diamond, and he had the eyes of a man who was ready for the butterfly net. Ditto for Mad Dog Coll and a hundred others. But not all their murders were for hire. Sometimes they killed for kicks, sometimes because they were confused.

A couple of months after I opened the Backstage Club, one of these wacks almost enrolled me in the Order of the Ventilated Forehead. It happened at the Polo Grounds one afternoon when the Giants were playing the Dodgers. As I settled back in a seat behind third base, a pock-marked gent next to me said, "Whatcha thinka Heinie Groh?"

Groh was the Giants' third baseman—a smart little ballplayer who held his bat short and usually hit the ball where he wanted to.

"He's pretty good," I said.

"Whatcha mean, pretty good?" said the stranger. "Groh'sa greatest ballplayer ever put on a mitt."

"All right," I said. "Groh'sa greatest ballplayer ever put on a mitt."

"Yer from Brooklyn, ain'tcha," said the Giant fan. "I don' like guys from Brooklyn."

I decided to needle Mr. Pock Mark and root for the Dodgers. If Groh fumbled or struck out, I'd let go with the long, loud cheer so popular in the Bronx. I figured that by five o'clock my next-seat neighbor would be ready for a psychiatrist.

But I never got around to this rib. Just as the first batter stepped up to the plate, somebody hollered, "That's him!" and three plainclothesmen lunged at the Heinie Groh admirer. Two of them grabbed his arms and the third snaked a long, blue pistol out of his pocket.

The papers that night were full of the capture of the man I was going to needle. He was a free-lance bootlegger named Paul Emanuel Hilton, and he was wanted for half a dozen murders. According to the cops, he was a crackpot, and whenever he got mad or confused he started shooting. Somebody had tipped off the police that he was a Giant fan and a great admirer of Heinie Groh, and plainclothesmen had been keeping an eye on the Polo Grounds, especially the section behind third base.

That afternoon Heinie Groh struck out twice and bobbled an easy grounder. On each occasion I probably would have yelled, "Back to the bushes, you bum!" If the cops hadn't arrested Hilton, I'd have had the satisfaction of getting the loony both mad and confused. In which case, I figured to get a small red hole in my head.

In the neighborhood where the Backstage Club was located, almost every apartment house had a pigeon coop on the roof. For reasons best understood by the psychiatrists, a good part of our hoodlum population raised pigeons and spent several hours a day up among the chimney pots.

The rooftop coop was their country club and many of these seedy psychos were completely ga-ga about their fantail buddies. Barrels of beer would be lugged up and consumed while the boys discussed the proper mixtures of buckwheat and barley, the respective merits of Pouters, Jacobins and Turbits, and the efficacy of tincture of aconite in treating pigeon catarrh.

It was a believe-it-or-not to see one of these plug-uglies anoint a pigeon's feathers with olive oil, and then wash the dust out of its eyes with rosewater. If a chesty little cake-walker sneezed once too often, the owner wouldn't hesitate to chew up the mash and feed it right out of the side of his mouth. During the cold months, some of the gangsters would even sleep in the coops because they believed that the human body gave off the right kind of heat for their strutting darlings.

Sometimes these devotees of the dove put the snatch on each other's prize specimens—birdnapping, they called it. I understand that at least fifteen deaths, listed in precinct-house records as accidental, resulted from one pigeon impresario nudging another off a roof.

I remember hearing a tender love story about one of these bums who owned four hundred birds. One day he got stuck on a chorus girl, but when he proposed, she said, "No thanks. I'm not spending my honeymoon up on the roof. It's either me or the pigeons."

The night of the wedding the bum went up on the roof for the last time. He couldn't stand the idea of another pair of mitts fondling his flock. He opened the door of the coop, lifted out a pigeon, and brushed it softly against his five-o'clock shadow.

"Goodbye, Gwendolyn," he whispered.

He twisted its neck and dropped it in a barrel. The

bum did this 399 more times. Then he went downstairs and climbed into his tux.

Besides this passion for pigeons, many of the hoodlums had a passion for singing. Their favorite entertainers were the minstrels who sang about home and mother. Some of them went a step further and did some plain and fancy yodeling themselves.

The tommy-gun tenor I particularly remember was a Chicago bootlegger named Jerry Dugan. I got to know him in a funny way. His favorite song was a bawdyhouse ballad called "Tonight You Belong to Me," and when he learned I had written it, he buddied up to me. He would hang out at the Backstage Club whenever he was in New York and the size of his tab depended on how often we let him sing with the band.

By shooting first and asking questions later, Jerry managed to live through Prohibition. I lost sight of him until a few years ago when I stopped off in Chicago on my way to the Coast. In the lobby of the Morrison Hotel, I saw him flanked by a couple of heavy-set gents.

"Hello, Jerry," I said. "How goes it?"

"Not so good," he said. "I'm on my way to Leavenworth to do a fifteen-year stretch."

"What did they get you for?" I asked.

"I socked a reporter."

"Fifteen years for that?"

"Not exactly," said Jerry. "They pinned an old homicide rap on me. But hitting the reporter was what brought it out of the files."

"Why did you hit him?" I asked.

"He snapped my picture as I was coming out of a movie theater," said Jerry. "Naturally, publicity isn't any good for a guy in my racket, and so I broke his camera and roughed him up a little. When the newspaper boys found out about it, they went to work on me and never let up."

One of the detectives looked at his watch. "We'll have to get going, Jerry," he said apologetically.

Dugan is still in Leavenworth. He wrote me recently that he still sings my song at the prison concert every year.

A few months after the Backstage Club opened, something happened which made me decide to get out while the getting was good. One night Waxey Gordon was entertaining some business associates. A harmless drunk stopped at his table and passed some remark. The heavy-set Waxey drove his knee into the drunk's stomach, and then proceeded to give him what is known as "the boots." This consists of driving the heel into a man's face and head, and kicking him in other tender parts of the anatomy.

I watched Waxey kick this man's face until there was practically no face left. Then I went into the kitchen and bawled like a baby. Next day I unloaded my interest in the club.

It wasn't until 1933 that I again got mixed up with the broken-fingernail set. One day a dress-goods manufacturer sent for me and said he represented a group of gentlemen who were interested in financing a nightclub. They had rented a theatre on West 54th Street and wanted to know whether I was available to stage the shows there.

As he talked, I got a notion. It was to combine a theatre, restaurant, and dance hall, and merchandise this three-in-one package at a price within range of the average purse.

When I asked who the other interested gentlemen were, he said the usual things about their being fine fellows and having plenty of money.

"What mob are you fronting for?" I finally asked him.
He admitted he represented a newly formed beer company which was looking for a prestige spot in which to promote its product.

I told him I would take the job, but only under certain conditions. First, the mob was to have nothing to do with the operation of the place. Second, they were not to interfere with rehearsals. And third, if there was any rough stuff after we opened, they'd have to get themselves another boy. The front man agreed to these stipulations, and next day they were incorporated in a carefully drawn-up contract.

On opening day, one of the hoodlums came to me and confessed that his combination hadn't been able to procure a liquor license—Police Commissioner Mulrooney didn't think well of the applicants and wasn't susceptible to Tammany pressure. I put on my hat and went down to Mulrooney's office.

"Who are these partners of yours?" asked the Commissioner.

"They're not my partners," I said, "I'm working on straight salary."

"What do you know about them?" asked Mulrooney.

"They're tough guys," I said, "and I think the Department has pictures of their thumbs."

Mulrooney smiled. "At least you're not lying," he said.

"I've got a contract to operate the place," I went on, "and as long as I run it, it will be a square joint."

"Okay," said Mulrooney. "I'll let you have a license."

And it was a square joint until I went to Europe the following summer for a vacation. During the six weeks I was gone, the dress manufacturer developed a Reinhardt complex and restaged the show. He fired Benny Goodman's band and let out Eleanor Powell because he didn't think she was worth $200 a week. When a representative of a new vaudeville union went backstage to organize the actors, he was kicked unconscious by one of the mob.

When I got back from Europe, I insisted on an immediate pow-wow with the backers. Walter Winchell was with me when I met them at 3 A.M. in the office over the café.

"You guys have broken my contract," I said. "It specifically states you are not to interfere with the operation."

The natty little Italian who headed the mob spoke up. "I wouldn't depend on that contract if I were you. While you were in Europe, I shot out most of the clauses."

"I'm pulling out," I said, "and I'm going to tell the papers I'm no longer connected with the joint."

"You're talking pretty big," said one of the boys. "Somebody might get sore and cut you down to size."

It was 5 A.M. when Winchell dropped me off at my house. I picked up the phone, called Mr. Baruch, and told him what had happened.

"Don't leave your apartment," he said. "I'm going to call Attorney General Cummings."

At 9 o'clock my bell rang and I let in three FBI men. I gave them the names and addresses of the men who had threatened me.

"Stay here until we get back," they advised.

At 3 that afternoon they returned. "Go about your business," they told me. "Nobody will bother you."

"What happened?" I asked.

"Nothing much," said one of the G-men. "We rounded up the boys, told them what the score was, and warned them that if you as much as slipped on a banana peel, it would be just too bad for them."

Months later I met one of the mob coming out of Dinty Moore's. "That wasn't nice," he said, "reporting us to the Feds."

"What did you expect me to do?" I asked him. "Wait around for one of your fifty-dollar punks to kick my head full of fog?"

"I guess you got a point," he said as he walked away.

A few months later I again came close to having my face air-conditioned. Late one night, Leonard Lyons and I were bisecting a blintz at Dave's Blue Room. The door opened and a gent with half a load on walked in. He was togged out in a camel's hair coat that the fussiest dromedary would be proud to wear. As he passed our table, he noticed I was staring at him.

"Whatcha lookin' at?" he snarled.

"I was admiring your coat," I said.

"Ya know somethin'?" said the drunk. "I don't think I like ya."

"Well, that's the end of a beautiful friendship," I said. "Why don't you run along, junior? This part of the room is reserved for grownups."

Suddenly Lyons yanked me to my feet and hustled me out the front door into a taxi. "Drive through the Park," he told the cabbie.

"What's the big hurry?" I asked the columnist.

"The fellow you were getting gay with," said Lenny, "is Pretty Boy Amberg."

"Step on it," I said to the cabbie.

"Amberg likes to do 'em up brown," the columnist went on. "After disabling a victim, he usually puts him in a car, pours kerosene on the floor, and throws in a match."

"It's a little hot in here," I said to Lyons as the cab stopped for a light. "Would you mind opening the windows?"

Lenny chuckled. "They're both open," he said.

The following year a nightclub owner in Chicago wanted me to produce a show for his cabaret. He asked me to come out and talk to him about it. I took a scenic designer named Clark Robinson with me.

Clark was mucho hombre. In World War I, he flew those wax-paper and chicken-wire planes. In World War II, despite a little snow around the temples, he flew again. This time he wasn't so lucky and was killed in a crash in India. Between wars, he designed a couple of Music Box Revues and most of the grandish scenery at the Old Roxy.

On the way to Chicago we stopped at Detroit, where a road show of mine was playing. My manager turned over the month's profits, about three grand, and I struck the bills in my cigarette case. I remember there was an usher in the office when the manager passed me the loot.

We got into Chicago about 5 in the afternoon, and I asked the hotel clerk to stash the three grand and the cigarette case in the vault. After dinner, Clark and I strolled over to see the cabaret owner. No deal. It wasn't much of a place and less of a proposition. Besides, I didn't fancy the assortment of broken noses at the ringside tables.

It was around midnight when we got back to the hotel. On the way to the elevators, I picked up the morning papers. Upstairs, I put the key in the door and opened it. The room smelled like an all-night card game. As Clark flipped the wall switch, a voice said, "Stick 'em up or I'll kill you."

There were two guys in our room, a stringbeanish gent with a handkerchief hiding his face, and a smallish character who looked as if he had never owned a handkerchief. The little one had the pistol—a big, ugly Luger. The floor was a mess of cigarette butts—the thugs had apparently been waiting for a couple of hours.

Clark chuckled. "You lads have been seeing too many movies," he said.

"Shut up," I said to the designer. I was afraid Clark might start throwing knuckles, and I knew knuckles weren't much good against a Luger.

"Hand over the cigarette case," ordered Handkerchief-on-the-Face. The usher at the Detroit theatre had obviously put the finger on me.

"It's in the vault downstairs," I croaked. "Want me to phone for it?"

"No phone calls," said the geezer with the gun. "Search them."

The big guy gave us a quick frisk. Between us we had twenty-four dollars and a gold watch they didn't want because it was monogrammed.

"That's malarkey about the vault," said Handkerchief-on-the-Face. "Maybe a bust in the head might help Rose remember where he bunked the case."

Out of fright I started talking. "I'd go easy on the rough stuff," I said. "I know a lot of fellows in this town, and they wouldn't like it if I got hurt."

"Who do you know?" asked the smallish character.

"Dion O'Banion," I said, picking a name out of deep left field. "If anything happens to me, his boys will go looking for you tonight."

The hoods looked at each other, and Dion O'Banion would have been proud of the weight his name carried. "Lay face-down on the bed," ordered the string-beanish gent.

We did. Again Clark chuckled. "Please," I whispered to him, "don't be brave."

The tall fellow took a roll of adhesive out of his pocket and taped us up. While he was putting on the adhesive, his partner was slamming bureau drawers and pawing over our luggage. Then the door quietly closed.

When we kicked free, I grabbed the phone and hollered for the cops. Clark eased off his shoes and picked up the morning papers I had dropped when I reached for the ceiling. For the third time he chuckled.

"What's so funny?" I asked.

Clark held up the front page. The big black headlines read:

ST. VALENTINE'S DAY MASSACRE
O'BANION MOB MACHINE-GUNNED
IN NORTH SIDE GARAGE

We caught a plane out at 4 that morning. For the next five years, when I had business on the Coast, I went by way of Texas. I wouldn't even fly over Chicago.

Around 1935, the New York tough guys began to run. They were running from a man with a little mustache. When Tom Dewey sent Lucky Luciano to prison, the gangsters realized they were up against a prosecutor they couldn't get to. And they couldn't get to a new mayor named Fiorello La Guardia either. I remember one of them telling me, "Do you know somethin'? If you took a wagonload of money down to City Hall, that little son of a gun would lock you up."

Encouraged by this exhibition of biceps, operators began opening nightclubs without hoodlum backing. The day after I opened the Diamond Horseshoe, an important mobster got me on the phone. He told me he stood ready to swap his influence and protection for a fifty percent interest in my club, and wanted to know where he could see me the following day.

"Tom Dewey's office at 12 o'clock," I purred. . . .

I didn't cross swords or paths with a tough guy again until 1939, when I was putting on the New York Aquacade. Out at the Fair Grounds I discovered that several of the contractors were former booze-and-bullet salesmen who had muscled into legitimate businesses after Repeal.

I had two choices. I could do business with these contractors, or I could spend the summer at Coney Island. And so, like everyone else on the Midway, I did business with them.

One of these contractors was a gent named Nicky Tullio, and he was as nice to have around as a black-widow spider.

The day before the Fair opened, he handed me a bill for $22,000. The job his men had done rated a zero less, but I gave him a check and got the bill stamped "Paid."

A week after we opened, Tullio walked into my office and handed me another bill for $15,000.

"What's that for?" I asked.

"Overtime and busted tools," he said.

"You see that big swimming pool down there?" I said. "Why don't you jump in and hand the crowd a laugh?"

"Very funny joke," said Nicky. "I'll see you again in a month. I think your show's going to make a lot of money, and maybe you'll feel different."

One evening a month later, I was hanging around the main entrance to the Aquacade with a friend of mine from Washington. He had come up to take a look at my show. We were standing there talking when I felt a tap on the elbow. It was Tullio. I asked my friend from Washington to pardon me and turned around to talk to Nicky.

"Understand your show's a big hit," he said. "How about the fifteen grand you owe me?"

"I don't owe you a thing," I said.

"I say you do," said Nicky, "and if you're a smart guy, you'll pay up and save yourself a lot of trouble. Don't forget I know where to find you."

My friend from Washington stepped up behind Nicky, swung him around and said, "Don't forget I know where to find you, Mr. Tullio."

Nicky hasn't bothered me in the past nine years. The friend who had come up from Washington to see my show was a gentleman named John Edgar Hoover.

No sirree, I can't go along with the nostalgic nonsense about the Twenties being the good old days on Broadway.

These are the good old days.

Clowns in Clover

UP TO THE TIME I was forty, my interest in trees was restricted to the ones that kept my shoes in shape.

One Sunday afternoon as we were walking through Central Park, Eleanor said, "Aren't those white birches pretty! How would you like to own some of them?"

"I would," I said, "if I were a lumber company. Why do you ask?"

"You'll find out," said my missus.

When we got back to the house, Eleanor said, "Hand me the real estate section of the *Tribune.* We're buying a place in the country."

"Not with my dough," I said. "Sunshine is for apricots."

The following Saturday I found myself sandwiched in a car, Eleanor on my right and two hundred pounds of real-estate agent on my left.

"What kind of place are you looking for?" asked the agent.

"About five rooms and an acre of garden," said my frau.

"None of that chicken-coop stuff for me," I said. "I want plenty of house and plenty of acres."

"Don't pay any attention to him," said Eleanor. "He likes elephants—even white ones."

The first place the agent showed us was the Walter Chrysler mansion on Long Island. It had a pipe organ in the living room. "This is something like," I said.

"Easy, Junior," said my missus. "We're looking for a home, not an Aquacade."

Eleanor fancied the next house we looked at. It was one of those clapboard bungalow jobs that are hot in the summer and cold in the winter.

"No dice," I said. "I'm not going to live in a bread-box."

Next week-end we inspected the Jacob Ruppert estate in Garrison, New York. The brewer had built himself a Nuremberg castle overlooking the Hudson. The estate featured a windmill, a suspension bridge over a hundred-foot stream and a complete menagerie like the one at Bronx Park.

"I'll settle for this," I said.

"How much meat does a lion eat?" asked Eleanor.

"About twenty pounds a day."

"Get into the car before I break your arm," said my spouse.

A hundred estates later, we came to the Schiffer place in Mt. Kisco. As we drove up the private road lined with pink and white dogwood, I got the feeling that this was the layout I had dreamed of when I was a kid on the East Side. But when we got to the big Georgian house and its white columns, Eleanor wouldn't even get out of the car.

"You're not saddling me with this," she said.

A caretaker showed me through. It was story-book stuff—full of eighteenth-century English furniture, and comfortable as an old slipper.

I went back to the car. "I'd look at it if I were you," I said to Eleanor. "If it isn't too rich for my blood, I'm going to buy it."

Just then Mr. Schiffer drove up. "How do you like the house?" he asked.

"I'm nuts about it," I said. "It's the most beautiful home I've seen in several months of looking."

"If you like it that much," said Mr. Schiffer, "you ought to own it. I'm selling it only because my children are married, and it's too much house to live in alone."

Mr. Schiffer told me how much he was asking for the place. It was four times more than I could spend and I told him so.

"Let me think about it over the week-end," he said. "Everybody who has seen the place so far has been cagey. You're the first person who has said nice things about it. That means a great deal to me because it took me twenty years to put it together."

Monday, Mr. Schiffer phoned and said he had decided to let me have the estate at my price. Two weeks later I took title.

Eleanor hardly talked to me during that fortnight. But a few days after we moved in, she handed me a present and said, "I was wrong, Pop. I'm as daffy about the place as you are."

That was the first and last time in our ten years together that my missus admitted she was wrong about anything."

"What'll we call the place?" I asked her.

"Let's put our names together and call it 'Roseholm,'" said Eleanor. "I'll give you top billing."

" 'Roseholm,' " I mused. "A little formal, isn't it? It sounds like knee breeches and a powdered wig."

"No use arguing," said Eleanor. "I've already ordered the sign."

"Now that that's settled," I said, "what's our next problem?"

"The walls," said my frau. "The ninety-six walls. What are we going to hang on them?"

I had three dandy suggestions—(a) railroad calendars, (b) paper them with old crackerjack boxes, (c) rent space to advertising agencies.

"Don't make bum jokes about our home," scolded Eleanor. "How about some modern paintings?"

"Too expensive," I said. "Besides, I don't want to wake up and look at a codfish playing the accordion."

"Well, then, let's do the house in reproductions," said Eleanor. "For ninety-eight cents up to twenty bucks, we can have our pick of cardboard masterpieces from Giorgione to Grant Wood."

"At least the price is right," I said.

Well, by the end of the summer, Roseholm looked like a wing of the National Gallery. Baby and I were breakfasting with Breughel and dining with Degas. And the total bill came to less than the cost of one original of a three-headed tootsie with an alarm clock in her tummy.

One afternoon a Broadway producer dropped in on us unexpectedly. This gent doesn't like me. He has me tabbed as one of those corny individuals who think this country is a pretty good place. I wouldn't call him a Commie, but if he doesn't get a check from Moscow every week, he's being robbed. You know the type: He signals the waiter and says, "Comrade, take back this lousy guinea hen under glass and tell our comrade, the chef, what he can do with it."

When the producer walked into the hall, he did a

double as he saw the Van Gogh reproductions. Having
read that I owned a few good pictures in town, he assumed the stuff in the country was the McCoy. As he
looked around my living room, I could read the first
three paragraphs of the Communist Manifesto in his
eyes.

"Only you," he snarled, "would have eight Renoirs
hanging in one room!"

I didn't know what to do. Should I kid him about not
knowing the difference between printing and painting?
Or should I keep mum and let him think I was a dirty
capitalist?

"Wait," I said, "and I'll get you a drink."

I found Eleanor and told her my problem. "Be a little gentleman," she said. "Say nothing till the bum
starts tripping over our furniture. Then throw him out."

Unfortunately, the pinko didn't drinko. When he left
an hour later, he hadn't tripped once. To this day, I'm
sure he thinks the makeshift masterpieces on my walls
are worth a million dollars. But it's a good thing for the
gentleman's blood pressure that he didn't see the maid's
room where I keep my Rembrandts.

After the producer had stomped out, I suggested to
Eleanor that we go to the village for a chocolate soda.
"I want to get that red taste out of my mouth," I said.

On the way back from Mt. Kisco, Eleanor said, "I
wish you'd learn how to drive. Every time you want
something, somebody's got to stop what he's doing and
chauffeur you into the village."

"Okay," I said, "if you'll play teacher."

Next morning I crawled into the car beside Eleanor.
"Just turn this jigger over," she began, "push in this
dingus, pull out this doohickey, step on this wing-
doodle, press down on this thingamabob, and you're
all set to go."

"What's this gizmo?" I asked.

"The hand brake," she said. "You throw it on quickly in case of emergency."

"What happens if the brakes don't work?"

"Hit something cheap," advised my spouse.

A moment later the car went hiccuping down the road. Then for a mile it went smooth as you please. A feeling of confidence came over me, the same feeling all new drivers get just before the lights go out. I pressed down on the gas.

"The pistons seem to be knocking," I said professionally.

"Pistons nothing," said Eleanor. "Those are my knees."

Everything went fine until we got to the traffic light in the village. I forgot to press the hickeymadoodle on the gilhooley, and the car stalled. The lights changed from green to red, and from red back to green. A cop came over.

"What's the matter?" he asked. "Haven't we got any colors you like?"

After switching the radio on and off, I suddenly pressed the right thing. In the order of the way it happened, I grazed the cop, skidded through the safety zone, clipped the fender on a bus, and came to rest with my bumper against a fire plug. The cop stalked over. He took a handkerchief out of his pocket and dropped it in front of the car.

"Lookit, Gene Autry," he said. "I wanna see you do that all over again, and this time pick up the handkerchief with your teeth."

Eleanor gave him the big smile. "He's learning to drive," she said.

"No kidding!" said the cop. "How long is this class going to last? Some other drivers would like to use this road when Sonny Boy gets through with it."

"What did I do wrong?" I asked the officer.

"Didn't you hear my whistle? Didn't you see my signal?" he demanded.

I shook my head.

The cop sighed. "I'd better go home. I don't seem to be doing much good around here."

I threw the car into reverse and backed away from the fire plug.

"If you're going to drive much," yelled the cop, "I'd have the car painted red on one side and blue on the other, so the witnesses will contradict each other."

"What kind of cops do they have in Mt. Kisco?" I asked Eleanor as we headed for home.

"I wouldn't know," she deadpanned. "Maybe he's Milton Berle's brother."

There are two stone posts flanking the drive which leads up to Roseholm. I got past them without a scratch —also without the rear bumper. That did it.

Since then, I've never been behind a wheel. When we go driving, I sit in the back seat and read the Burma Shave signs. The only concession I've made to the Automotive Age is to learn how to fold a road map.

Speaking of road maps, one of these days I'm going to send out for two weeks' provisions and learn how to read one. At least a dozen times since we've been summering in Mt. Kisco, I've found myself in a car with a fellow who (a) knew short-cuts, and (b) wouldn't ask directions.

About a year after we opened Roseholm, Eleanor and I were invited to a wedding at New Hope, Pennsylvania. Bernie Hart, who was spending the week-end with us, offered to drive.

We started out about 10:30 in the morning. Outside of New Brunswick, New Jersey, we came to one of those every-which-way traffic circles.

"There's the sign," said Eleanor. "Turn left."

Bernie swung right. "I know a short-cut," he said. "I've got a road map in my head."

"I don't doubt it," said my missus, "but it's awfully dark in there."

We went through an underpass, crossed a railroad and, after a couple of miles, hit a dirt road which would have shaken the Siamese Twins apart.

"Are those our springs," asked Eleanor, "or am I hearing jungle drums?"

The dirt road petered out and we found ourselves in a pasture. I spotted a farmer and went over to him. "How do we get to New Hope?" I asked him.

The farmer pondered. "If I was going to New Hope," he finally said, "I wouldn't start from here at all."

As I walked back to the car, Bernie was holding a wet forefinger up to the wind. "I've got my bearings now," he said.

After another half-hour of flying blind, we finally saw some houses. "See?" crowed Bernie. "We're coming to a town."

We passed the local firehouse. By threatening him with a tire iron, I got Bernie to stop. A fireman came out of the building and looked us over.

"If ya got a fire, won't do ya no good," he said. "Chief's got the engine out tractorin'!"

As we drove off, Eleanor yelled, "Please notify the Bureau of Missing Persons. When last seen, Mr. Rose was wearing a desperate look."

Around 3 o'clock we came to a city. "Amazing what standardization has done to the American town," I said. "This place looks just like New Brunswick."

"Standardization your grandmother," said Eleanor. "This *is* New Brunswick."

Several turns later, we passed a State Trooper. "We want to go to New Hope," I hollered.

"You have my permission," grinned the cop.

"How far is it?" I asked.

"The way you're going, 24,960 miles. Forty, if you turn around."

"Milton Berle must have a lot of brothers," I told Eleanor.

I looked at my watch. It was almost 4 P.M. I knew the ancient words had been spoken, the bride kissed, and the punch bowl emptied.

A sign shaped like an arrow loomed up. "To New York," it read. Well, I can take a hint as well as the next fellow.

It was getting dark when we stopped to pay toll at the Holland Tunnel. As I handed my four bits to the officer I said, "As far as I'm concerned, you can close the border to immigration."

When we got back to Roseholm, we found our week-end guests had guests. Half a dozen couples had driven up from New York and the gang was on its fourth pitcher of Martinis.

"Don't start crabbing," said Eleanor. "Everybody's having a good time."

I had a bite in the kitchen and went up to my room. After my trip with Bernie Hart, I was in no mood to listen to a lot of alcoholic jabberwocky.

Why didn't I join the crowd and have a few drinks? For two good reasons. First, hard liquor tastes to me like something you take for the grippe. Second, I've been selling it in my nightclubs for years, and taking on a cargo of lightning bugs has no glamour for me. It would be like a soda jerk going on a walnut sundae binge.

But before the Anti-Saloon League sends around that long, white ribbon, let me say I don't object to other people drinking. There's only one drink at which I draw the line. That's the Martini.

Scotch and soda is a lullaby that puts you to sleep in easy stages. The Martini is a baseball bat to the base of the skull. Eight ounces, and dowagers do the bumps.

This yellow mixture had spoiled my first two summers at Mt. Kisco. Our week-end guests had been witty and civilized folk, and I had enjoyed their company very much—during the day. But around 7 P.M., these arthritic athletes would come off the tennis court and congregate in the game room for what they called "Happy Cocktail Hour." Eleanor, always the good hostess, would have a big pitcher of Martinis waiting.

During the first couple of drinks, everybody would have a good time, including me. And then—whammo! Martini number three would take hold. From then on, everyone would have a good time, excluding me.

By the time we hit the dinner table at 9, our guests would be more bleary than bright. And for the rest of the evening, I'd be the sober little guy in the corner everybody felt sorry for.

"Once and for all, I've got to slug it out with Mr. Martini," I said to myself. And the following summer I did.

I started by holding a stop-watch on my guests. Few of them consumed more than two Martinis the first hour. I realized that if I could throw some hot soup into them before they buddied up to the third Martini, everything would be all right. The problem was how to get my guests to the dinner table an hour earlier.

The plan I finally evolved darn near broke me. It was to build a small movie theatre and substitute Ginger Rogers for gin, Veronica Lake for vermouth and Olivier for the olive. This meant ripping the stalls out of the stable, bringing in half a mile of electric cable, building an asbestos booth, buying a couple of projectors, and bulldozing the film companies out of their new pictures. I finally finished it late in July, and George Jessel christened it "Loew's Rose."

If peace of mind is worth anything, the theatre paid for itself the first month. The day it opened, I casually remarked at lunch, "We're showing the new Bing Crosby movie tonight. We'll have to start dinner early because the operator lives in Mt. Vernon."

Nobody squawked. And so, instead of sitting down at 9 with a bunch of howling hooligans, I picked up my soup spoon at 8 in the company of reasonably reasonable people. Marc Connelly was there that evening, and it was nice to hear him talk like Marc Connelly.

And it's been that way for the past seven summers. After the movies, the guests usually come back to the game room. And if they feel like a Martini, it's all right with me. My bedroom is on the other side of the house.

In the summer of 1943 I played another trick on my guests. But this one was for flag and country.

That spring, the Department of Agriculture had appealed to all large-scale users of food to plant Victory gardens. This included me, on account of because I owned the Diamond Horseshoe.

When I told Eleanor, she was all for it and immediately had Hattie Carnegie run her up a pair of overalls. I had once raised some geraniums in a window-box on 54th Street, and figured farming was pretty much the same thing, only more of it. The only skeptic was the farmer who takes care of my place.

"I hope you know what you're letting yourself in for," he warned me.

At the local hardware store I picked up one of Mr. Burpee's seed catalogues, illustrated with pictures of pumpkins big as Cinderella's coach and lima beans the size of footballs.

The day after we planted the seeds, I got up early

and went out to look at my garden. Nothing. Next day, likewise.

When the first bit of green peeked out of the ground, Eleanor had to stop me from pulling it up and pressing it between the pages of my diary. When the first green button appeared on a tomato plant, I began inquiring about the nearest county fair. I could hardly wait for what was going to come up.

What came up was Japanese beetles. I went after the shiny monsters with insecticide, but they lapped it up and looked around for a chaser.

In spite of hell and no water, the stuff began to ripen. I was especially proud of the cabbages. "So round, so firm, so fully packed," I told the boys at Lindy's.

One morning, Eleanor told me I'd have to hire some hands to pick the crop. I ran an ad in the White Plains paper, but no migratory workers showed up. I guess they were all busy telling their experiences to John Steinbeck.

Just as the crop was ready to be picked, I got a brain wave. "We clutter up the house every week-end with guests," I told Eleanor. "Let's make them work for their keep."

And, brother, they did. Every Friday night, after throwing a big meal into them, my missus would ad lib, "I've got a cute idea. Let's get up early tomorrow and pick vegetables."

Next morning, while the sun was still snoring, the guests would be herded into the fields. And what a sight it was. Guys like Jimmy Stewart and Orson Welles wound up with blisters as big as the electric lights which spell out their names. Moss Hart, Max Gordon, Lou Holtz—these palefaces had never picked up a tomato without whistling at her first. And the mosquitoes which bit them generally lost blood on the deal.

That summer my garden was the conversational tidbit around Broadway. George Jessel described it as a place where "the sparrows had to kneel down to eat the corn." Quentin Reynolds spread it around that I had to lather the fields with shaving soap before I could cut the wheat. Ed Wynn reached back and came up with the one about some of my potatoes being as big as marbles, others as big as peas—and then there were the little ones.

Actually, we raised enough stuff on fifteen acres to keep my nightclub in fresh vegetables all that fall. The combination salad I sold for ninety cents may have cost four bucks to raise, but I figured it was worth it when I thought of the manicured fingernails I had helped ruin.

Since then, I haven't had much ear-time for fellows who tell jokes about farmers. In my book, anyone who can produce things to eat at a profit rates with Einstein and Houdini.

Max Dreyfus, the music publisher, agrees with me. He has a dairy farm not far from Roseholm. Recently I dropped in to see him.

"How about a drink?" he suggested.

"Fine with me," I said.

"What'll it be," he asked, "milk or champagne? They both cost me the same."

When we first moved up to Mt. Kisco, some of our neighbors dropped by to pay their respects. I didn't encourage these visits. The landed gentry of Westchester are nice enough folk, but they don't talk my lingo. Besides, I see no point in cultivating people who think it's smart to chase a fox.

But a little down the road from us live a couple I cultivate as often as they'll have me. Their names are Fred and Jane Newell. I met them through Eleanor two years ago, and I'll never forget the first night we had dinner at their house.

Jane answered the doorbell. She was pretty all over, and I liked her right away. "Excuse the peasant skirt," she said. "I have a baby penciled in for the fall."

Fred was in the living room listening to the radio. He had the tweedy look of the good guy in the women's magazine stories. We talked for a couple of minutes before I realized he was blind. He told me he was a writer, and answered my unspoken question by explaining he dictated his stuff to his wife.

It was a fine dinner and a fine evening. Jane carried her child as if baby-having were some kind of party. Around 11 o'clock, Fred said to Jane, "Maybe the Roses would like some ice cream."

"Maybe they would," said Jane, "but we haven't any. I'll drive down to the village and get some."

"I'll go with you," I said, "just to make sure you don't forget chocolate."

On the way to the ice-cream parlor I said, "Tell me something. What makes you kids act as if you had a gold mine in the cellar?"

Jane smiled. "I don't know. I guess we've been pretty lucky."

"Lucky!" I said, and then stopped, embarrassed.

"It's all right," said Jane. "Of course, it would be nicer if Fred could see, but neither of us thinks that's very important."

"How'd it happen?"

"War stuff," said Jane. "Fragments of a land mine on Okinawa. We weren't married then. Fred was moved to a hospital in San Francisco. The first few letters he sent me weren't in his own handwriting. He explained that he was dictating to a nurse because he'd been wounded in the right hand.

"At the time, he still had some hope that a special operation might restore his sight. He didn't want to tell me about his eyes until he knew for sure.

"Well, the operation was a complete miss-out. When Fred knew he'd never see again, the darn fool wrote me that I was free to marry anybody I liked. Of course, I hopped a plane to San Francisco and got my fella."

"Atta girl," I said. "Now tell me to shut my face if I'm out of line, but doesn't it ever bother you—I mean, making this sacrifice?"

"Sacrifice, my foot," said Jane softly. "Look at it this way. I'm two years away from thirty. In ten years, I'll be two away from forty. When Fred went off to war, I was twenty-three. Real roses in the cheeks. Probably the best I ever looked in my life.

"From here in, no matter what happens to me— wrinkles, dry skin, gray hairs, babies—Fred will always see me as the fresh-faced kid he kissed goodbye at Penn Station in '42. For the guy I'm crazy about, I'll be twenty-three the rest of my life. Is that bad?"

"No," I said. "That isn't bad at all."

The day after we dined with the Newells, Ben Hecht telephoned me. "Gene Fowler is in town," he said, "and so is Jimmy Durante. Why don't you invite the three of us up for the week-end?"

"Consider yourselves invited," I said.

When I told Eleanor who was coming, she said, "Wire them we've gone to South America. Those professional katzenjammer kids will tear this house down, brick by brick."

"You've been reading their press releases of twenty years ago," I said. "Relax. They're old parties now."

When the boys came up late that Friday evening, I said, "What's your pleasure, gentlemen? What would you like to do tomorrow?"

"I'd like to go fishing," said Hecht.

"There's a pond about a mile from the house," I said.

"We're not interested in minnows," said Fowler. "Ben is talking about deep-sea fishing."

"But we're two hours from the ocean," I said.

"Well then, let's go to sleep early," said Ben. "We'll get up at three, drive to Long Island and rent a boat there."

Next morning, we had to pull the sheets from under Durante to wake him. On the way to the garage, I noticed he was smacking every tree he passed. "When I'm awake," Schnozzola explained, "no boid sleeps."

At Bay Shore we chartered a boat and tackle from a blood relative of Captain Kidd. Ben elected himself captain and took the wheel. Fowler, who knew how to bait a hook without laying open his thumb, took care of the tackle. Durant fished a deck of cards out of his pocket and the two of us started a game of nickel casino. A mile out, I began to lose interest in the cards. Maybe it was the four seasickness remedies I had taken. I looked at Jimmy's famous nose. It had turned a delicate shade of chartreuse.

"Can I get you anything?" I asked him.

"Yeah, an island," he moaned.

Three miles out, Fowler asked if I wanted to cut up some clams for bait. I shook my head. Then I stopped—but my head kept shaking. I stretched out in the bottom of the boat and Jimmy joined me.

Fowler looked up from the bait cans. "Don't worry," he said. "Nobody ever died of seasickness."

"Don' say dat," croaked Durante. "Oney da hope a' dyin' is keepin' me alive."

We putt-putted until I figured we were off the coast of France. Then we dropped anchor and the boys began to fish. An hour later Durante looked up long enough to say, "If dey're bitin' today, dey mus' be bitin' each udder."

Again we putt-putted and again we stopped. "Time to eat," said Hecht. He and Gene went to work on a liverwurst which looked like a policeman's club. Durante paled. I closed my eyes. When I opened them, Fowler was wolfing a dill pickle. I closed them again.

"Look! There's the *Queen Elizabeth!*" yelled Ben.

"Call me when ya see a bus," gasped Durante.

After lunch, the boys started fishing again. That's what they called it. Bait-drowning would be more accurate. Late in the afternoon, Jimmy and I got steady enough to take rods.

"Get in dere an' fight," Durante told his bait as he dropped it in the water.

A second later he screeched, "I godda bite!" He cranked away as if he had Moby Dick on the line. He brought up a little fish and kept reeling until it was at the tip of his pole. "Whaddo I do now?" he hollered.

Fowler looked thoughtful. "You might climb up the rod and strangle it to death," he suggested.

The fish flopped itself off the hook and dropped back in. Hecht was disgusted. "Where did you learn how to fish?" he sneered.

"Venice," said Durante, "where dey fish oudda da windows."

"There's nothing around here," said Fowler an hour later. "Let's go out further and try for sharks."

"*Why?*" I screamed.

Nobody could think of an answer, so we headed back. When we got to the pier, Durante and I knelt and kissed the planks.

On the way home, we stopped at a fish store. Jimmy bought six flounders. Then he asked the proprietor to throw them at him one at a time.

"What's the big idea?" asked the fish store man.

"I promised my wife I'd catch her some fish," flipped Schnozzola, "an' I don' believe in lyin' to da missus. Hink-a-dink-a-doo. . . ."

As I write this, my calendar tells me it's April 29th. In a few days, Eleanor and I will lock up our little house on the East River and move to Mt. Kisco for the summer. And I can hardly wait.

The kick I get out of tramping around my own land is something only another kid who was raised in the dust and thunder of an East Side slum can understand. My trees, lawn, gardens, bridle paths—the road map says they're forty miles from the cold-water flat where I was born. But the road map doesn't know what it's talking about. The distance is more like forty million.

Many a night Eleanor and I have taken the long walk to the movie theatre in our stables. As we strolled past boxwood hedges and banks of rhododendron, I've often asked myself, "What are you doing here? Don't you know this setup was intended for people with long, thin faces and stylish ancestors? Better watch yourself. Any minute now, a guy with a badge is going to pop out from behind a tree and chase you and the fire chief's daughter off the grass."

Many a night I've sat on the edge of the pool and watched Eleanor swim by moonlight. "He might chase you," I've mumbled, "but he's certainly not going to chase her. No Whitney or Vanderbilt ever looked that good in a swimming pool."

Many a night Eleanor and I have sat out on the porch and heard our guests laughing in the game room—laughing the way you're not supposed to laugh in Georgian houses with white columns. Quentin Reynolds, the writer; Lou Holtz, the vaudevillian; Deems Taylor, the composer; Gordon Carroll, the editor; and Benny Goodman, the clarinet player—clowns in clover—all of us a generation or two removed from another kind of world.

Last fall, Eleanor and I rented a couple of horses and took some riding lessons. This summer we're planning to make a regular thing of it. Had anyone prophesied this thirty years ago, I would have thought he was kidding. In my neighborhood, a horse was something that wore a straw hat over its ears and pulled a wagon.

Wouldn't it be a nice twist if I were to wind up chasing a fox myself?

WITNESSETH

AGREEMENT made this Ninth day of April, 1948, between BILLY ROSE, hereinafter referred to as the "Husband," and ELEANOR HOLM ROSE, hereinafter referred to as the "Wife":

WHEREAS it is a matter of common knowledge that the Husband is a blabbermouth and given to hogging the conversation at his dinner table, and

WHEREAS the Wife knows the Husband's marathon yarns by heart and can recite them syllable by syllable, and

WHEREAS their friends are beginning to turn them down when invited to the house to lacerate a herring, and

WHEREAS the Wife has served the Husband rice pudding six nights in a row and on recent occasion sent him to work wearing one black sock and one brown,

NOW, THEREFORE, it is hereby agreed between the parties hereto that the Husband shall bunch his coffeetime tales into the following chapter, and never repeat them again in the presence of his wife or her dinner guests. The Husband further agrees to make available one (1) copy of this book which the Wife may keep to the left of her salad fork, and bounce off his head any time he clears his throat and says, "Did I ever tell you the one about . . ." *

Signed: *Billy Rose*

Signed: *Eleanor Holm Rose*

Witnessed by

Fred Allen

Paul Ross
NOTARY PUBLIC, STATE OF NEW YORK,
RESIDING IN N. Y. CO., NO. 285, REG.
NO. 720-R-9, COMMISSION
EXPIRES MARCH 30, 1949

* The Husband, however, reserves the right to tell the one about the elephant and the amorous mouse.

Poor Eleanor Knows Them by Heart

❀ ❀

I'm not much good at telling stories, but ...

During the closing days of World War I, I took the President of the United States out of play for fifteen minutes. I did it with my little shorthand pencil.

At the time, I was working for the War Industries Board in Washington taking shorthand notes and running out to get chocolate sodas for Mr. Baruch, its chairman.

A few days before the Armistice, a Board executive handed me a letter and told me to deliver it to the proper party. The proper party was Woodrow Wilson.

The White House that day was a jumble of senators, Cabinet members, ambassadors, and important brass. News of the Armistice was expected any hour, and the tension was like the last few seconds of the Dempsey-Firpo fight.

I handed the letter to one of Mr. Wilson's secretaries, and was asked to wait in case of a reply. A few minutes later the secretary returned, looking puzzled. "The President would like to see you," he said.

I got trembly inside. I was pushing eighteen at the time—fresh out of the East Side, and also plain fresh. But my dealings with Presidents had been limited to the one I had seen on dollar bills.

Mr. Wilson smiled when he saw me. "I understand you're quite a shorthand writer," was his greeting.

111

My trembles vanished. I knew the President was a shorthand writer of sorts—the tachygraphy magazines were always bragging about it. "I hear you're pretty good yourself, Mr. President," I blurted out.

Mr. Wilson blushed prettily. "I don't get much chance to practice these days," he said, like a fisherman apologizing for a six-inch fish. "Mr. Baruch tells me you can write two hundred words a minute. I wonder if you'd give me a little demonstration."

He handed me a pad and a pencil, and picked up a New York newspaper on his desk. Then, in his clipped, precise speech, he read one of the editorials at about a hundred and fifty words a minute. When he had finished, the President said, "Now let's hear you read it back."

Well, as every stenographer knows, it's the reading back that counts. I shot the editorial back at him a good deal faster than he had dictated it. And then I started at the bottom of the page and read the editorial backwards.

Wilson chuckled. He asked me questions about Gregg shorthand—he was a Pitman writer. By this time, I was patronizing him a little—the caddie who shoots a sixty-nine isn't self-conscious when he discusses mashie shots with a Rockefeller.

I picked up the New York paper and handed the pad and pencil to Mr. Wilson. "I wonder if you'd mind writing for me, Mr. President," I said.

Wilson rubbed his glasses on his sleeve. "Don't go too fast," he warned.

I read the editorial at about one hundred words a minute, and then asked him to read it back. When I told him he had made no mistakes, the President sighed like a kid who has just finished playing "The Elves' Waltz" for Paderewski.

I picked up his notes. "If you don't mind, sir," I said, "I'd like to keep them."

Woodrow Wilson reached for my shorthand notes: "We'll exchange," he said.

I walked out of the White House and floated back to my office via the rooftops. I had no sooner gotten to my desk than the phone rang. "Mr. Baruch wants to see you," said his secretary.

"Pretty good for Delancey Street," I said to myself as I walked down the hall. "Woodrow Wilson and Bernie Baruch in one hour."

The girl in Mr. Baruch's office looked up as I bounced in. "The boss wants you to get him a chocolate soda," she said.

If you think that's funny, wait till you hear this one . . .

Back in the Twenties, Harry Houdini appeared in a benefit show at the Winter Garden, and it was one of those nights oldtimers are forever talking about. Joe Cook imitated four Hawaiians, W. C. Fields did his poolroom act, and Al Jolson got down on one knee and sang "Mammy."

Then came Houdini's turn. After doing everything but escape from an iron safe personally locked by J. J. Shubert, Harry announced a new trick—one he had been working on for fifteen years.

"I shall place a dozen needles and some loose thread in my mouth," he said. "Without using my hands, I will thread all the needles in one second."

Today this stunt is in the repertoire of every club-date Merlin, and you can buy it in magic stores for a dollar. But twenty years ago, it was wonder stuff.

"I need a volunteer," Houdini told the audience. "I want him to examine the needles and thread, then look

in my mouth and make certain I have concealed nothing
there."

The magician ran his eyes over the front rows and
rejected the celebrities whose glamour might detract
from his trick. Finally he spotted a little man sitting
on an aisle seat.

"You, sir," said Houdini. "Would you care to volunteer?"

The little man got to his feet and climbed up on stage.

"Kindly examine my mouth," said the magician. "Do
you see any needles or thread hidden under my tongue?"

The little man peered into the magician's mouth.

"Don't be frightened, my good man," said Houdini.
"Please tell the audience what you see."

"Pyorrhea!" said the little man.

The audience laughed for five minutes. The magician
went ahead and did the trick on which he had worked
for fifteen years, but nobody paid any attention.

Poor Houdini! Out of sixteen hundred people at the
Winter Garden that night, he had to pick on Groucho
Marx, whom he didn't recognize without his mustache!

I wouldn't want this to get around, but . . .

When I first hit Broadway, I had a big crush on a gal
named Peggy, who did a little modeling for whoever
was the John Powers of that year.

One evening she fixed dinner for me on the one-
burner gadget in her flat. When I saw her with her hair
mussed, in a green organdie apron with an appliqué
rose, I made up my mind to get a permanent option on
her services.

That week end, Peggy's mother came in from Syracuse
for a visit, and what a shock I got when I saw the old
girl. She was a dead ringer for Peggy, but she weighed

about two hundred and fifty pounds. Alongside her mother, my girl reminded me of the old cigarette ad, "Coming events cast their shadows before. . . ."

I squired Peggy and her mom around town that week end, and it was startling how alike they were. They had the same trick of listening with their heads cocked to one side. When I suggested the vaudeville show at the Palace, they chirped in unison, "That'll be yummy," and when I took them to an ice-cream parlor after the show, they both ordered double banana splits.

Peggy's mother cooked Sunday dinner for us, and when I saw this mountain of a woman wearing her daughter's organdie apron, I got frightened. "That's your girl ten years from now," I said to myself.

A month later Peg and I had cooled down to room temperature, and it wasn't long after that she went back to Syracuse and married a druggist.

One day last spring the box office man at the Ziegfeld phoned to say there was a lady at the window asking for me who said she was from Syracuse, her name was Peggy, and I would know. I sent my secretary down to get her, and ducked into the bathroom to slick up.

"Remember your manners," I said to myself. "No cracks about the hummingbird that turned into a hippopotamus."

When Peggy walked into the office, she was wearing a tailored suit and a silly, wonderful hat that was all net and flowers. Soaking wet, my used-to-be wouldn't have pushed the scale past a hundred and five pounds.

"Let me look at you, Peggy," I said. "Walk around a little."

She pirouetted like a model and said, "How's that for the mother of two and grandmother of one?"

"Wonderful," I said.

She told me she was in town to do some shopping,

had passed the theatre, and thought she'd stop in to say hello.

"Do you still have the organdie apron with the rose on it?" I asked.

Peggy didn't even remember it.

After a bit she looked at her watch. "I've got to run," she said. "I'm meeting my son-in-law for cocktails at the St. Regis."

I took her to the door, and she looked at me for a long moment.

"You're the same Billikins," she said. "But if I were you, I'd watch my diet. You're beginning to look like my mother."

With that, and a twinkle, she was gone.

This is strictly off the record, but . . .

One of Florenz Ziegfeld's greatest successes was the original production of *Showboat* in 1927. Oscar Hammerstein II wrote the libretto and lyrics, Jerome Kern wrote the music.

Showboat averaged better than $50,000 a week for a hundred weeks, but Ziggy had so many other things to do with the dough that weeks would often slip by without the authors getting their royalty checks.

One day Oscar and Jerry got tired of waiting for their royalties and decided to have it out with Mr. Z. They drove up to the great showman's estate at Hastings-on-the-Hudson, a layout that would make Mount Olympus look tacky. As a Wodehouse butler was bowing them through the hand-carved doors, Flo stuck a lather-covered face out of an upstairs window and shouted, "Come on up, boys. I'm shaving."

Oscar and Jerry stormed up to the bathroom—and

then stopped. Chatting with Flo in the little boys' room was a distinguished-looking gent.

"Hello, boys," said Ziggy, casually. "Shake hands with the King of Greece."

And darned if it wasn't!

Oscar and Jerry stayed for lunch—the appetizer was terrapin flown up from Baltimore by special plane. And when they left late that afternoon, they thanked Mr. Ziegfeld for a most charming day. Naturally, they never mentioned money. As Oscar put it, "How can you dun a man who has the King of Greece sitting on the throne? . . ."

This one's right from the horse's mouth . . .

I never counted them, but over the years I must have employed at least fifty fortune tellers in my nightclubs, and I never met one who could even prophesy where his next job was coming from.

But every rule has its exception, and the exception is a gal named Tilly Tomorrow who used to run a mitt joint on the East Side. I knew Tilly when I was a kid on Allen Street; I met her again when she was catering to seer suckers at the Chicago World's Fair, and our last meeting took place recently in my office at the Ziegfeld.

In the days when I was pitching pennies outside her store on the East Side, Tilly was a very special kind of fortune teller. She serviced the most superstitious people in the world—the two-bit racketeers, dips, grifters and second-story men who frequent what slick-paper writers call "the twisted alleys of the twilight world."

The toughies in our neighborhood always dropped around to consult Tilly before they went out to crack a safe or a head. The ritual was always the same. The lawbreaker would extend his pitted palm, Tilly would examine it, and then retire to the back room to meditate with weather reports and the moon charts in *The Farmer's Almanac.*

By suggesting moonless nights for outside jobs and thunderous ones for ventures involving dynamite, Tilly kept many a broken nose from getting more broken and many an undertaking from winding up at the undertaker's.

Her fees were reasonable, and with reason—for if the job was successful, her appreciative client generally did what was right and proper. And so, if I may be pardoned a bit of bum alliteration, this cut-rate Cassandra probed the pre-ordained prospects of punks and prospered. . . .

When Tilly Tomorrow dropped in to see me recently, we exchanged the usual lies about how the years had not affected each other's looks.

"Have you read any good crooks lately?" I bad-joked.

"I went straight years ago," said Tilly. "Right now, I'm looking for a job."

"What happened to your old grift?" I stalled nervously. "Did the bad boys get smart and start buying their own *Almanacs?*"

"I was blacklisted by my clientele because of one mistake," said the palmist. "A fellow who was going to do a warehouse job came in for consultation, and I advised a Thursday when the moon was full. Somebody tipped the cops, and when the chase got under way, they had a trillion-watt floodlight to help them. My client got a chunk of lead in the leg and fifteen years in prison."

"How come you slipped up?" I asked. "Did you pick up the *Racing Form* instead of the *Almanac?*"

"I never play the ponies," Tilly reminded me. "While I was examining this client's palm, I noticed a strange

tattoo on his forearm. It was a heart with the initials
B. T. and A. N. inside."

"Did you recognize them?"

Tilly nodded. "B. T. were the initials of a fellow
named Ben Turchi, and A. N. were those of Amelia
North. Turchi married her forty-five years ago and they
had a child. It wasn't a happy marriage—Turchi drank
a lot and beat her. When the kid was five, Turchi disappeared and it was rough going for mother and daughter the next ten years."

"You must have known him pretty well," I said, "to
remember the tattoo."

"It was an especially heavy hand," said the fortune
teller, "and I started feeling it at the age of four."

"Neat story," I said. "The gal was your momma and
you were the kid. When you advised a night with a full
moon, you were squaring an old grudge."

There was a long silence. Finally Tilly said, "You
don't believe this story, do you?"

"It's a wild yarn," I said, "but most of the pieces seem
to fit."

"Well, every word of it is a lie," said Tilly. "I made it
up because I want you to give me a job."

"Sorry, honey," I said, "but I'm not using fortune
tellers in my café this season."

"I wasn't after that kind of job," said the palmist.

"What did you have in mind?" I asked politely.

"Making up stories," said Tilly Tomorrow. "This is
a sample of the kind I could make up for your column."

I'd rather you didn't tell it around, but . . .

I was walking up Broadway one night when I felt a
hand beating a paradiddle on my collarbone. It was
Harry the Hat.

"Glad I ran into you," said the Broadway haberdasher. "Do you know anything about the Amazon?"

"Which one?" I asked. "The river, or Lois De Fee, the strip-teaser?"

"The river," said Harry. "I'm leaving for Brazil next Saturday."

"Let's talk this over in my office," I said, steering him into Lindy's. "Are you going to bring back a wild Stetson alive or did you fall for that oldie about the beautiful white princess?"

"Neither," said the Hat. "I'm going to South America to see an old friend. The last I heard he was living with a native tribe."

"Begin at the beginning," I said.

"The beginning," said Harry, "was up at Columbia University, where two fellows and I roomed together. We became great pals—wore each other's neckties and talked big about going into business together when we finished college.

"Of course it didn't work out that way. One of my buddies—Mac—got a job selling insurance. I took over the hat shop when my uncle died, and Marty—the smartest of the trio—hooked up with an engineering outfit. A few years ago, his company got a contract to build a road over the Tumuc-Humac Mountains and Marty was sent down to supervise the job.

"Last fall, Mac came into my store with a copy of the *National Geographic Magazine* which he had stolen from his dentist's office. 'There's an article in it by Marty,' he said.

"That night I read the piece and it was a lulu. Marty described the habits of the headhunters in the village where he was working, and how they would hollow out a head and put hot pebbles in it to make it shivel up. He said that when these savages weren't killing each other, they were quite congenial, fond of their children and always glad to lend a wife to a lonesome traveler.

"Marty seemed particularly impressed by the chief of the tribe, a fellow named Pujabima. This savage was a friendly cuss and, within the limits of his environment, something of a scholar.

"Well, I read the article and forgot about it until a few weeks before Christmas, when Mac dropped in to see me again. 'Let's send our old friend a silk topper,' he said. 'It's the one present Marty can't possibly use down there and he'll get a laugh when he opens the package.'

"That afternoon I had one of the clerks pack a high hat and ship it off to Brazil. But when several months went by without an acknowledgment from Marty, I wrote and asked if the topper was the right size. Well, I finally got an answer, and that's why I'm sailing Saturday."

"I don't get it," I said. "Why so much fuss about a silk hat?"

"Maybe you'll understand when you read this letter," said Harry, handing me a piece of yellow paper.

"Dear Sir," it began. "On behalf of your friend, I am acknowledging receipt of the hat. You will be pleased to know it fits his head perfectly." The letter was signed, "Pujabima."

"I still don't get it," I said. "If the chief says the hat fits Marty, what are you worried about?"

"Well," said the haberdasher, "I checked with the clerk who packed the hat, and found that by mistake he had sent one of those miniature toppers we use for window displays."

I don't like to interrupt, but . . .

There's an impressive house about two miles down

the road from our place in Mt. Kisco, and for years Eleanor and I have been wondering who lived in it. Recently we found out.

In the mail one morning was a note from its owner, a Mr. James Belding, inviting us to an anniversary party.

That Saturday we put on our number-one clothes and drove over to Mr. Belding's. He turned out to be a gracious old gent and his guests looked as if they had stepped out of a center spread in *Town and Country.*

After coffee we adjourned to one of those paneled living rooms you see in English movies, and a butler passed around the benedictine and brandy. The talk was mostly about taxes and the difficulty of making an honest million dollars these days. Around ten o'clock our host silenced us. "With your permission," he said, "I'd like to play my anniversary song."

He went to a trophy cabinet and took a silver cornet out of an expensive leather case. The guests looked at their shoes enthusiastically—they had evidently been in on this ritual before. Then Mr. Belding stepped to the center of the room and played a chorus of "There'll Be a Hot Time in the Old Town Tonight."

"Did you hear what I heard?" I whispered to Eleanor. "We're in a loony bin."

"Sssh," said my missus. "It's probably an old hunting song."

When he had finished playing, Mr. Belding came over to me. "Do you think you could use me in your cabaret?" he asked.

"Sure," I said. "What other songs do you know?"

"You've heard my entire repertoire," smiled the old gent.

"What do you celebrate at these parties?" I asked.

"The anniversary of the night this cornet saved a couple of hundred lives," said my host. "About fifty years ago, I was a reporter for a New York paper. When the Spanish-American War broke out, the editor assigned me to cover the naval part of the conflict. Along with a lot of other correspondents, I was on the dispatch boat that followed our fleet and when we'd get a good story, we'd put in at a port where there was a cable station.

"When I left for Cuba, my mother presented me with the cornet and a booklet of five easy lessons, and to kill time during the trip, I practiced quite a lot. The first four lessons were scales and runs. The fifth lesson was 'Hot Time in the Old Town Tonight.'

"Well, after hearing me play that song a few hundred times, the other reporters began to talk about giving me a permanent bath. Being outnumbered, I locked the cornet in my trunk.

"One night when we were off the Isle of Pines, a storm came up—one of those tropical affairs with almost continuous lightning and so much wind it knocked the waves flat. In the middle of it an American destroyer pulled broadside to us a hundred yards or so away.

" 'What's the name of your ship?' we heard someone shout.

" 'The *Sally J.*,' our captain yelled back. 'Press boat.'

"The voice from the destroyer bellowed, 'Answer or we'll fire.'

"We knew we were in trouble. The wind was blowing our words back at us. And what was worse, the *Sally J.* was about the same size and shape as a Spanish blockade runner.

"Suddenly there was a puff of smoke from one of the destroyer's guns, and a shot sailed over our heads. 'That's to show they mean business,' said our captain. 'Boat stations, everybody!'

"I ducked into my cabin and got my cornet and stuck it through a porthole. Then I went into 'Hot Time'—

and I don't think Sousa's Band ever played it any louder. After the first chorus, the destroyer signaled okay. The Navy knew darn well that only a fellow American would know that glorious tune."

"Lucky thing for all concerned that your mother gave you that cornet," I said.

"Yes," said my host, "and it was even luckier that the fifth lesson wasn't the 'Toreador Song' from *Carmen. . . .*"

Speaking of strange experiences . . .

I remember a certain night when sleep was the most important thing in the world. It was back in 1945 when I was jeeping through Germany, inspecting our Army recreation facilities.

I hadn't slept much for a month. At night, my head was full of what I had seen during the day—garbage piles which had once been cities, concentration camps with their rows of ovens, and the endless processions of punched-out people going nowhere.

The trip from Nuremberg to Salzburg had been particularly rugged. Every few miles along the Autobahn, we would get to a blown-up bridge, and the driver would have to ad lib a detour. And to make it more complicated, it was snowing and there were no chains on the jeep.

At Army headquarters in Salzburg, I was welcomed by a young Special Services captain. "How about some dinner?" he said.

"Thanks," I said, "but if you don't mind, I'll have dinner for breakfast. Where do I sleep?"

He showed me to a double-decker wooden bunk and pointed to the top tier. The mattress would have stopped an .88.

"I get air-sick up that high," I said. "Can't you find me a sissy bed—one with sheets?"

The captain thought a minute. "I think I know one," he said, "but I'll have to get an okay from G-2."

Five minutes later he was back. "You've got yourself a bed," he said.

He drove me to a large villa about ten miles outside Salzburg. On the second floor he opened the door into a huge bedroom. "Sweet dreams," he said. "I'll come by for you in the morning."

The bed was the biggest and loveliest hunk of sleeping equipment I had ever seen. I ripped off my clothes, slid under the covers, and a few seconds later I was in a moonlit world where silver birds were singing like Lily Pons.

Twelve hours later the captain woke me. "How about lunch?" he said. "Feel better?"

"I think I'll live," I said. "Incidentally, this is the finest bed I ever slept in. Whose is it?"

"I'm glad you didn't ask last night," said the captain. "On the way out, you mentioned you'd been to Dachau, and you might not have slept so well had I told you that this was Himmler's house and you were sleeping in Heinrich's bed."

I'm not one to exaggerate, but . . .

Somewhere on the isle of Manhattan lives a man by the name of Szymon Szwarc. On the same island live Hyacinth Muckle, Weda Yap, Inga Wank, John T. de Blois Wack, Renietella A. Wapples, Hatzala Vaad and a gent named Frank Ix.

If you think I'm kidding, open the New York City Telephone Directory and check me. And while you're at it, look sharp and you may spot one of these awesome monickers yourself. If you do, extract a drop of blood from your thumb, dip your pen in it and letter the name out on a piece of tissue. You will then be a full-fledged member of the Ancient and Honorable Order of Cognomen Collectors.

Name collecting, I hasten to add, has always been the noblest of hobbies, and the practitioners of it are a loyal and enthusiastic group. When one of them returns from a field trip, which generally consists of trekking through phone books and cotillion rosters, he will spend weeks exhibiting his specimens to brother connoisseurs and basking in the warmth of their I-don't-believe-its.

One expert I know has been dining out for the past six months simply because somewhere in the fastnesses of the African veldt he had bagged one of the rarest specimens of all time, Theanderblast Mishgedeigle Sump, Esq.

Like all sports, name collecting has its tall tales which are told wherever the fraternity gathers. My favorite is the one about a magazine writer with the unlikely name of Joe Smith.

Several months ago, a Hollywood studio brought Joe out to work on a scenario. He was given an office, a desk, a phone and—you guessed it—a directory of Greater Los Angeles.

For two days, Joe worked at his typewriter, conscious of the big salary he was receiving. But try as he would, his eye kept straying to the plump, promising volume on the window sill. On the third day he took the phone off the hook, lowered the shade, placed the book on his eager knees and opened it. The first name that caught his eye was Gisella Werberzerck Piffl.

"This I can't believe," he said to himself. "Even in Hollywood such a name is impossible."

But Joe was wrong. It so happens there really is a Gisella Werberzerck Piffl in Los Angeles. Before the war, she was a character actress in Austria, and at that time her name was simply Gisella Werberzerck. Subsequently she married Herr Piffl, and when Mr. Hitler took over, she and her spouse fled to Hollywood. Here, because of her heavy accent, this talented actress has had to content herself with playing bit parts.

Joe Smith, of course, knew none of this. He stared at the name for a long time, rolling its rich, succulent syllables on his tongue. Then suddenly he picked up the phone and dialed the number.

"Hello," he said tremulously. "Is this—uh—Gisella Piffl?"

"Yah," a pleasant voice answered.

"Gisella *Werberzerck* Piffl?"

"Yah, das iss she."

Joe didn't know what to say next. "Gisella," he ad libbed, "this is an old friend of yours, Theanderblast Mishgedeigle Sump. I used to go to the University of Wisconsin with you, remember?"

"Nein," said the voice. "Vass neffer in Vischkonzin the schdate, ledding alone Vischkonzin the schkool."

"I'm terribly sorry," said the writer. "It must be another Gisella Werberzerck Piffl."

This one'll kill ya . . .

A couple of years ago, a Señor Rubio González y López called on me and, in an accent you could cut with a rusty machete, informed me he represented important interests planning a world's fair in Mexico City. Would Señor Rose be interested in heading up this peso-laden proposition? Could he leave for Mexico immediately?

I told his excellency that Señor Rose would be in-

terested indeed, but before investing carfare, he wanted
an official invitation from the Mexican Government.

"But of course, *amigo*," said the ambassador. "And
when the exposition opens, I trust you will not forget
the man who brought you this bonanza."

A week later the mailman dropped off an envelope
large enough to hold a high-school diploma. The invitation was signed by the brother of a former Mexican
President and the most conservative sentence informed
me that all Méhico awaited my arrival.

"Pack your huaraches," I told Eleanor. "We're heading for the border."

When we climbed out of the plane at Mexico City
a few days later, I could feel my hatband giving way.
Waiting to glad-hand us were Señor González y López,
three generals, and six motorcycle cops. González
handed Eleanor enough gardenias to blanket a gangster's grave, and then let go with a few thousand words
on Pan-American cultural relations.

"Aren't you glad that you married me?" I whispered
to my missus.

"There may be less to this than meets the eye," said
Eleanor.

We got into a long, black, supercharged something,
and with the sirens open, were driven to Hotel Reforma.
"I hope Señor Rose will not be offended if I place my
car and chauffeur at his disposal," said González.

"Señor Rose is not easily offended," I assured him.

González informed me he had arranged an appointment with the Governor that afternoon. "It is important
that you arouse his official interest," said the caballero.

"I don't get it," I said. "I thought official interest had
been aroused. Anyway, I ought to see the fair site first."

After lunch, González, Eleanor and I set out for the
site. A few miles south of the new bull ring, we turned
off on a dirt road and headed into open country.

"It's a little cooler here," said Eleanor. "I think we just passed the Equator."

Several hundred bumps later, we got to a hill which featured an interesting assortment of sun-baked rocks, and found ourselves looking down on a dried mud valley.

"This is the site," said González.

"An interesting location," I said, "but how will the customers get here?"

"That is why you must see the Governor," said González. "He must build roads."

"An exposition uses a lot of water," I said. "I don't see any pipes."

"Maybe there is water beneath," said González.

"How about sanitation?" I asked. "You'll have to get rid of thousands of tons of refuse every twenty-four hours."

González thought for a moment. "We can throw it away," he said.

"A world's fair costs a hundred million dollars," I said. "Where's the money coming from?"

"From America, of course," said González. "General Motors and General Electric will rent space for exhibits."

"Very neat," I said. "Incidentally, who owns this land?"

González brightened. "I do," he said.

"Take your hat off," whispered Eleanor. "You're in the presence of one of God's true noblemen."

On the way back to Mexico City, I told González that world's fairs were essentially civic enterprises run on a non-profit basis. When I said, "Non-profit," the entrepreneur winced as if I had called his mother a bad name.

As we shook hands at the hotel, González prophesied I would some day regret my decision not to speak to the

Governor. And a minute later I did. When the Señor left, the car and chauffeur he had put at my disposal left with him.

As I was telling my wife last night . . .

I first met the late Fred Bissel twenty years ago when he was head box-office man at the theatre which housed my first musical, and during its entire run, I never saw him crack a smile.

"What's eating Fred?" I once asked his assistant.

"He's always been that way," the assistant said. "I guess it's because he's married to a dame who never stops talking, and his only son is a bum."

A few years later, when I produced *Jumbo,* Bissel was one of the men in the Hippodrome box office. Shortly after the show opened he asked me to give his son, Harry, a job.

"I hear he's bad stuff," I said.

"You haven't heard the half of it," said Fred. "If you don't watch him, he'll walk away with the theatre."

"That's quite a recommendation," I said. "If I hire Harry, will you keep an eye on him?"

"I'll try," said Bissel, "but it'll be like trying to keep an eye on a three-card monte dealer."

A month after I hired Harry, his father came to my office. "I think you'd better fire him," he said. "He's booking horses in the balcony, and having a thing with one of the lady acrobats."

I let Harry out pronto. From what I had heard around the theatre, it was only a matter of time before his thumbs would be *objets d'art* to every police photographer in the Union.

Last September I read in *Variety* that Fred Bissel had died, and the following month his son walked into my office, wearing a suit with fifty man-hours of hand-stitching in the lapels alone.

"I'm opening a ticket agency," said Harry, "and I was wondering if you'd fix me up with some down-front locations in your theatre."

"What makes you think you rate it?" I asked.

"I'm not saying I rate it," said Harry. "I only came around because you were fond of my father."

"Leave your dad out of it," I said. "He didn't have much use for you."

"That's what I thought," said Harry, "until the family gathered to hear the reading of his will. The first paragraph cut off my old lady without a penny. It explained that Pop had hated every minute of his married life—the bum meals, the nagging and the eternal giving-in.

"The second paragraph left every dollar—seventy thousand—to me. All his life, Pop said, he had wanted to do the things I'd been doing—dames, dice, horses, and booze. Consequently he was leaving his dough to the one person who would blow it in like he had always dreamed of doing. He said he expected me to wind up in the gutter, and regretted he couldn't be there with me."

"Nice third-act curtain," I said. "How much of the seventy grand have you got left?"

"Practically all of it," said Harry. "At first, I went nuts—bought a dozen suits, a convertible, and called a lot of phone numbers. Then I got to thinking and realized I wasn't a kid any more, and that if I didn't watch out, I'd wind up like my old man said I would. That's why I've latched onto this ticket agency proposition."

I walked over to the window and looked down on Sixth Avenue. "Poor Fred Bissel," I thought. "He couldn't even go on a binge by proxy."

You probably won't believe it, but . . .

One June day I was sitting in Central Park when a wispy little geezer who looked as if he had come out second best in a bout with a moth sat down on the same bench. He opened a bag, took out a peanut and tossed it to a squirrel.

"That reminds me," he said in a friendly voice, "have you heard the one about the mouse who fell in love with the elephant? But of course you haven't. Well, it seems a mouse became enamoured of an elephant . . ." And then he told me a joke which I couldn't repeat here without getting this book banned from the mails.

"Funny story," I said. "But what made you so sure I'd never heard it?"

"Because I just made it up," he said.

My ears perked like Peter Rabbit's. "I suppose you also made up the one about the octopus and the bag-pipes?" I said.

"Certainly," said the little man. "I make up all the dirty jokes."

For thirty minutes I third-degreed him, going all the way back to the one about the traveling salesman and the farmer's daughter. He popped out the answers like a square slot machine.

I realized I was in the presence of the greatest comic mind in the world—the man who wrote the dialogue for stag parties, ladies' bridge sessions, and the preliminaries before presidents and prime ministers sit down to make history.

"Can you write clean jokes?" I asked him.

"Of course," he said, "if I have to."

"Are you interested in a million dollars?"

"Not particularly," he said, but I noticed he swallowed before he said it.

I went to work on him and pointed out how much

money Fred Allen, Bob Hope, and Jack Benny were making. I told him that any time a producer had four fresh jokes, he'd put a $200,000 musical into rehearsal. I assured him that if he cleaned up his nifties, he could make enough money in six months to last him the rest of his life.

While he was wavering, I eased him into a taxi and shanghaied him up to Mt. Kisco, where I gave him pencil and paper and locked him in the attic. And there I kept him for three months while he finished two-thirds of the funniest show in the history of the spoken word.

But one morning I unlocked the door and took him back to town. I realized I had made an earth-shaking blunder—that cut off from its supply of rowdy humor, the world was rapidly going to pot.

That month Molotov had met Marshall in London. "Have you heard the one about the fat lady in the taxicab?" the General began.

"Three months ago!" snapped Molotov. On that note they went into conference, and ten minutes later they were throwing chunks of Europe at each other.

The Seaman's Union had met with the shipowners. "Have you heard the one about the soldier who wouldn't take a medal from the King?" asked a shipowner.

"That's as old as your theories of economics!" snarled a labor leader. And next day, thousands of men were on strike and ships were collecting barnacles in the harbors. . . .

Well, you'll be glad to know I saw the wispy little geezer not long ago on the same bench in Central Park. He was feeding the squirrels and chuckling softly.

So don't let the front pages scare you, my friends. He's on the job again, and I can see nothing but sunshine and roses.

Cross my heart and hope to die . . .

One night last summer I was walking up Fifth Avenue with my old friend Mike Romano, the detective. As we got to the sedate 60's, we passed an impressive residence in which the shades were up.

"Looks as if one of our Republican friends is spending the summer in town," I said.

The detective shook his head. "That's Nancy Harrington's house," he said, "and Miss Nancy would no more summer in town than she would eat domestic roquefort."

"Then how come the blinds aren't down?"

"They haven't been down in ten years," said Romano. "There's a cute yarn behind those window shades."

"Give," I said.

"Well," said the detective, "to hear old-timers tell it, Nancy Harrington was quite a gal around the turn of the century. She was the good-looking daughter of one of the town's classiest couples, and her debut got almost as much space as the Hudson-Fulton Celebration.

"The only person who wasn't impressed by the Harrington family tree was Miss Nancy, and for years she scandalized the society columns by her lack of respect for the right and proper. And then, to top it off, in her mid-twenties she eloped with a French swindler a few hours after she met him on a train going up to Saratoga.

"For three heady years, Nancy and her good-looking bum followed the sun and had themselves a time at the swank watering places. Then one day, the Sûreté Générale in Paris arrested her husband for peddling phony castles in the Loire Valley, and held Nancy as accomplice. Her pop, of course, came to the rescue, but by the time his daughter was out of pokey and divorced from the Frenchman, it had cost him half a million of those old two-dollar bills.

"Miss Nancy came back to Fifth Avenue but never married again. After the kiss-your-hand-madame swindler, I guess she couldn't get steamed up about any of the coupon-clippers who came a-courtin'. Today she's an old lady with a houseful of fine paintings and a fondness for escargots Provençals."

"Get to the window shades," I said.

"I'm coming to them," said Romano. "Ten summers ago, another good-looking Frenchman popped up in the old girl's life. This one called a few days before she was due to close her town house for the summer and introduced himself as Henri La Roche, representative of the company which insured Miss Nancy's art collection.

"'We're interested in how you protect your treasures against thieves while the house is shut,' he said.

"As you've probably guessed, La Roche was a crook, and his technique was as amiable as it was airtight. Working in cahoots with a minor official of the insurance company, he would inspect a house, examine the locks, doors and burglar alarms, and even get the owner to point out what was most worth stealing.

"Miss Nancy took La Roche on a tour of inspection. When it was over, the young man suggested that before she left, she make certain that deliveries of milk and newspapers had been stopped. 'Such articles,' he said, 'piling up on the doorstep, are an invitation to any thief who happens to pass by. I'd also advise that you do not pull the window shades down. Drawn blinds are responsible for a considerable percentage of all burglaries.'

"'Thank you, young man,' said Miss Nancy. 'You seem to know your business. What did you say your name was?'

"'La Roche,' said the crook. 'Henri La Roche.'

"'Henri,' mused the old dame, 'You must be French.'

"'I was born in Brittany,' said the phony inspector.

"The afternoon after Miss Nancy left town, Henri broke into her house, pulled down the shades and wrapped up half a dozen of her finest paintings. But as he let himself out the front door, he stepped into the arms of a couple of cops with drawn guns.

"'I'll go quietly,' he assured them, 'but would you be good enough to tell me how you knew I was in there?'

"A policeman pointed to the lowered blinds. On each one, printed in bold, white letters against the dark green background, were the words, 'Burglar Inside.'"

Don't quote me, but . . .

One afternoon not long ago I was walking along 50th Street when I saw a sign on a second-floor store window—"Budnick's Chess Club." I walked up. Like the East Side coffeehouse here I learned how to play, it featured a low ceiling and a set of high foreheads.

At a couple of long tables, half a dozen housemen were taking on all comers. If you lost a game, it cost you a quarter. If you won, you paid nothing.

I plopped down in a chair opposite one of the pros.

"Want to move first?" he said, lighting a brown-paper cigarette.

"Anything you say," I answered.

"Take the white and move," he said. "It's your quarter."

I tried a fancy opening—tournament stuff out of the book. Around the fourth move I got the feeling the pro didn't recognize the gambit. He moved his men quickly, almost carelessly—and chess is a game where players have been known to wear out a two-pants suit between moves.

The first five minutes I thought I was doing fine. I knocked off two of his pawns and a bishop. But suddenly, from way out in left field, his queen came into play and, protected by a knight, dusted off the pawn to the left of my king. "Check *and* mate," said the pro. "Want to try another?"

I tried six others, but it was like Mortimer Snerd arguing relativity with Einstein. By game No. 7, I was so confused that I fell into the old trap—The Fool's Mate in four moves.

I got up from the table feeling pretty low. "Not my day, Capablanca," I said.

"That's five games you owe for," said the pro.

"Seven," I corrected.

He took out a pencil stub and a pad. He put down 25 and under it a 7. He multiplied and got $1.25.

"You're cheating yourself," I said.

He tried again and got $2.25. Then he did a lot of crossing out. Finally he put down 25 seven times and added. This time it came out right—$1.75.

I took out a $5 bill. He frowned and went back to the paper. He wrote down $5.00 and put $1.75 under it with a big minus sign. The answer came out $4.85.

The pro looked up wistfully and said, "I don't think that's right. Haven't you got the even change?"

I laid the five on the chessboard where I had been humiliated. "Keep it," I said. "I feel a lot better now."

I'm not at liberty to mention names, but . . .

One night a few weeks back, I was clinking coffee cups with an actor who had just arrived from Hollywood. He's not much of a talent, but he has one of the best leers in show business, and is always in demand to play the villain in shoot-'em-ups and whodunits.

But the night we met, his expression was more Bette Davis than Bela Lugosi. "What's the matter?" I asked. "Wife trouble?"

The actor nodded.

"Tell papa," I said. "On a columnist's word of honor, I'll keep your secret."

The actor bit his lip, but an audience of even one was more than he could resist. "My troubles," he began, "stem from a Swami."

"Swami River?"

"Swami Ali Ben Ashi," said my friend. "He's head of the Temple of New Truth in downtown Los Angeles.

"Shortly after I got to Hollywood, I met a very pretty girl who was a member of the Swami's sect, and when I proposed marriage, she accepted on condition that the wedding take place in the Temple.

"Well, as Durante used to say, I was in no mood to dicker. At the ceremony, Ali Ben Ashi painted the symbol of Om on our foreheads and gave us a small vial of colorless liquid. He assured us that as long as we were faithful, the liquid would remain clear, but if either of us cheated, it would turn black as ink."

"Did you believe this mumbo-jumbo?" I asked.

"Of course not," said the actor, "but to please my wife, I kept the vial on the mantelpiece as a symbol of our love.

"One day last month, my wife told me she was going to Pasadena to spend the night with her mother who wasn't feeling well. That night I had some of the boys from the studio in for a game of stud. When one of the gang noticed the vial and asked me about it, I repeated what the Swami had told me.

"While I was in the kitchen fixing the drinks, the boys decided to have a little fun. They emptied the vial and filled it with black ink. I noticed the switch as soon as I came back into the room, and made a mental note to replace the ink with water when the game was over. But it was 3 A.M. before the game broke up, and by that time I was woozy. I dropped off to sleep and forgot the vial completely.

"Soon as I got up next morning, I remembered it, and rushed downstairs to change the ink back to water. But I was too late."

"I get it," I said. "Your wife got in early, saw the vial, accused you of infidelity and walked out."

"It was worse than that," said the actor. "When I got downstairs, my wife was fixing herself some breakfast. She put her arms around me and kissed me a little too tenderly. On the mantel was the vial—filled with a colorless liquid."

Stop me if you've heard this one . . .

A few months ago, I wrote a column about the ten dream sweeties in my life—the girls with whom I wouldn't mind sharing my orange juice if I hadn't married Eleanor. My list of crushes ranged from the pigtailed pretty I used to make eyes at in grammar school to the top tantalizer of them all—Greta Garbo.

Most of my dream sweeties wrote me that they had no objection to my adoring them—at a distance. In addition, I got quite a few letters from fellows who enclosed their own lists. But the best letter of all came from a gent in Whippany, New Jersey.

Dear Billy,

Last Monday night, my wife laid down the evening paper and asked me if I had read your column—the one about the crushes. "Yeah," I said. "What about it?"

"Well, I was just wondering," said my missus, "whether there were any dream sweeties in your life—girls in your memory book who give you goose bumps."

"No," I said. "You're the only girl I ever cared about."

My wife put her thumb to her nose and saluted me with her fingers.

"Okay, Baby," I said, "I'll come clean. Once—a long time ago—I was dead stuck on a girl. And if you must know, I still think of her now and occasionally."

"That's better," said the missus. "Wait till I pull up a chair."

"You don't need a chair," I told her. "Sit on my lap and I'll tell you how it happened. One night while I was still going to high school I opened a copy of *Collier's* and saw a girl winking at me in four colors.

"Was she beautiful? Lover, she was goddess-like. Long black hair and one of those gulp-gulp figures. But even with all that architecture, there was something pert and teen-agey about her. You know, like a kid who is wearing her first pair of high heels.

"For one hour I sat there transfixed. When I came to, I cut out the photo and put it in my wallet. And next day I went to every newsstand in Whippany and bought all the copies of *Collier's* I could lay hands on. I pasted up half a dozen of her pictures in my bedroom and slipped the rest of them into my textbooks. And for the rest of the year, my teachers complimented me on the way I kept my nose buried in my lessons.

"Well, I suppose I would have gone on mooning about this girl all my life if you hadn't come along, Baby. But when I met you, I scraped her pictures off the walls and burned the ones I used to keep in my books. That was almost fifteen years ago—"

"The crying towels are in the bathroom," my wife cut in. "And after you've stopped blubbering, why don't you write Billy Rose a letter about your crush?"

"I've got a good mind to," I said, "because the memory of Eleanor Holm in a bathing suit still sends my blood pressure no place but up. . . ."

Next time I see you, remind me to tell you the one about . . .

Somebody Hold My Coat

EVERY NOW AND THEN I write a serious column.

When I do, a baby blizzard of letters hits my office, and in angry words my correspondents inform me that serious questions should not be discussed by a Broadway clown with breakaway suspenders and a nose that lights up.

Well, maybe the letter-writers are right, and then again maybe they're wrong. Perhaps I ought to confine my writings to razzle-dazzle and razzmatazz, and let the Thinkers do the thinking—but I'm not so sure. Where does it say you have to take fencing lessons before you can stick pins in balloons? Where does it say you have to have an FBI badge before you can holler, "Stop thief?"

Of course I know how easy it is for a fellow with a syndicated column to become deafened by the thunder of his own thoughts. I've seen it happen to several gents I know, and I'm not saying it can't happen to me. However, I don't think it will. Nine columns out of ten, I expect to be peddling that ever-lovin' popcorn and doing my old soft-shoe dance. But now and occasionally, when I feel like hollering I'm going to stand up on my hind legs and holler.

I'm not saying that my palaverings rate being carved on the pyramids. But I am saying that I have as much equipment for palavering as most of the practicing experts: a typewriter, a byline, and a hell of a nerve.

Will somebody please hold my coat? . . .

For openers, let me tell you about a letter with a Brooklyn postmark which I recently got in the mail. The envelope contained a sheet of ruled yellow paper—the kind that sells for a nickel a pad. Across the sheet an unprintable racial crack was lettered in red crayon. There was, of course, no signature.

When I was younger, I used to get mad at these anonymous attacks on Jews, Catholics, Negroes and Protestants. But no more—I've boned up on the hate hucksters and I know what's bothering them. I know that they're sick, that they've got big miseries in the head, and that when they write their little murder notes they're looking for relief, much as you do when you reach for an aspirin.

Another reason I can't get mad at an anonymous correspondent is that I've known him all my life. When I was a kid on the East Side, his name was Albie. He was a frustrated little cuss—not very bright in his studies and not enough of an athlete to make any of the teams. And to add to his miseries, his old man drank a lot and sometimes would kick him around for the fun of it.

Albie started getting even with the world by beating up kids smaller than he was. I was one of those kids, and he gave me a rough time until I attached a hunk of iron to a sewing-machine strap and belted him on the head with this ad-lib weapon.

A few years later I changed schools, but Albie was still in my class, except this time his name was George.

Once he threw a rock at my grandfather. I remember the old gent coming home with blood on his cheek and protesting it was just a scratch. When I started out to avenge the family honor with my trusty strap, he stopped me. He said George was suffering from an old sickness, and that I couldn't cure it by hitting him over the head with a hunk of iron.

When I went to high school, George went right along with me, but this time he had still another name—Otto. One day, in front of other kids, Otto tried to pin a murder rap on me. I told him I had an airtight alibi: I wasn't anywhere in the neighborhood when *He* was killed, and I had witnesses to prove it.

Otto was calling himself Frank when I met him five years later. He was wrapping bundles in a downtown wholesale house, and he told me the reason he couldn't get a decent job was that the bosses were all Catholics or Jews. When I offered to introduce him to a Presbyterian boss, Frank said they were the worst of all—slave drivers.

During my first twenty years in show business, Frank wrote me once a month. But to keep me guessing, he used different names and different styles of penmanship. Sometimes he made it even more complicated by mailing his letters from cities like Boston, Detroit, and Scottsboro, Alabama.

I didn't see Frank again until we met in Germany in 1945. His name now was Vic, and he was a Special Services officer. He told me how much he was impressed with the cleanliness and good manners of the Nazis, and confided that we had fought the war on the wrong side. When I asked him about Dachau, Buchenwald and Auschwitz, he assured me it was a lot of propaganda.

Since he got out of the Army, Vic has stopped signing his letters. This worries me. It means that my old

buddy is sicker than ever, and that in addition to thinking like a rat, he's now hiding out like one. Poor little
spiritual numskull—when his head fills up with more
hate than it can hold, the only way he can stop the
pain is to get out his red crayon and nickel pad of paper.

Sometimes he mails his bile and bilge to a priest.
Sometimes the address is the home of a colored family.
Sometimes it's me. . . .

The other day, as I was about to toss his latest letter
into the wastebasket, I happened to notice the stamp
on the envelope. It was a stamp I hadn't seen before—
one that the Post Office Department had just put out. It
showed four men, their arms linked, standing on the
deck of a sinking vessel. It commemorated one of the
great war stories—the four chaplains aboard the troopship *Dorchester* which was torpedoed in the North Atlantic in 1943.

Two were Protestant ministers, one was a Jewish rab-
bi, the fourth a Catholic priest. When they found there
weren't enough preservers to go around, these men of
God handed over their life-belts to soldiers. And when
last seen, they were knee-deep in water on the sinking
ship, each praying in his own language and according
to his own faith:

"Our Father, Who art in Heaven . . ."
"Miserere mei, Deus, secundum magnam miseri-
    cordiam tuam . . ."
"Shma Yisroel Adonoy Elohenu Adonoy Echod . . ."

As I sat there looking at the scrawl in red crayon and
the canceled stamp, I felt like the mathematics teacher
who, discouraged by a pupil's inability to add 2 and 2,
suddenly remembered that the human race also produced Einstein.

It's a good thing for my friend in Brooklyn that he didn't send along his name and address. Had he done so, I would have mailed him a story about Flatbush which might have confused him even more. . . .

Last summer while driving past a church on St. Felix Street, I heard a set of chimes that did nice things to my ears. They were unusually good chimes, and figured to have cost a lot of money. Naturally, I wondered how they happened to be in the belfry of a modest church in a modest neighborhood.

"What's the church with the chimes?" I asked a newsstand proprietor.

"Methodist," he said. "Hanson Place Central Church."

"Have they had those chimes long?"

"No," said the newsie. "They put 'em in last spring."

Next day I did some telephoning, and I liked what I found out.

When Rev. John Emerson Zeiter heard about a new type of electrically-controlled chimes called Carillonic bells, he told his congregation about them and said it would be a nice thing for the neighborhood if people going to work in the morning and coming home at night could hear those beautiful chimes. He told his flock the bells cost a lot of money, and suggested they contribute a little something from time to time. Maybe in a year or so, the church could afford the bells.

Next day a member of his parish phoned. "I've been discussing the bells with my partner," said the parishioner, "and we'd each like to donate a third of the cost. But there's a hitch."

"What is it?" asked the Reverend.

"Well, my partner is Jewish," said the businessman, "and we were wondering if that would make any difference."

Reverend Zeiter said it wouldn't make any difference at all.

"We think," continued the businessman, "that it would be a good idea to find a Catholic to put up the other third. After all, people of all faiths are going to enjoy these bells."

Next day a Catholic in the neighborhood offered to put up his third, and the bells were ordered. At the dedication ceremony a couple of months later, a plaque was put up on the wall of this Methodist church, and inscribed on it were the names of the Catholic, the Protestant, and the Jew. . . .

Do I think that the story of the Carillonic bells would have straightened out the twisted mind of my anonymous friend? Of course not. Do I think the people in Flatbush who hear the chimes are going to be kinder and more tolerant? Again, of course not.

Why, then, do I bother mentioning the bells? Well, I guess it's because I'm chump enough to think that even one drop of clean water falling on a dusty street is important. It may clean up an inch of ground and give somebody else an idea. One of these days—and I don't expect to be around to see it—a lot of drops of clean water may fall and a lot of dust may be washed away.

Speaking of dusty streets, let me tell you about a very famous one that could use a little clean water—Broadway.

Ninety-nine times out of a hundred when a Negro goes up to the box office of a legitimate theatre and asks for a good ticket, he's told, "Sorry, we're all sold out." If he waits around, however, the colored man may be treated to the exquisite humiliation of seeing the next fellow in line buy the ticket he was told wasn't in the rack. The Negro can see the show, but only if he's willing to settle for something high in the balcony, a row or two below the level where you start receiving spirit messages.

What happens when he presents a ticket he bought through the mails? They let him in, but only because there's a state law which makes the operators liable to prosecution if they don't. Can the Negro buy orchestra seats to our flop shows? Sure—but so can anybody without a scarlet-fever sign on his chest.

Am I accusing our high-minded playwrights and producers of setting up a color bar at their box offices? I am not. However, I am accusing them of doing nothing to lower the bar that has always existed. I'm accusing them of failing to instruct their box-office employees to look only at the color of a man's money, and not at that of his skin. Such instructions—and a little watching—are all that is necessary to get our New York theatres in line with the Thirteenth Amendment.

If the lads I'm leveling a finger at tell me that this comes as a surprise to them, I'm going to be suspicious. Surely they are aware of the widespread discrimination practiced by Manhattan headwaiters, room clerks, cocktail-lounge hostesses, and rental agents. Surely they can't be naïve enough to think ticket-sellers are functioning on a higher level.

I have no quarrel with the box-office boys themselves. They're doing what they're doing because it's been handled that way for years, and because they think it will please the boss. But once the boss tells them different, that'll be the end of it.

When we've straightened out the Jim Crow situation in the New York theatre, we can tackle some of the other cities in the glorious free states of the North— Boston, Philadelphia, Pittsburgh, Cleveland, Detroit, and Chicago. But before we start pointing fingers at the South, let's make sure our own fingernails are clean. . . .

Another thing about intolerance in New York that worries me is the hold it has on kids. I get a little sick whenever I read about grade-school youngsters defacing synagogues and ganging up on classmates of a different color. It means that these children are learning the *five* R's, with Race and Religion as the added starters.

And I'm not blaming their teachers. I know that these poor devils are doing the best they can with the little they have to work with. But I *am* blaming the politicos and public who keep pigeon-holing the complaints about outmoded textbooks and overcrowded schools.

Not long ago a kid offered to bet me a quarter that the population of New York City was four million. I told the tot it was closer to eight million, and asked him where he got his information. He told me in his geography book.

When I asked the child some questions about American history, he knew all the answers up to Teddy Roosevelt and Admiral Dewey. That was as far as his history book went, he said.

I went around the next day and took a look at his school. The walls hadn't been painted in twenty years. Only a few rooms were equipped with electrical outlets. For six hundred kids, there was one faucet for drinking and washing. The paper-towel container was empty and there wasn't any soap. When I asked how come, one of the teachers told me the city budget didn't provide for such luxuries.

As I walked home I remembered a line about kids in the Constitution of the United Nations: "Since wars begin in the minds of men, it is in the minds of men that the defenses of peace must be constructed."

When I got home, I phoned the Public Education Association, a voluntary group trying to improve the New York school system, and asked for some facts and figures. Well, I almost wished I hadn't. They made me ashamed of the town I'm always bragging about. . . .

There's a building up in Harlem that used to be a

prison. Twenty-five years ago the Police Department decided it was unsafe and abandoned it. Today it's called P. S. 125. The school kids eat their lunches in the cells. The wealthiest metropolis in the world hasn't even bothered to remove the iron bars.

P. S. 86, erected in 1889, has a seating capacity of 2,059. It's a 6-B school—kids five to twelve. To get to a lavatory, the youngsters have to go down to the basement through an unheated passage. These lavatories have no flushing facilities, and there isn't a sink in the entire building.

P. S. 16 in Brooklyn has its toilets in the yard. Ditto for P. S. 127 in Manhattan. And double ditto for 26 other schools.

By modern standards, 287 of our schools, attended by 150,000 children, are firetraps. P. S. 58 has exits on only one side of the building. And if that side caught fire, it would be just too bad.

According to education experts, New York needs 9,000 more classrooms and 10,000 more teachers, plus 600 assorted doctors, nurses, and dental hygienists. Not to mention modern textbooks, workshops, gyms, musical instruments, and some decent furniture. . . .

If this condition exists in a fifty-billion-dollar town like New York, it's reasonable to assume that it's a lot worse in a lot of other places.

The English are skipping plenty of meals these days, but they're spending twice as much of their national income on education as we are. And the Russians are spending six times as much, proportionately. Next time you stand up and sing "The Star-Spangled Banner," remember we're spending 6 percent of our national income for booze and smokes—but only 1½ percent to teach our kids to think straight.

While we're on the subject of kids, you might be interested in a letter I wrote recently:

The President of the United States
The White House
Washington, D. C.

Dear Mr. President:

It isn't often a fellow gets a chance to do something nice on a big scale. Well, you've got that chance.

As you probably know, there's an awful lot of kid-hungry people in this country. One out of every nine marriages is childless, and there just aren't enough kids up for adoption to go around.

I got a dramatic reminder of this not long ago when some papers around the country printed that my wife and I were planning to bring over twenty-five European orphans. For days, the postman laid stacks of letters on my desk from couples in every one of the forty-eight states. They told me how lonesome they were, and how much it would mean to them to have one of these children. They even mailed in snapshots of the spare rooms where the kiddies could sleep and the toys they could play with.

Of course, Mr. President, your State Department wouldn't let me bring the twenty-five tots in, but if I had brought in twenty-five thousand, I could have placed every one of them in a fine home. Evidently a lot of would-be pops and moms want something around the house that makes noise besides the radio.

Well, I know where there are enough kids to go around twice—and you do too. They're the war orphans in the DP camps of Europe—Belgian, Polish, Jewish, Dutch, French kids. And I think you'll agree that they're the thing most worth salvaging out of the scrapheap that used to be Europe.

I got a close-up of these small fry a few winters back when I was in Germany, and I particularly remember some I saw at Landsberg. A full-scale Bavarian blizzard was doing its stuff as I trudged past the shacks in which sixty-five hundred DP's were waiting for the world to make up its mind what to do with them.

Off in a corner of the camp, I heard laughter coming from one of the shanties. I walked in, found myself in a makeshift laundry and ducked under some wet clothes hanging over a dirt floor. Near the washtub, a bunch of kids were playing with a doll they had made out of knotted rags. And they were laughing—laughing like kids anywhere laugh. As I stood and watched them, I'm afraid I wept a little, because I couldn't think of any set of kids in the world who had less to laugh about.

Under our present quota system, it takes up to eight years for such youngsters to get visas—years when they should have somebody to wipe their noses, dab Mercurochrome on their knees and buy them red wagons for Christmas.

These kids wouldn't compete for anybody's job, and they wouldn't know a foreign ideology if it came up and bit them. There are organizations standing by to pay their passage, post the necessary bonds, and arrange for legal adoptions. And the whole program could be so administered that the children wouldn't be dropped into our congested cities.

There it is, Mr. President. Thousands of people hungry for kids, thousands of kids hungry for people. Surely there must be some way to get these two lumps of loneliness together.

Respectfully,
Billy Rose.

Of course I never got an answer to this letter. Presi-

dent Truman had more important things to think about—
like building an extra porch on which to sun himself.

Around that time I sent an open letter to another
busy gentleman, but unlike Mr. Truman, this chap
didn't neglect his mail. My letter was promptly answered
on the front pages of *Pravda* and *Izvestia*, and the answer was full of words like "provocateur," "white slaver,"
and "yellow journalist." Here's the letter which inspired
these compliments:

Premier Joseph Stalin
The Kremlin
Moscow, USSR

Dear Mr. Stalin:
Every now and then, you throw knuckles at the American press and say it ought to be muzzled. On your drop-
dead list are certain newspaper and magazine publishers, including, of course, Henry Luce, bossman of
Time and *Life* magazines.

If you can spare the time, I'd like to tell you a story
about this Luce gent. It involves Henry, me, *Time*, a
kidney-shaped desk, and what the fancy-adjective boys
call "the freedom of the press."

Some time back I wrote a column about an old lady
whose corpse got mixed up with the corpse of a two-
star general. Shortly after it appeared, one of *Time's*
research girls phoned me. "Is it true," she asked in a
station-wagon voice, "that the desk in your office is
kidney-shaped?"

"What's it to you," I asked, "whether my desk is
shaped like a small intestine or a big toe?"

"Oh, we just wanted to know," said Miss Station
Wagon. "We're doing a piece about that switched-

corpse story you wrote. It's been around for quite a while, you know."

"I get it," I said. "Your magazine is going to hang me out to dry again. This will make the third time in as many months that you've used me for the back end of a shooting gallery. Well, I know a juicy item about one of your editors, and I wonder how he would like it if I spit in his eye all the way from the Mexico City *Herald* to the Paris *Herald Tribune*?"

"I don't think he'd like it at all," said the *Time* tot. "Let me call you back after I've talked to the head of my department."

When an hour went by without my phone ringing, I called a Park Avenue hotel and got Henry Luce. "Mr. Luce," I said, "it's about time your gang stopped using me for target practice. I understand that *Time* is going to run a piece about my pitching chestnuts instead of horseshoes, and I'd appreciate it if you'd tell them to lay off."

Mr. Luce said he'd look into the matter, and ten minutes later my phone rang. It was T. S. Matthews, managing editor of *Time*.

"Mr. Luce called me," he said, "and told me about your request. The story you're sore about isn't much of a story, but if I kill it, I might as well put on my hat and walk out of this office. I'm either editor of this magazine or I'm a trained seal."

And that's all there is to this yarn, Mr. Stalin. *Time* printed the story the following week, and when the boys at Lindy's kidded me about it, I took refuge in Ben Hecht's old line—"Never mind what they say about you in a newspaper. Tomorrow someone will wrap a herring in it."

Why do I bore you with this trivial tale, Mr. Stalin? Well, I guess it's because it may have something to do with the freedom of the press around here as compared with what it is in your country. It's a safe bet that if the Russian equivalent of Henry Luce were to tell one of the hired help at *Pravda* to kill a story, there wouldn't be any back-talk about putting on hats and walking out of offices.

Am I trying to say that stories never get slanted or killed in the American press? Certainly not. There will be different slants as long as there are different publishers, and there will be pressure to slant and kill stories as long as there are readers and advertisers.

But around here it's not just one big pressure—it's a lot of little pressures working in different directions. The results may not be perfect, but, kidding aside, don't you think our newspapers are a lot better than they are in countries where the blue pencils are all in one pocket?

Sincerely,

Billy Rose.

The Russian reaction to my letter to Joe Stalin wasn't any more violent than my own reaction the other day when I read an article by a man who said he was in favor of slavery, and was willing to start the ball rolling by becoming a slave himself.

No, this piece wasn't written a hundred years ago. It appeared in a recent issue of *Commentary* magazine, and its author is Pinchas Goldfeder, who has been a DP in a German camp for the past three years. His proposition is simple. He will sell his sinews and soul to any American who will pay his passage, and provide him with a roof and three squares a day. He says he has nothing to lose by such an arrangement—not even hope. That disappeared long ago.

In addition to several hundred thousand DP's, Mr. Goldfeder says there are 50,000,000 Frenchmen, Dutchmen, Englishmen, Italians and Central Europeans who would be interested in a similar arrangement. These people, he claims, would rather live as 1,500-calorie-a-day slaves than die as 600-calorie-a-day freemen.

Mr. Goldfeder estimates that at least 15,000,000 could be comfortably enslaved in the United States, with benefit to all concerned. To begin with, 5,000,000 could be used to do the dirty jobs the average red-blooded American doesn't relish—street-cleaning, janitoring, ditch-digging, coal-mining and the like. Another 5,000,000 could be used as domestics, so that in addition to two cars in every garage, we could have two slaves in every garret.

American industrialists, says the author, could put the remaining 5,000,000 to work as laborers and agriculturists in the various undeveloped areas of the world. What's more, they could be carried as assets on company books and, of course, depreciated yearly.

But most important, the cost would be low—probably no more than $200 per slave, f.o.b. New York or San Francisco. And by using low-grade foods, the cost of maintenance per head would be little more than the upkeep of a six-cylinder car.

Mr. Goldfeder says he's fed up with slogans about freedom, equality, brotherhood and humanity. Slaves, he points out, could be brought in without changing our immigration quotas, and without our having to use the dirty word, "immigrant." He maintains that all this would be thoroughly in the American tradition, since we once carried on a brisk traffic in white indentured servants and Negro slaves.

Mr. Goldfeder calls his scheme "A Practical Plan to Settle the DP Problem, with Malice to None, with Profit to All. . . ."

All right, gentle reader, you can relax now and unclench your fists. I've taken you in, just as *Commentary* magazine took me in. You see, when I got to the end of

this article, I found that the author was not a foreigner
at all, but an eminently respectable Pennsylvania Quaker
named Herrymon Maurer, who says he chose to write
in this vein about the DP problem because "sometimes
you are faced with an injustice so monumental as to
make ordinary arguments seem useless."

His piece reminds me of one written by Jonathan
Swift back in 1729, which he called "A Modest Proposal
for Preventing the Children of Poor People from Being
a Burden to Their Parents or the Country, by Fattening
and Eating Them."

Shortly after Swift's satire appeared, an eminent
English writer reviewed it and said it made him ashamed
of his country.

I don't know about you, but Mr. Maurer's piece affects
me the same way.

Confetti on the Brain

ALL THIS STUFF about my being an expert at picking
pretty girls is so much smoke from a press agent's pipe.
And the same goes for Sam Goldwyn and the late Earl
Carroll. Anybody who can cross the street without a
Seeing-Eye dog can pick a pretty girl.

When it comes to judging beauty, the wolf whistle
is much more important than the tape measure. The
experts tell you that a girl should have a 24 waist, 34
hips, and 34 you-know-whats. Arkus-malarkus! If she
gives you goose bumps, hire her.

The key to collecting cuties is the same as the key to
so many other problems—money! What you're willing

to pay is ninety-nine percent of it. The other one percent is an eye sharp enough to read the top line on an optician's chart.

Let's see how Ziegfeld, the all-time boss of the beauty business, used to go about getting his girls. When the Equity minimum for show girls was thirty dollars a week, Ziggy was paying Gladys Glad and Lillian Lorraine as much as three hundred. When his competitors were spending sixty dollars on a girl's costume, the Great Glorifier was dolling them up in a thousand dollars' worth of beads and baubles.

No one ever scared off a honey by offering her clothes and money. Soon every girl with straight legs, straight nose and carfare headed for Ziggy's office. When the Great Man issued a chorus call, they had to summon the riot squad to keep the babes from taking his building apart. His competitors, paying a fast thirty a week, had to content themselves with seconds, thirds and twelfths.

A few years back I put on a revue called *Seven Lively Arts*. There was plenty of disagreement on the show's merits but none on the showgirls. People kept asking me where I got them. I winked and played genius.

Let me 'fess up. After several disappointing chorus calls, I dropped in to see Harry Conover, the model agent. I told him I was willing to pay a hundred a week for real sigh-catchers. The next day his magazine-cover girls mobbed me. Herbert Hoover could have taken it from there.

What did I look for as they paraded around the stage? The same things you look for when you're standing on a windy corner.

Picking actresses, of course, is something else again. An interesting chest and a mess of grapefruit-colored hair aren't enough. If I were a theatrical agent trying to build up a stable of actresses to support me in my old

age, I'd look for two things in the girls who applied—
(1) talent, and (2) toughness.

By toughness I don't mean talking like a top sergeant
and forgetting what Mommy said about strange men.
That kind of toughness winds up in a beanery dealing
them off the arm, or down in South America pleasuring
the coffee-planters.

The kind of toughness I'm talking about is compounded of ego, energy, and a white flame in the vitals.
It's the kind of toughness that makes a gal sing her head
off on a three-dollar club date at Botchi Galoopo's Bar
and Grill. It's the kind of toughness that shrugs off
walking to save carfare, sorry-you're-not-the-type-leave-
your-name-and-address, and the other assorted kicks in
the slats.

A couple of centuries ago the babe who had this
combination of talent and toughness was the person
to see when you wanted a favor from the King. In our
time, she gets to be an actress, a playwright, an editor,
a designer, a Congresswoman.

I hardly know Joan Crawford, but I've been watching
her ever since she did the Charleston in a nightclub
across the street from mine, back in the jazz-and-juniper
days. I saw her go to Hollywood, scratch her way to
stardom, do a fadeout when talkies came, learn how to
act with words, and then storm back to the top over
mountains of younger flesh. That's a toughie for you.

It was only a few years ago that I was paying Betty
Hutton sixty bucks a week for kiyoodling with Vincent
Lopez's band at one of my cabarets. I've enjoyed seeing
this babyface bite, kick, and somersault into an eminence
which not long ago commanded $28,000 for seven days
at a Boston theatre. Another pistol-packer.

I once bit chunks out of an orchestra seat while Tallulah Bankhead held up a dress rehearsal to make sure
she was lighted properly. While stagehands played

pinochle and the company went out for coffee, Tallulah made certain no unflattering shadow would hurt her appearance. The rehearsal cost me a lot of dough, but I couldn't help admiring this Humphrey Bogart in lace panties.

When I call these girls tough, I mean tough in the way a great fighter is tough. Not mean, not dirty—but slick, strong, smooth, and determined to be champ. Unless a gal has that kind of toughness to go with her talent, I think she'd better stay home, marry the butcher's son, and live in luxury forever after.

In addition to being talented and tough, it also helps if you're a bit of a screwball. A lot of people want to go on the stage. If you're one of them, I suggest you ask yourself seven questions before you leave home:

1. Are you normal? If you are, I don't think you've got much chance. What do you do in a thunderstorm— duck under a tree? Well, then, you're wrong for show business. An actor, when he hears thunder, stands there and takes bows.

2. Are you truthful? If you are, join the Boy Scouts. A trouper lies like a trouper—it's the nature of the animal. If an audience snickers, he tells you he fractured 'em. If an audience laughs, he'll tell you they had to be carried out on stretchers. The lowest gross in show business was chalked up a few years ago in Pittsburgh during a flood. By actual count the box office took in $6. The star of the show told the story this way: "We played to the smallest gross in history—$7."

3. Are you modest? Well, then, work in a coal mine. Do you walk into a room like people, or must it always be a Big Entrance? Wallace Reid, the silent-picture star, came late to the Dempsey-Carpentier fight. Just as he walked in, Carpentier drove Dempsey to the ropes and thirty acres of spectators went crazy. Reid bowed,

turned to a friend, and said, "Isn't that nice of them?"

4. Are you reasonable? When you miss a short putt, do you blame yourself or some other fellow? Willie Collier was once in a show that opened Thursday and folded Saturday. His comment was: "The play was a success, but the audience was a failure." Marlene Dietrich once complained to a photographer that his pictures of her weren't as glamorous as those he had taken some years back. The tactful cameraman replied, "You must remember, Miss Dietrich, I was eight years younger then."

5. Are you humble? Can you walk out on a stage, face a thousand strangers, and say with your eyes, "I'm wonderful. Love me!" Do you think you'd make a superb King Lear because you once made offstage noises in a high-school drama? Can you live up to the traditions of the actor on the ocean liner who fell overboard one stormy night? The ship stopped and its searchlight picked him out in the water. As he was going down for the third time, the hambo shouted, "Make that an amber spotlight!"

6. Are you romantic? Are you prepared to swap the cottage with the roses for the trunk with the stickers? Would you trade your girl for an electric sign? Do you prefer billing or cooing? If you hesitated for a moment on *this* question, don't bother answering.

7. Do you know when it's time to quit? If you do, I don't see much future for you. You've got to have the instincts of the fellow who gave up acting to become a surgeon. He removed an appendix so skillfully that the doctors watching him started to applaud. Whereupon he bowed and cut out the man's gall bladder for an encore.

If your answers to these seven questions indicate that you're wacky, a big fibber, swell-headed, bull-headed and fat-headed, then come to Broadway. There are about five hundred jobs available each season. You can be one of the ten thousand trying to get them.

One other thing before you start packing. Do you realize you're going up against a business in which good looks plus talent doesn't necessarily equal employment? Has anybody told you that most of the fellows who do the hiring on Broadway are dopes? Well, most of them are.

Take me for instance. My press agent is forever sending out stories about the stars I've discovered. Malarkey! When it comes to sitting down in a noisy rehearsal room and picking the star of tomorrow from fifty shaky youngsters, I'm as blind as Justice. As for instance:

Metro owns a couple of stars named Van Johnson and Esther Williams. Esther swam for me in the Aquacade at the Golden Gate Exposition. Van was a chorus boy at one of my cabarets in New York. Did I foresee that Van Johnson and Esther Williams would become two of the most valuable entertainment properties in the world? All together now—*in a pig's eye!*

When I was auditioning acts in Fort Worth in 1936, a girl warbled a chorus of an unhappy song called "Gloomy Sunday." I advised her to get married and tend to her dishes and diapers. A few years later a lovely in a Mainbocher gown came up to my table at the Stork Club and kissed me on top of my head. Sure, it was the same girl—Mary Martin—the biggest hunk of musical comedy talent since Gertie Lawrence came over from London with *Charlot's Revue,* in 1924.

Danny Kaye worked for me a few years ago. He stooged for a hoofer named Nick Long, Jr. I paid Danny $75 a week and permitted him to say exactly three words—"Soft and mellow." Betty Hutton worked at the same cabaret. While the trumpet player rested his lip, I used to let her sing a chorus with the band.

Where was Joe McGenius when all this talent was jiggling around his joints? Why didn't I sign these hot kids to long-term contracts? Well, I guess I was too busy reading the scrapbooks where it says I'm a smart showman.

A succession of press agents have claimed I gave Benny Goodman his start. Don't believe it. It's true I gave his band its first job at the Billy Rose Music Hall, but it only filled in while the other band was catching a smoke in the alley. When the whole country went crazy about B. G. and his Cats, I took a few bows here and there, but I never knew what all the hollering was about.

Louis Prima, the Andrews Sisters, Vera Allen, Abbott and Costello, Virginia Mayo, they all did bits in my shows before anybody realized they were anybody. I used them and forgot about them until their names exploded all over twenty thousand marquees.

Which all adds up to this: If you come to Broadway and have a tough time getting started, don't jump on a train—or in front of one. The producer who turns you down may be as big a dope as I am.

A few hundred words back I said there were only about 500 acting jobs each season. I wasn't kidding. We aren't producing as many shows as we used to. We can't afford to. Twenty years back, you could ring up the curtain on a legitimate show for $10,000. Today the same show costs $60,000. And when it comes to mounting a musical, it's plain astronomy.

Recently I turned down the chance to produce a tune-and-tinsel frolic which had all the earmarks of a hit. A minute with a pencil showed it would cost over $200,000 to put it on. The show would have to gross better than $25,000 a week to cover operating expenses. I decided not to do it, and have a good season.

What makes these cardboard-and-rhinestone *Schauspiels* cost so much? Why should a stage kitchen cost more than a home in Long Island with real plumbing? Why does an obscure hoofer who's on stage twenty-four minutes a week earn more than a fine painter like Thomas Benton?

Well, to begin with, show business isn't a business. It's a crap game. And there are no small salaries around a gambling house.

The showgirl costume that cost me a hundred bucks a few years ago now costs five hundred. Scenery, props, electrical equipment—you'd think they came from Tiffany's. The average teamster, stagehand, or musician earns more than a lot of our big-league ball players.

The economics of producing are so daffy these days that a show can run a year and lose a bundle. For instance, was *Showboat* a good show? Try to think of a better one. It grossed more than two million when it was revived at my theatre. Yet it wound up $160,000 in the red.

Another thing that makes producing a treacherous business these days is the thousand tired people who attend the opening night of a Broadway show.

For a lot of years now, I've been one of that thousand. The same bunch of us show up first night after first night in our penguin suits. We've eaten too much and generally have a few brandies under our belts. Another show to us is like another book to a librarian. It's my guess that not more than a hundred of us give a damn about the play.

Let's look at a typical opening night audience as it files into the theatre. First in their seats are the four people who don't consider themselves celebrities. Next come the relatives of the cast. Their prolonged applause for a bit player will again prove that blood is thicker than billing.

Taking their seats now are the actresses who read for
the part but didn't get it. It's all right with them if the
chosen one trips on her gown and falls into the orchestra
pit. The closer her acting gets to Bernhardt, the closer
they'll get to heartburn.

For every girl who didn't land the part there's an
agent who didn't land the commission. He comes disguised as a human being, and he'll hate the play only
ten percent as much as his client.

The theatre is beginning to fill up. Here come the set
designers who didn't get to do the show. The only time
they ever noticed the actors was the night *Our Town*
was presented on a bare stage.

In the aisle seats you can pick out the critics. They
usually eat a light dinner so as to leave room for the
playwright.

Scattered through the audience are talent scouts from
the gold-plated popcorn machine called Hollywood.
These gents are merely killing time until intermission,
when they will rush backstage and disrupt the company by offering some actor ten times as much as he
is worth.

Down front are the rival producers, who look at the
other fellow's play like a crocodile watches Tarzan trying to swing over a stream. As they come in, they wish
the producer luck, the liars. The producer manages a
tired quip: "What have I got to lose—only a lousy fortune!"

The author stands at the back, stabbing latecomers
with his eyes. He wishes he had a machine gun as he
watches them trample all over the first half-hour of
something that represents a year's work.

By the time everyone is seated, the first act is over.
The entire audience tries to crowd into a lobby hardly
big enough for Sydney Greenstreet. The wits and
clamor girls take over:

"I've had a lovely evening, but this isn't it."

"If anyone in the audience had a fish, what was he waiting for?"

"She's been playing ingenue parts since 34th Street was uptown."

A buzzer announces the second act. They stamp out their cigarettes and go in, having ruined the carpet and a dozen reputations.

About seventy-five shows open each season. Perhaps a baker's dozen successfully run the first-night gantlet. Every producer wishes he could unveil his show to the public and sidestep these cats-and-yammer kids. But I'm afraid there won't be any change in this setup until some inspired fellow figures out a way to open a show on the second night.

Of course I realize that the rusty harpoons I'm throwing at the legitimate theatre aren't going to stop anybody who really has what it takes. As long as one Barbara Bel Geddes can happen, a thousand would-be Barbaras are going to keep punching. They know that the payoff for the few who make good in the theatre is a fantastic one, not only in money but in prestige.

For reasons that are two thousand years old, the theatre has what the movies have never been able to buy—manners and tradition. The boys in the Beverly Hills bungalows may not like this, but to the acting profession, Hollywood is still the awkward newcomer to the show-business banquet—red-faced, bumbling, and waving money bags to hide its embarrassment. The performer knows that the runaway tailors on the West Coast haven't produced a writer in thirty years fit to shine the shoes of Sean O'Casey of the little Abbey Theatre in Dublin.

For years I've been listening to Hollywood actors

cuss out the flicker factories which keep them in cookies and convertibles. For years I've watched $2,000-a-week script writers pant for a chance to get back to Shubert Alley with that play they've been writing on M-G-M's time.

I know what is biting them. Like everybody else, they yen to be involved in classy goings-on, and no matter how much Louis B. Mayer pays them, he'll never get it out of their heads that the theatre is the Rembrandt of show business. . . .

I'd like to wind up this chapter by telling you a little story. If you have a record of Irving Berlin's "There's No Business Like Show Business," it might be a nice touch to play it as background music.

When I got into trouble with my first musical back in 1931, I decided to kiss the theatre goodbye. Late one night at the old Friars Club, I told George M. Cohan what I had decided. The Yankee Doodle kid said, "I don't blame you, Billy. I think you've made a smart decision.

"Your hard luck this season reminds me of another hard-luck showman I happen to know of. When he took out his first show—and it wasn't much of a show by our standards—he was twenty-six years old.

"His first stop was a small town in Massachusetts. The hotel in which his troupe was staying caught fire that night and some of his costumes were burned. Then at the next stop, a hell-fire-and-brimstone parson ran him out of town.

"A bit discouraged, he headed south. In Roanoke, Virginia, it rained so hard he had to cancel his show. The owner of the hotel where the performers were to have stayed threatened to have the producer jailed unless he paid for the three meals and lodging which had been arranged for. The producer paid up—but only after his company ate the three meals at one sitting and lay down on the beds for half an hour to soil the sheets.

"In South Carolina, his star colored singer walked out. The producer rubbed some burnt cork on his face and did the fellow's numbers himself. As he came off, he heard an argument between his ticket taker and one of the natives. The producer, still blacked up, butted in and talked tough.

"The Carolinian whipped out a pistol. No colored man was going to get uppity with him. The producer had to roll up his sleeves and show his white skin to keep from getting shot.

"One night the magician's assistant didn't show up. The producer crawled into the trick compartment under the table and handed up the props which the magician was supposedly producing out of thin air. One of these props was a live squirrel. It bit the producer in the soft part of the back. He leaped out of the compartment and ran ki-yi-ing through the audience. The crowd threatened to break up his show and he had to give their money back.

"Down in Mississippi he picked up a showboat—not the one they sing about, but a beat-up hulk which would have turned over if fifteen people leaned against the same rail. The second day out, one of his minstrels fell over the side and drowned.

"For the next few weeks, whenever the producer ran short of cash he would sell a piece of his show. I don't mean a financial interest—no one would buy that. I mean a curtain, an old trunk, or one of his musicians' instruments.

"By the time he got to New Orleans, there wasn't much left of the show. He traded what remained for a few kegs of blackstrap molasses.

"The producer swore he would never mess with show business again. And he didn't—until the following season.

"Unlike you, my dear Billy, P. T. Barnum didn't know enough to quit when the quitting was good."

Love Begins at 8:40

❧   ❧

PROFESSOR KINSEY recently set up shop at the Astor Hotel, and interviewed scores of actors and actresses. According to his press releases, he was compiling statistics on the sexual behavior of people in show business. Meaning no disrespect to the Boswell of the boudoir, I think it was a waste of room rent.

To begin with, few of the people on Broadway were born there. Turn the average customer at El Morocco upside down and acorns will fall out of his pocket. And if the Professor doesn't think so, let him count the people who cry in their whiskey when the orchestra plays "On the Banks of the Wabash."

It's my hunch that the naughty numbers which the Professor's adding machine punched out at the Astor will be a lot like his statistics for Sequatchie County, Tennessee. What Sequatchie lacks in hotel rooms, it more than makes up for in haystacks.

I've spent a lot of years around here watching the mazdas and moonbeams play peek-a-boo. I've also spent part of my forty-eight years in the forty-eight states, and it's my experience that sexual behavior is about the same around Lindy's as it is in Louisiana. It just gets a bigger play in the papers.

In the chapter which follows, I've translated some Broadway sex statistics into case histories of a few hundred words each. In deference to the family trade, I've eliminated the lustier scenes. However, those who letch for the lascivious may read between the lines. To do this, dip the chapter in Chanel No. 5. Under a purple light, the four letter words will come to the surface.

Are these case histories true?

Well, let me answer it this way. They're as true as most of the confessions Professor Kinsey heard at the Astor.

WRONG NUMBERS DON'T COUNT

Did you know a giraffe has the same number of vertebrae in its neck as you have? Well, neither did I until I met Roy McClean back in 1933.

Roy was a newspaperman with a trick memory for trivia. Whenever the make-up man was stuck for a three-line filler at the bottom of a column, Roy would rummage around in his head and tell him that the Simplon Pass in the Alps was the longest tunnel in the world, or that the crocodile's teeth are picked for it by a little bird.

One thing in Roy's mind, however, didn't come under the heading of trivia. That was a photographer's model named Jan Morrison. A columnist once cracked that A. T. & T. should have paid for the privilege of installing Jan's telephone.

Roy fell in love with her at a cocktail party between the first and second Manhattans. Over the third, he asked her to marry him.

"I like you," said Jan. "But I'm not ready to give up my seat on the merry-go-round. Besides, I'm leaving for Hollywood next week. Got a year's contract with Paramount."

Roy was at the station to see her off. That night he wrote her the first of 365 letters. On the day she got the 365th, Jan was already packed to go back to New

York. All she had to show for a year in pictures was a suntan and a few jiu-jitsu holds she had learned saying "No" to assistant directors.

Roy was waiting for her at Grand Central Station. He did the right things by her luggage and taxied her to her apartment. "It was sweet of you, taking care of the sublet and getting the place cleaned up," Jan told him. "What's new in the old town, newspaperman?"

"You," said Roy. "I know an aisle nobody will be using next Sunday. How about marching down it with me?"

"Thanks for the offer, pal," she said. "But I've been away for twelve months, and I've got a lot of catching up to do. Ask me again in a couple of years."

"That's 730 nights away," Roy protested.

Maybe it was the excitement of getting back to the Big City, but Jan got a little boastful. "This is my town," she said. "I don't intend to, but I think I could date a different beau every one of those 730 nights."

Roy smiled. "There's a new crop of chicks in town, and more coming in on every train. Your old playmates have a lot of new phone numbers in their little books."

"Maybe so," said Jan. "But I wrote some of the old bunch I was getting in today and I'll bet you my phone rings a dozen times tonight."

"I'll bet you," said Roy. "But let's make the bet interesting. Will you marry me if nobody phones you for a date by midnight?"

"Done and double done," laughed Jan. "I'll hold the stakes."

"Wrong numbers don't count," said Roy, "and you're not to call anybody yourself. I'll be around to collect at midnight." The newspaperman picked up his hat and left.

A few minutes later the phone rang. Jan winked at herself in the hall mirror as she skipped to answer it.

"Is Mrs. Morley there?" a voice asked.

"Wrong number," said Jan.

By the time she had finished unpacking it was almost seven. "Pretty late for a dinner date," she told herself. "I suppose I'll have to settle for the theatre."

She laid out the Adrian gown she had brought from California, then turned on the radio and sat down at her dressing table. The face that had sold a hundred carloads of toothpaste looked back at her. She smiled —and then the smile cracked. What was that near her eyes—a wrinkle? She switched off the radio and finished dressing. The phone remained black and silent.

She picked up a book and started to read, then slammed it shut. The clock on the bureau told her the curtain was going up in thirty theatres.

She decided to take off the Adrian gown and keep it fresh. In the closet she found an old woolly bathrobe and put it on over her slip. Back at the mirror, she took a long look.

"Some glamour girl!" she told her image. "In this bathrobe, you could understudy Lionel Barrymore."

She went to the window and looked out. It seemed to her there were more taxis than usual on the street. She heard a phone ring, started, and then stopped—it was in the next apartment.

"Easy does it," she said. "Still time for the Stork Club."

Suddenly Jan began thinking about the girls she knew whose phones didn't ring—about their solitary movies, their Ry-Krisp and lettuce lunches, their evenings with the book from the circulating library. From an apartment down the hall, she heard the rattle of ice in a cocktail shaker and the beginning of a party. She began to cry.

How sure was she of Roy? The new crop of chicks he had talked about—did *he* have any of their numbers in his book?

At twelve a bell rang. She ran to the phone, then realized it was the door. She opened it, and fell into Roy's arms—bathrobe, tears, and all.

They drove to Maryland and got married that night. I've seen them around town for the last dozen years, and they look as happy as two kids in a jam closet.

But I sometimes wonder if Roy ever told Jan this interesting bit of trivia: That back in 1934, if you dialed a telephone in New York—and then kept your receiver off the hook after the other person hung up—the other person's phone was dead to incoming calls.

HAPPY MATCH

One night I walked into Rudy's rum-and-ravioli parlor on 45th Street. In one of the booths a girl was having trouble keeping her fingers out of a fellow's hair. A quart of bubbly was on the table.

"Who are the lovebirds?" I asked Rudy.

"You ought to know them," said the proprietor. "Hogarth and Harriet. They do a mind-reading act. Been doing it for years."

"Aren't they a bit old for that lovey-dovey routine?" I asked.

"Could be," said Rudy, "but this is an anniversary."

"Hope your sprinkler system is working," I said as the pair went into a slow-motion kiss. "They may set fire to your joint."

"Funny you mentioning fire," said Rudy. "That's what the anniversary is about."

"I'll have an iced Moxie," I said, "and the details."

"It's a cute story," said my friend. "They first met at the old Keeney Theatre in Newark. Hogarth was doing a standard mind-reading turn and Harriet was thrushing with a Paul Specht unit. They got married and started doing a two-act.

"For the next five years it was what you writer fellas call sweetness and light. Uppers, lowers, meals off greasy one-arm chairs, and living with the clock upside down. They beefed about it like all show people, but finally did what few of them do—quit."

"Don't tell me they built that dream house and settled down in New Rochelle," I said.

"Hackensack," said Rudy. "And they didn't leave the cottage for days at a time. Harriet baked deep-dish apple pies and Hogarth ate them. Real B movie stuff.

"I didn't see them for almost a year, and then Hogarth started dropping in again. First for a quick one, and then for some that were not so quick. After a while he was opening and closing the joint with me. One night he walked in with a suitcase and told me it was all over between him and Harriet. Here's how he explained it.

"In show business a husband and wife are riding the pink horse. Most of the time they see each other with the make-up on. A guy doesn't get to know what kind of a cook his missus is because she has no place to cook, and the wife doesn't realize what a slob she married because he's throwing ashes on somebody else's carpet.

"But cooped up in that dream cottage—well, that was something else again. Instead of 'Who was that lady I saw you with?' Hogarth got to saying, 'And that goes for your aunts and uncles too.' And Harriet had that snappy nine-word comeback, 'I hate you, I hate you, I hate you.'"

"Good background stuff," I said to Rudy. "When do the fire engines arrive?"

"Right now," said my host. "One evening Hogarth was working his way through a bottle when I was called to the phone. Some lady in Hackensack said to tell the performer his house was on fire. When I yelled the news, Hogarth didn't budge. 'Let it burn,' he said. 'I hate every board and cockeyed petunia in that dump.'

"Well, I couldn't go for that, so I made him get into my car and we drove out to Hackensack. But by the time we got there, there wasn't enough dream house left to roast a marshmallow. A fireman told Hogarth his wife was in the house next door. We found Harriet in an upstairs bedroom. 'Sorry I couldn't save anything,' she said to her husband.

"And then a funny thing happened. They both began to laugh like crazy. I didn't get it until Hogarth picked up the phone and called his vaudeville agent. 'He says we can open next week in Schenectady,' he told his wife after he had hung up. 'And wait till I tell you about that new piece of Yogi business I've got to finish the act.'

"When I tiptoed out, they were kissing like in a Lana Turner movie."

I finished my Moxie and took a last look at the couple. The girl was still having trouble keeping her fingers out of the fellow's hair.

"Nice story," I said as I paid the tab. "And tonight they're celebrating their wedding anniversary?"

"Nope," said Rudy. "Their house-warming."

TATTLE-TALE RED

Hugh Taylor is a fattish, balding little man, and a sucker for an inside straight. Maybe you've seen him on the stage. He usually plays the sad-eyed shorty who winds up with the neck of the chicken. He has made a lot of kopecks playing these roles, and has a house and ten acres in Westchester to prove it.

There has only been one clam shell in his chowder— Mrs. Hugh Taylor. In most ways, Ruth is a nice gal. She keeps the house clean and has a light touch with a strudel. But she hasn't made Hugh happy.

Shortly after they were married, she developed a fixation that her husband wasn't to be trusted. When Hugh was a few minutes late getting home from the theatre, she would sniff at his coat for tattle-tale perfume. When he was playing cards with the boys at the Lambs Club, she'd call every hour to see if he was really there.

Recently the actor arrived home an hour late. He told his wife that the stage manager had kept the company after the show to brush up a scene. While Hugh was in the kitchen uncapping a bottle of beer, Ruth sneaked out to the car to look for evidence of philandering. She found none. Even the ash tray was empty. But fixations are funny things. Ruth marched into the kitchen and said, "You cleaned out the ash tray to get rid of the evidence."

Our nag-happy hero sighed and finished his beer. Then he did what he had done in the third act of so many of his plays. He went to his room, threw some things into a bag and left.

"Good riddance," thought Ruth. "No man is going to two-time *me*."

Next day she located him at a hotel in White Plains and went about getting evidence for a divorce. A week and $200 later, a detective reported that his snooping had only uncovered a tryst with six poker players.

A month passed and no word from Hugh. Ruth began to lose interest in the divorce evidence. Rattling around the house alone wasn't much fun. One night she got Hugh on a backstage telephone and told him she wanted to talk things over. The actor told her he'd rather skip it.

That night Ruth looked up at the ceiling until she knew every brush mark in the paint. By 5 A.M., she dressed and phoned for a cab. But at the door of the hotel in White Plains, she lost her nerve. For the next hour she walked up and down, trying to figure out what she'd say to Hugh when she saw him. Then she spotted his car in the parking lot, climbed in and decided to wait for him.

In the car, Ruth found the evidence she had always been looking for. The ash tray was loaded with lip-sticked butts.

There it was. No doubt about it. Her sad-eyed kewpie doll looked good to some woman and had gotten himself involved. For quite a while she sat and sizzled. But about the time White Plains woke up, so did the lady with the fixation.

Hugh had been unfaithful. So what! Somehow it didn't seem important. What did seem important was that some other gal had discovered how cute he was.

At 10 A.M., when Hugh opened the door of his car, Ruth was still waiting. "To what do I owe this honor, Mrs. Taylor?" the actor asked.

"I've been sitting here since 5 o'clock," said his wife. "I'd like you to drive me home."

Hugh liked what he saw in Ruth's eyes. It reminded him of the first days of their marriage. "How about this other woman stuff?" he asked cautiously.

"I know there's another woman," his wife said, "but I don't care."

"Maybe I could break it off," said Hugh, "but it'll take time."

Late that afternoon he kissed Ruth goodbye and set out for the theatre. But just before he got to the parkway, he stopped at a bungalow and picked up a middle-aged woman.

"I can't tell you, Mr. Taylor, how much I appreciate these rides," she said. "When I took the job as wardrobe mistress, I didn't know it included a ride into town every night with the star."

The wardrobe lady mashed a lipsticked butt into the ash tray. "I hope you don't mind my smoking," she said.

The actor grinned. "Not at all, Mrs. Wilson," he said. "In fact, I love it."

AFTERNOON OF SUCCESS

I'm going to call him Caldwell Kane—as pseudo a nym as you'll find anywhere. For the past quarter-century, he has been a matinee idol, and it wouldn't be cricket to use his right name. For one thing, he's on the wrong side of fifty. For another, a lot of young girls occasionally see one of his twenty-year-old photographs in the paper and still think of him as Mr. Glamour. Why blow the whistle on a guy who's enjoying what somebody once called the Afternoon of Success?

One evening, Caldwell Kane was sitting alone in a midtown cocktail lounge. He was studying his reflection in a Martini and hoping the greenish tint came from the olive and not from his complexion.

A girl came hurrying toward him. She was slender and very young. The actor didn't rise. "You're five minutes late, my dear," he said.

"I'm terribly sorry," said the girl. "I came early and stood at the bar so I could see the looks on people's faces when you walked in. I almost lost my nerve. . . ."

"Sit down, Miss Brown," said the actor in those purring decibels which had saved many a bad second act.

As the girl sat down, the actor looked her over. The only thing missing from his eyes was a jeweler's glass.

"I knew you couldn't ignore my letters forever," said the miss. "When a girl bares her heart on paper again and again . . ."

"I know, I know," the actor cut in. "You write a good letter, and you're quite presentable, but we'll have to do a lot of work on you. To begin with, a new hair-do and some proper clothes. And then an acceptable name —Jennifer, maybe. That out of the way, I'll have my press agent fake up a background for you. I'd look ridiculous if it got out I was marrying the daughter of a man with a milk route."

The girl reddened. The actor continued talking. "You remind me a great deal of my first wife," he said.

"Your first—"

"Yes, there were five altogether. But Cynthia was the most helpful. Without her on my arm that night, I don't think I'd have gotten a second glance from Frohman. And Frohman, you know, was the producer who gave me my first break."

"And what—happened to Cynthia?"

The old matinee idol sipped his Martini. He had neglected to order one for the girl. "I wouldn't know about Cynthia," he said absent-mindedly. "After our divorce, she was no longer my responsibility."

The girl stared at him. Her fingers played "Here's the church and here's the steeple" in her lap. "And the others?" she asked.

"Don't bother your pretty head about them," he said. "Let's talk about us. And let's be practical. As my sixth wife, you'll meet a great many of my friends. I'd prefer they didn't know we were married. If I introduce you as my private secretary, it'll make for gossip. And gossip is good for a man in my position."

The girl looked as if someone had broken her doll. She got up slowly. "Excuse me for bothering you," she said and went straight out the door.

The actor drank up and left. Outside he hailed a cab and rode crosstown to a small bar and grill. A comfortably padded woman of forty was waiting inside for him. "How did it go?" she asked.

"One of my top performances," he said. "Too bad the critics didn't catch me."

"I hope you didn't let this one down too hard," said the woman.

"You've got to let them down hard. I don't think we'll be getting any more mail from Miss Elizabeth May Brown."

The woman played with the gold band on her third finger. "What was she like?" she asked.

"Real cute," said the actor. "Nice pair of legs. And by the way, I made it five wives today instead of the usual three."

THE MAN THEY CALLED "SPORT"

"Up two hundred," said the man in the blue suit—the one they called "Sport."

"I drop," said Mike Harris, the booking agent.

"Me too," said the next two men around the poker table.

"It's up to you, kid," said the dealer to Danny Dowling.

The vaudevillian squeezed his five-card spread open. The first four were jack, ten, nine, and eight of diamonds. "I raise it a thousand," he said.

"Too rich for my blood," said the dealer, dropping his hand.

The man they called Sport lit a cigarette. "Sonny Boy is throwing his weight around tonight," he said. "Just to separate the men from the boys, I'll see that thousand and raise five thousand."

The vaudevillian looked at his chips. There was about fifty dollars left. "I don't have enough to cover the bet," he said. "But I know where I can get it. Would you gentlemen mind waiting while I make a phone call?"

"Go ahead," shrugged Sport, "but remember it's two in the morning."

The vaudevillian stepped to a wall telephone a few feet away and dialed a number. "Hello, Myra? This is

Danny. Of course I'm all right. Listen, honey, this is important. I'm in a poker game at Dinty's. I want you to get that money I drew out of the bank today and have your brother bring it around. It's in an envelope in the bottom bureau drawer."

He turned his back to the table and lowered his voice. "Please, honey, don't argue. I tell you I'm not going to lose the money. The new house means as much to me as it does to you. When we go to the real-estate office in the morning, the money will be in my pocket. Atta girl!"

He hung up. "It'll be about twenty minutes," he announced. "Meanwhile, how about a drink?"

Half an hour later a waiter stuck his head in the door. "There's someone downstairs to see you," he said to the vaudevillian. "Shall I bring the party up?"

"It won't be necessary," said a voice. A slender brunette brushed past the waiter and came in.

"Myra, you shouldn't have—" Danny began.

"You're forgetting your manners," said his wife. "You haven't introduced your friends."

The men nodded as Danny called off their names.

"Glad to meet you, gentlemen," said Myra. "Now, Danny, perhaps you'll tell me what this is all about."

The vaudevillian handed her his cards. She spread the hand open. Jack, ten, nine, eight of diamonds. As the fifth card appeared, a big smile lit up her face. "But of course, baby," she said.

She took a brown envelope from her bag and handed it to her husband. Danny took out a packet of bills. "There's ten thousand here," he said. "I'm calling Sport's five thousand and raising another five."

The dealer counted the money. "You're two hundred light," he said.

Danny remembered the two hundred he had left with the real-estate agent that morning as a binder on the house. But before he could speak, Myra had slipped her wedding ring off. "It cost three hundred," she said, throwing it in the pot.

The man they called Sport studied his cards. "You win the marbles, Sonny Boy," he said finally, laying down his hand. Danny Dowling handed the ring back to his wife and cashed in his chips.

"I've always heard you were a tough man to bluff, Sport," he said. "This may interest you." He laid his hand on the table—jack, ten, nine, eight of diamonds—and the five of spades.

Sport smiled. "Well, there's always a first time, Sonny Boy," he said.

"That was a mighty fancy piece of play-acting, Mrs. Dowling," said the dealer. "Ever been on the stage?"

"Yes," said Myra, "before I married Danny. You might have seen me in *The Doughgirls*."

"I didn't," said Sport, "but I sure would have liked to."

As they were leaving, Myra turned to the players. "If you ever get out to Kew Gardens," she said, "drop in and see our new house."

After the couple had gone, the booking agent said to Sport, "Mind if I look at your cards?"

"No objections," said Sport.

The agent turned them up. The first card was a ten of clubs. The next four were aces.

"You must be nuts," he said to Sport, "letting that vaudevillian chase you out. On percentage, it was a million to one against him filling a straight flush. He stole the pot."

"It wasn't a very big pot," growled Sport. "Besides, what would I do with a wedding ring?"

The booking agent put on his hat. "And I used to wonder why they call you Sport," he said.

DEAREST MARYA

It happened in Vienna, where so many other memorable love scenes have been played. Our romantic lead is a novelist and playwright. If you read three books a year you've heard of him. Let's call him Rudolf Gans.

I don't know how old Rudolf was when he fell in love with Marya. He had written and lived enough to be a hundred. Actually, I suppose he was half of that—and looked it. If you dine well every night for thirty years, and your only exercise is throwing epigrams around, chances are you'll be pudgy at fifty. Well, Rudolf was pudgy.

But the great women of Central Europe adored him. If his ex-sweeties had formed a sorority, there would have been chapters from Constantinople to Cherbourg. It was an old joke in Vienna that one of Rudolf's novels had sent the Austrian birthrate up eight percent.

And then one night Rudolf met Marya at a party. Of course, she was beautiful. Of course, she was gay. And of course, she was married to a man whose idea of romance was to buy her a vacuum cleaner for her birthday. After chatting with Marya for five minutes, Rudolf walked her into the garden and announced he was in love with her. Marya laughed and left him standing there.

For days, the playwright wooed her with books, roses, and baskets of Viennese bon-bons. But Marya didn't even acknowledge them. Rudolf began to lose his famous appetite. One night at a café he was out-epigrammed by a playwright with only one success to his name.

Right around this time a new actor appeared on the scene—Hitler. Anti-fascist Rudolf decided it was prudent, even urgent, to leave Vienna. But to leave without Marya was unthinkable.

So this master of dramatic invention devised a plot. He invited most of the celebrities of Vienna to what he announced was his going-away party. Marya and her husband received an invitation. They almost didn't go, but in Vienna a party at Rudolf's was not to be missed.

It was the kind of evening where the man at the piano playing Rachmaninoff *is* Rachmaninoff. About midnight Rudolf stilled his guests and walked to the phonograph.

"I would like to play something for you," he said. He placed a record on the turntable and inserted a new needle. From the phonograph came a voice—the voice of Rudolf Gans. "Dearest Marya . . ." it began.

Nobody remembers the exact words on the record. But it was not the talk of a pudgy man with a short breath and a fondness for schnitzel. It was a great heart in love. For the next few minutes, with some of the most famous artists in Europe gasping on the sidelines, his voice made unashamed love to Marya.

It was in turn humble, gay, tender. It made sly fun of her husband. It promised skyrockets instead of security, poetry instead of laundry lists.

Those who heard it swear it was the greatest bit of love-writing since "Song of Songs." At the end, the voice commanded Marya to leave her husband, marry Rudolf, and go with him to America.

Well, if you stand at the 59th Street entrance to Central Park late any afternoon, you're apt to see a monocled old boy arm-in-arming it with a Viennese beauty. When they pass, tip your hat. You're looking at the third act of my favorite love story.

SUGAR O'HARA

Some years back when I was running one of those big, brassy cabarets that Kokomo Joe confuses with New

York night life, one of the guys who used to bounce in and out of my office was an old-time press agent named Tim O'Hara. If you were doing a movie about O'Hara you'd try to get Barry Fitzgerald to play him.

O'Hara was always pooh-poohing the modern public relations counselor. He kept reciting the exploits of the old space-pirates who had Anna Held bathe in milk, and smuggled lions into the Astor to ballyhoo a Tarzan movie.

I liked Tim the Talker, but I couldn't afford to like Tim the Press Agent. Hoaxing an editor these days is as smart as picking a cop's pocket. You may slip one fakeroo past the city desk, but from then on, even your legit stories wind up on page none.

O'Hara used to tell me about his daughter, Katherine. Said she was a great beauty. I dismissed it as another of the old boy's build-ups. But one day Katherine came to see me, and she lived up to her old man's advance notices. I changed her first name to Sugar and put her in the chorus. And in opera-length hose and spangled fluff, she was that sighful little eyeful they sing about.

The second night, one of the customers got stuck on her. He was a good-looking kid, and out of one of those Back Bay families whose ancestors ate at the captain's table on the *Mayflower*. Tim told me about Sugar's beau and referred to him as "Charley Crew-haircut," but I could see he was impressed. A month later, Tim told me the kids were going to get married as soon as the boy finished Harvard.

Now here's where our little story sits down on the chewing gum.

One night after the show, some of the boys in the band took a couple of the chorus kids up to Harlem, and Sugar was one of them. They wound up in one of those joints which stay open later than the license says it should.

At 5 A.M. somebody said something to somebody, and a fight started. The cop on the beat blew a whistle and soon they backed up the wagon, and everybody—Sugar included—was taken to the station house. There, a detective found marihuana on one of the musicians.

It was the kind of story that tabloid editors cried for in those days—Chorus Girls! Harlem! Slugfest! Narcotics!

At 6 A.M. my doorbell rang and I let Tim O'Hara in. He gave me the story in half a dozen fast sentences. "If this gets out," he said, "the boy's folks up in Boston will call off the marriage. Sugar's stuck on that kid, and it mustn't happen."

"Wish I could help you," I said. "I could call some of the city desks, but I don't think it would do any good. This kind of story sells too many papers."

"I'm not asking you to do anything," said O'Hara. "Just let me be your press agent for an hour."

The old boy sat down at my phone. The first number he called was Cortlandt 7-1212. "*Journal?*" he said. "This is Tim O'Hara. I'm doing press for Billy Rose. Got a pip of a story for you. A couple of his chorus girls just got arrested in a Harlem dive. Big fight, marihuana all over the place. One of them is engaged to a Boston blueblood. Send a photographer right up and I'll get her to pose for some leg shots."

He hung up and winked at me as he started dialing the *Telegram*. And then I got it.

Sugar's father knew no city editor would print that kind of story if it came from an old phony like Tim O'Hara.

PICK-UP

Every so often I take my appetite to a small café off Lexington Avenue. It has two attractions—(a) six fiddles, and (b) meat balls that speak with an Hungarian accent.

One night I was dining there when a good-looking woman walked in. The headwaiter sat her down at the table next to mine and I inventoried the newcomer. Thirtyish—good profile from head to toe, and togged out in the kind of clothes everybody's missus would like to wear.

On the other side of the napkin-sized dance floor, I noticed a middle-aged gent sharing my interest in the gal. When she looked in his direction, he smiled at her. The unattached lady smiled back, and the gent got up and walked out. A minute later he returned with one of those cellophane-wrapped orchids that the pros in our better men's rooms carry as a sideline.

"Here it comes," I said to myself. "A pick-up."

And a pretty pick-up it was. The gent scribbled something on a menu. A waiter delivered the menu and the orchid to the lady. The lady read the message and smiled a yes to its sender. The gent walked over, bowed, introduced himself and sat down.

"This is very kind of you," I heard him tell her. "It's not much fun dining alone. Will you permit me to choose the wine?"

"A smooth operator," I thought. I saw the headwaiter watching the couple and wondered when he was going to tell Romeo that a pick-up might jeopardize the joint's liquor license.

"I've been seeing you around town," the man on the make continued. "I didn't quite know how to go about meeting you."

The lady smiled. "It was very thoughtful of the Duke of Cumberland to introduce us," she said.

The wine steward brought in the ice bucket and popped the cork.

"Roederer '26," said Pick-up Pete. "This is a special

occasion, my dear, and a toast is in order. Here's to the two of us over the years."

The tzigane orchestra went into an old Franz Lehár song. The gent rose, bowed, and asked his lady if she'd care to dance. Old World stuff, but I had to admit they looked pretty good together on the dance floor. When they sat down, I heard him whisper something about not wanting the night to end too soon.

"Operetta dialogue," I said to myself, and asked for the check.

On my way out I passed the headwaiter. "What gives here?" I asked. "You saw what happened. How come you didn't break it up?"

The maître d' smiled. "It's been going on for a long time," he said. "On the same evening every year, Mr. Coddington and the lady come here and re-enact the same little scene, and they've been doing it ever since he first picked her up in this restaurant back in 1936. Last year I got up enough nerve to ask him why. He told me it kept them both young."

"Who's the lady," I asked.

"That's no lady," grinned the maître d'. "That's his wife."

LOVE'S OLD SWEET SONG-AND-DANCE

The dance director felt like doing a buck-and-wing as he got out of the elevator and walked down the hall to his apartment. It was nice to have Miriam home again. A fellow always appreciated his missus more after she'd been gone for a while. The potted steak with mushrooms was going to taste pretty good after a month of catch-as-catch-can eating.

As he dug into his pocket for the key, he decided not to kid Miriam about her show folding so fast. Sure, he had told her he didn't like the script, but why rub it in?

This was her third out-of-town flop in a year. Maybe she'd stay home for a while now and stop trying to be Judith Anderson.

He pushed open the door and waited for the perfume of the potted steak, but the perfume wasn't there. Maybe Miriam had missed her train. "Honey?" he called.

Miriam answered from the living room. "I'm in here," she said. She was sitting on the edge of the lounge— sitting a little primly, he thought.

"Aren't you going to make with the kisses?" said the dance man.

"Sit down, Clark," said the actress evenly. "I want to tell you something and then get out of here. Right after I got in this evening, the phone rang. Before I could even say hello, a dame's voice said, 'Why didn't you call me last night, Clark? It's pretty lonesome without you.' When I asked who was calling, the dame hung up."

The dance director knew his wife wasn't acting. Miriam wasn't that good an actress.

"I'm not going to take it," continued his wife. "When someone calls a guy by his first name on an unlisted phone, I don't need a blueprint. Tomorrow my lawyer will fix it so you can go on playing pattycake with the new dame."

Miriam picked up her valise and started for the door. "You admit I'm right, don't you?"

The dance director didn't look up. "I think you had better go," he said quietly.

"Then you admit it," said his wife.

"I admit nothing," said Clark. "I don't know who made the phone call, but it isn't important. The important thing is you no longer trust me. It's been pretty nice around here for five years. We believed in each other. But that's out the window now. From here on in, you'd always be suspicious. You'd always be looking for something, and I guess a person can find anything he wants to find."

"But the dame . . ." his wife began.

"I have no idea who she was," said Clark. "Probably a gag, but why discuss it?"

The actress set her valise down. "I'm sorry I blew my top," she said. "Kick your shoes off, honey, and I'll fix some dinner. I'll be back from the store in a minute."

Clark waited for the elevator door to snap shut, then picked up the phone and dialed a number. "Hello, Doris?" he said. "That was a brainy stunt, calling me. I told you my missus was expected back. If I hadn't said the right things, I'd be minus a wife now."

He paused. "Not tomorrow," he said. "Nor the day after. Yea, I like you fine, monkey, but I like my wife better." He hung up.

The actress's arms were full of paper bags as the elevator brought her back to the floor of their apartment. "You must be nuts," she told herself. "Suppose he had let you walk out? Then what? Why don't you get wise to yourself, chum? You're stuck on the guy. What it takes to make you purr, he's got."

As she fished in her pocketbook for the key, another thought hit her. "I wonder," she said to herself, "if the dame was a blonde or brunette?"

STRIKE WHILE THE ACTRESS IS HOT

This love story, like most love stories worth telling, concerns itself with a girl, a poor boy, and a rich boy.

The girl is an up-and-coming actress. She isn't a Helen Hayes, but then—who is? I'll call her Nancy Booth.

The poor boy is not too poor. He's one of the expert stage managers around Shubert Alley, and his weekly take-home is considerably above union scale. Let's call him Bob Martin.

The rich boy is really something. He's Latin and his family owns half the cows in Argentina. We'll call him Manuel Ortega.

Manuel came up to New York and fell in love with our tall buildings and beautiful women. Three days later he had narrowed down the beautiful women to Nancy Booth.

Nancy at the time was rehearsing in a show. After five years of walk-ons and bit parts, she had finally gotten the second lead in a play by one of America's top dramatists. She had a chance to get angry in the first act, and a big death scene just before the final curtain.

Bob Martin was stage manager of Nancy's show. He took a shine to her the first day of rehearsal, and well he might. Nancy was part Irish, part firecracker. The second day he handed her a container of coffee during a rehearsal break.

The third day Ortega went into action. At lunchtime a hamper of goodies arrived from the Colony. As rehearsal broke, a chauffeur brought in the forty-buck orchid from Schling's and an invitation to join Manuel for supper at the Pavillon.

Within a week Ortega had bought a piece of the show so he could hang around rehearsals, and he was on the train when the company left for the out-of-town tryout. Opening night in Boston, Nancy got a good-luck telegram from Bob. A minute later she received a box from Ortega which contained a ruby big as a gumdrop.

Opening night in New York, an hour before curtain time, Bob was tacking up a notice on the call board backstage. Ortega came in. He was wearing a thousand dollars' worth of evening clothes and looked the way the headwaiter at El Morocco wants all the customers to look.

"Robert," he said to the stage manager, "I am giving a little party after the show. Nancy tells me you two are big friends. Will you come? I am hoping to announce our engagement."

Bob hammered in an unnecessary tack before he answered. "Have you proposed to her?"

"Not yet," said Ortega. "I will ask her at the party."

Bob's stage sense took over. "That's bad timing," he said. "Nancy is an actress and likes to dramatize everything. She's going to be a big hit tonight, and when she comes off after the final curtain, she'll be all emotion. Ask her then, and I think you're a cinch."

"Wonderful idea," said Ortega.

Bob added the final Lubitsch touch. "Tell you what," he said. "As Nancy goes into her death scene, slip out and come backstage, and I'll plant you in the wings. The second she comes off, kiss her and propose, and don't let her out of your arms until she says yes."

"You must have Latin blood," said Ortega. "Thank you."

"Don't mention it," said Bob.

Between-acts chatter in the lobby that night had the electric excitement you feel when a hit is unfolding inside. Talent scouts were making check marks on their programs next to the name of the blonde who was playing second lead.

In the last act, Nancy hit them right between the eyes. As she went into her big death scene, Ortega squeezed out of the fourth row and tiptoed up the aisle.

Nancy played the death scene like a Barrymore. The curtain came down slowly. No one breathed until the tassels touched the floor. Then the house went crazy.

Behind the curtain, Nancy jumped off her deathbed and skipped to the wings, all set for the bows she had been dreaming of for five years. As she came offstage, Ortega grabbed her, gave her the Gaucho kiss and in too many words asked her to marry him. Nancy kicked and struggled, but the Latin held on.

The curtain went up and down half a dozen times. Bob Martin trotted the other players out to smile and bow. The audience bravoed and then went home.

I hear Manuel is back in Argentina. The scratches on his face have probably healed by this time, but I doubt whether the playboy of the pampas will ever understand why Nancy burst into tears and snarled, "Go 'way, you baboon! You walk out in the middle of my big scene and charge up the aisle like one of your father's cows. Then you smear up my lipstick and keep me from taking the most important curtain call of my life. I never want to see you again!"

A nice way to finish this story would be to say that Bob took Nancy out after the show, proposed, and married her the next morning. But I can't write it that way. His wife and two kids out in Flatbush wouldn't like it.

THE BLONDE LIKED STRAWBERRIES

Barry Draper, the songwriter, was finishing his steak. He washed the last bite down with coffee, and turned to the dessert—vanilla ice cream and strawberries. Fresh strawberries in December! Irene would have liked that. . . .

Strawberries were the first thing he ever gave her. It was the night they met. He took the big blonde away from a fellow who was too drunk to care at one of the stay-up-lateries. They walked down Fifth Avenue. In Hicks' window, there were boxes of out-of-season berries.

"Buy me some of those," said Irene.

Hicks' was closed, so they taxied to the all-night produce market on Washington Street. The songwriter jollied a wholesale merchant into selling them a box by telling him Irene was going to have a baby and had a craving for strawberries. On the way back to his apartment, they stopped at a twenty-four-hour drugstore and bought a quart of vanilla ice cream.

While Irene cleaned the berries, Barry played his songs on the piano. The big blonde recognized some of them, and the cash register in her mind started adding and subtracting.

The songwriter and his lady got along fine for several months. He bought her a wristwatch and a lot of silk pretties. Every so often she'd touch him for a hundred for cigarettes and incidentals. Which was okay with Barry as long as he had it.

Then one day a French music publisher sued him for plagiarism and tied up his song royalties. The Paris firm claimed that his tune, "Ever After," was a note-for-note steal of one of its copyrights.

Barry knew they'd beat him in court. Like some other fellows in the music business, he was better at remembering than creating.

Irene wasn't very sympathetic. The first time he didn't have the hundred for the cigarettes and incidentals, she pulled a long face. The second time, she said, "Fine songwriter you are! You couldn't write your name unless somebody played it over for you first."

One night he came home and found her dressing to go out. "I don't feel much like traipsing around tonight," he told her.

"You don't have to," said Irene. "Somebody else does."

She left around eight. When it got to be midnight, Barry went out and poured a few drinks into himself. For the next couple of hours, he phoned the apartment every fifteen minutes. Then he walked to 58th Street, picked up a box of strawberries at Reuben's, and went back to the apartment.

It was morning when Irene finally got in. She had been

drinking. Her mouth looked as if somebody had been kissing her.

"I got you some strawberries, honey," said Barry. "And there's ice cream in the refrigerator."

Irene poured herself a drink. "Why don't you and that nickel box of berries get lost?" she said.

"Take it easy, honey," said Barry. "Haven't I been good to you?"

"What's good about it?" sneered the blonde. "A pack of cigarettes here and a hamburger there. I'm sick of this setup."

She went into the bedroom and brought out a suitcase. "Where are you going?" he asked her. Irene swept the box of strawberries off the table and put the suitcase on it. The red berries rolled all over the carpet.

Barry tried to put his arms around her. She laughed at him. He grabbed at her. Irene slapped his face. Underfoot the berries were being crushed. They made a splotch like blood on the floor. Then suddenly the whole floor was red. . . .

A lot had happened to Barry since that night. He was tired of thinking about it. There was a French-fried potato left on the plate. He picked it up and nibbled at it.

Down the corridor, someone started to sing. It sounded like a colored boy. The song had no words, but it had the rhythm of an old work song, full of ancient sadness.

"That's a good tune," Barry told himself. "As good as 'Blues in the Night.' Might sell a million copies."

The singer stopped. Barry was afraid he'd forget the melody. There was an old magazine on the floor. He leafed through it till he found an ad page with a lot of white space. He took a pencil out of his pocket and ruled out the five lines of a staff. He whistled the tune softly and decided to put it in F.

Suddenly the door opened and several men entered. Barry looked up. He crumpled the paper and got to his feet.

The colored boy started singing again. Barry and the men walked slowly down the corridor to a room with a green door. He could still hear the song as they strapped him to the electric chair.

Iron Butterflies

Mr. Louis B. Mayer
Metro-Goldwyn-Mayer Studios
Culver City, California.

Dear L. B.,

The last time I saw you in New York, you offered me a job. I explained that I was working on a big popcorn deal and asked for a raincheck. You told me that if I ever hit on a good movie idea to get in touch with you. Hence this letter.

I have a notion which ought to keep the M-G-M lion in tenderloins for a long time to come. It's a plan for a cycle of movies called "Iron Butterflies."

I don't have to tell you, L. B., that cycles make plenty of shekels. When the Brothers Warner were producing biographies of doctors and inventors, they had money in all six shoes. And when the same brothers arranged for Alexis Smith to marry every composer from Gershwin to Gounod, they needed hip boots to hold the dough. But before I blueprint the "Iron Butterflies" cycle, I think it only fair to say that it's going to cost you a pretty penny—or rather, a pretty painting.

Some years ago, I saw a picture by Rembrandt at the Knoedler Galleries on 57th Street. It was called "Aristotle," and the catalogue said it was owned by a Mrs. Erickson. Since that time I haven't been able to get the painting out of my head. I want it like Caesar wanted Gaul, like Stalin wants Oak Ridge, like boy wants girl.

So here's my proposition: Get me the picture that doesn't move and I'll present you with four pictures that will.

The flickers I have in mind are made to order for your dream factory. They're full of maids, music, madness and malarkey—the four M's that Hollywood would do well to rediscover. I think you'll agree, L. B., that it's about time your writers stopped looking into the crystal ball and shifted their gaze to the navel. An occasional political picture is fine, but it will never replace the fluttering eyelash and the half-minute clinch.

The cycle I have in mind concerns itself with the lives of four talented, tough, and tetched babes who did all right for themselves in the four big branches of show business—opera, circus, theatre, and dance. The opera singer was as dizzy as the heights she scaled. The circus performer was a mixture of sugar and dynamite. The actress—the only member of the quartet still functioning—can do more with an audience than Georgie Jessel can with a date. And as for the dancer, the lady may have said "yes" too often, but she never took "no" for an answer.

I call this cycle "Iron Butterflies" because the gossamer wings of these ladies are made of spun steel and the ends of their feelers are tipped with molybdenum. (Incidentally, the phrase "Iron Butterflies" isn't mine. Some syllable-happy guy once bestowed it on your old artiste of the aria-ways, Jeanette MacDonald.)

Getting these four scripts in shape shouldn't be much of a problem. You have a building full of writers who are kept in sterile compartments and forced-fed on the hour. Though these script-writers are shy on plots, they're long on pencils, and when given something to write about, they turn out many a pretty participle.

In this cycle, they won't even have to dream up those torrid touches which sell tickets. Their only problem will be to get the scripts down to shooting size. In fact, you may have to caution them not to dip into their adjective bags at all, for gilding the lives of these four dillies would be like adding salt to the Atlantic.

The heroine of the first picture is Mary Garden, the opera singer. If Lana Turner has stopped making like a B movie, she should be ideal for the role. And don't tell me she can't sing. They said the same thing about Larry Parks, and look how he sang in *The Jolson Story*. . . .

We pick up Mary Garden in Scotland where she was born in 1877. (Business of bagpipes and heather on the hill.) When she was six, her family moved to Chicopee, Massachusetts. (Snowstorms and her first plate of baked beans.) Next Chicago, where she gave a violin concert at 12. Then Paris and the Left Bank. (Students, sidewalk cafés, and talk about an upstart named Debussy.)

The next sequence is pretty corny but surefire. The date—April 13, 1900. Scene—the Opéra Comique. Mademoiselle Rioton, the star, collapses during the second act of *Louise*. Without an orchestra rehearsal, Mary Garden is rushed onstage. Sensation! Flowers, diamonds, supper at Maxim's. Mary continues in role for a record two hundred performances.

Our heroine becomes "The Toast of the Continent." She is tall, bosomy, and beautiful. Kings sit in boxes and applaud, and queens give them a good talking-to when they get home. (Fadeout on this sequence with King

George of Greece giving Mary a necklace worth
$100,000.)

1907. (Establish by fluttering pages of calendar.)
Oscar Hammerstein's grandpappy engages Mary for
season of opera in New York at $1,800 a night. Mary
opens in *Thaïs*. Critics not overly kind, but audiences
go mad about opera singer with only one derrière.
(Better check on this with Eric Johnston office.)

Miss Garden's antics in the next couple of reels will
have to be played down to make them believable. Especially her flair for publicity. In *Louise* she introduces the
twenty-five-second kiss. When a steampipe bursts backstage of the Manhattan Opera House, she continues
singing and averts a panic.

In Boston, she announces she will appear in *Salome*
without benefit of veils. Beantown bans the show, but
it sells out in sixty-one other cities. The following year,
she climbs Mont Blanc, and on her first day back in New
York, poses with Andrew Carnegie. That evening she
meets the press and says, "American women don't wor-
ship their men. They merely skin them."

For the next twenty years, our heroine is seldom off
the front page. (Suggest you let Vorkapich montage
this.) Show Mary Garden giving out statements about
caring more for art than men. Then letting it leak out
that she's going to get married. Then announcing she's
going to become a nun. Show her introducing the hob-
ble skirt, kissing seventy Shriners at a banquet, carrying
a cane full of liquid dog food for her pooch, paying
$7,600 for eight hats, and telling reporters she yearns
to meet a cold-blooded murderer.

During World War I, there's another socko sequence.
When the shooting starts, Mary disguises herself in
Zouave garb and tries to enlist in the French Army as
a boy. When her curves give her away, she turns her
Versailles home into a hospital for wounded soldiers.

And now for the wow finish, which is worth a million domestic, L. B., because it's got a moral.

When Mary gets into the big dough, her father insists on his share of the loot. Says it's coming to him for the piano lessons he once staked her to. Mary is a good girl, and rather than bite the hand which once walloped her with a hairbrush, she kicks in regularly. At one time she's making as much as $200,000 a year. But the more she makes, the more her old man demands as his cut. (If Bela Lugosi will work without makeup, he'd be dandy for the father.)

Whatever money Mary Garden manages to hold out, she invests in the stock market. Then comes the crash of '29. She's wiped out. And by this time, her voice has developed some rough edges and good paying jobs are none and far between.

Mary writes her father and asks him to come to see her. She's almost glad of the chance to tell the old buzzard the well has dried up. But before the postman can deliver the letter, her father ups and dies. A few days later, his lawyers notify Mary she is his only heir and he has left her well over a million dollars!

It's the same money, of course, that her father had whined and wheedled out of her over the years. The old man had always been haunted by the story of the star who ends up broke.

Mary Garden is still living. In 1942, the papers said something about her writing an autobiography. Your Paris office can check on where to contact her. You might open the picture with a shot of the Mediterranean, the sun sinking in the sea, and the old opera singer signing a contract to let M-G-M make a picture of her life.

The second picture in our cycle is about a queen—the only one I ever knew. Her name was Josie De Mott

Robinson and she was the greatest equestrian star in the history of the Barnum & Bailey Circus. I think Judy Garland could play Josie beautifully. You can use a double for the bareback riding and get around the thrill sequences with long shots. (There are quite a few horses in this movie, L. B., and what you haven't got in your stable you can always borrow from Harry Warner.)

I first met Josie in 1934 when I was lining up a cast for *Jumbo*. The Hecht-MacArthur script called for some old-time circus stars, and Nagafy the Fire-eater suggested I look up Josie De Mott.

"She's past seventy," said the diavolo, "but don't let that throw you. She can still do more tricks on a horse than I can on a sidewalk."

I dropped Josie a note and she showed up a few days later at the Hippodrome—a gray-haired kewpie doll about five feet tall.

"Can you still ride?" I asked.

Josie smiled a sweet-old-lady smile. "Try me," she said.

We went down to the basement where the horses were stabled and she selected a dappled percheron. Rehearsals stopped in the arena as the old girl went into her audition. I looked and blinked. The three-score-and-tenner was performing with the same limp, kittenish speed that had been hers as a girl. I got the feeling she was doing more than ride the horse—she seemed to inhale the darned thing through the soles of her feet.

When Josie dismounted, the performers and roustabouts addressed her the way I imagine Elizabeth's husband addresses the Queen Mother. I got an even better idea of what Josie meant to circus tradition when Dick Maney, my press agent, brought me the *Jumbo* program copy to okay. This flinty Broadway broadsider had devoted as much space to the has-been as he had to Durante and Whiteman, and he had written about her with a degree of feeling and respect I never knew was in his typewriter.

Josie De Mott was born a sawdust princess, and no Bourbon or Hapsburg had a better background. Her ancestors were doing horseback high-jinks when the center box was reserved for Napoleon I.

Josie made her debut at three in her father's horse-drawn caravan. According to the yellowed clips on my desk, the audience at first thought the tot was a mechanical doll. By the time she had galloped into her teens, she was a headliner with Barnum & Bailey. Swedes toasted her in glogg, and Mexicans in tequila. She was as well-known in Paris as she was in Paterson.

In 1890, Josie fell in love with Charles Robinson, part owner of the Robinson Brothers' Circus. Everyone thought it was a fine match—the impresario and the star. But it didn't turn out that way. The impresario got interested in politics and became a gillie (a gillie is a person who thinks there is something in the world more important than the circus). For fifteen years, Josie did her best to be a gillie too, but she never quite made it.

One day she got stuck on a cream-colored gelding pulling a milk-wagon, bought him, and went back into training. Robinson divorced her. Nobody had ever come back to bareback riding after a fifteen-year lay-off, but Bailey, who owned 90 percent of the Barnum Circus, gave her a contract.

A month before the circus was to open at the old Garden, Josie missed a somersault and broke two ribs. The doctors taped her up, and the morning after opening night she was again the biggest five feet in Circusdom.

That is the saga of the sawdust sweetie who performed for me at the Hippodrome and went along with the troupe to Fort Worth when I presented *Jumbo* at the Centennial. And now, L. B., for one of those vignettes which explains why we're both in show business.

One spring evening a few years back, I went to the opening of the circus at Madison Square Garden. As Merle Evans picked up his baton for the preliminary fanfare, he turned, faced a center box and bowed. Then, as the performers trotted out for the opening spec, I noticed their eyes were on the same box.

The riders saluted with whips as they pranced by. The aerialists signaled a jaunty two-fingered hello, and the clowns did an extra flip. Prodded by their trainers, even the elephants waved their trunks.

"What gives?" I asked myself. "Is the President in the house?"

I followed a Crackerjack salesman down the aisle to the box. Seated in it was you-know-who. Her white hair had been primped and curled until it looked like a platinum tiara.

After the finale, I went backstage and looked up Pat Valdo, who has been major-domoing the Greatest Show on Earth for a quarter of a century. "Who arranged the big fuss for Josie?" I asked him.

"Nobody arranged it," said Valdo. "It's been happening like this for years."

"You mean Josie attends every circus opening?"

"Yes," said Pat, "and all the other performances too. You see, the old lady lives in a hotel down on 23rd Street. Not much of a place—one of those bed, dresser and chair jobs. The walls are covered with her old circus posters, and on the mantel are the decorations she won—the medal from the President of Mexico, the miniature horse presented by Edward of England.

"Every year when the Big Show plays New York, Josie puts on her best dress and hires a limousine. She doesn't have any trouble getting into the Garden—she still has the gold lifetime pass that Barnum himself gave her. The management reserves the center box for her, and every afternoon and night for six weeks, Josie is in that box. And if she wasn't, I guess the performers would get worried and figure something was wrong. . . ."

When the Barnum show opened at the Garden this year, L. B., I was there as usual with peanuts, popcorn, and pennant. But Josie De Mott Robinson wasn't. She had died a few weeks before.

And what happened at the Garden that night would make a fine closing sequence for your movie. Throughout the show, the performers played to the center box as usual, and at the finish, nodded their heads in memory of a lady whose life was a little sad, a little gallant and a little remarkable.

You won't have to go off the lot, L. B., to cast the heroine of the third picture in our cycle. Greer Garson should be able to do a fine job as Gertrude Lawrence. And if you don't think Greer can handle the songs, you can always use Gertie's voice on a sound track—that is, if you want to get documentary all of a sudden.

Gertie was born on July 4, 189— none of your business. Before the braces were off her teeth, she was doing pirouettes on the sidewalks of Clapham (wherever that is) and turning a pretty ha'penny at it. Between semesters at the Convent of the Sacré Coeur, she was a child dancer in a pantomime called *Babes in the Wood.*

But this babe didn't stay in the woods long. At the age of 15, she played a white-robed, gilt-winged angel in a Gerhart Hauptmann opus. The angel next to her was a lisping adolescent named Noel Coward. A few years later she was featured in Max Reinhardt's London production of *The Miracle.*

New York fell in love with her in 1924 when she sang "Limehouse Blues" in *Charlot's Revue.* In 1926, she played Kay in Gershwin's *Oh Kay.* Two years later she

was the star of *Icebound*, which won the Pulitzer Prize.
In 1931 she played opposite Noel Coward in *Private
Lives* and teamed up with him again five years later in
To-Night at Eight-Thirty.

Some of her other successes include *Susan and God*,
Liza Elliott in *Lady in the Dark*, and the street girl in
Pygmalion. She's been married twice and, according to
her autobiography, has had several stylish sweeties.

Recently I caught Gertie in a revival of *To-Night at
Eight-Thirty*. As I watched her take charge of the audience, I asked myself:

"What makes this babe worth five thousand a week?
Is she funny? Yes, quite funny, but Nancy Walker is
funnier. Can she act? Sure, but not any better than a
little gal named Barbara Bel Geddes. Is she a great
singer? Well, it's a matter of taste, but personally I prefer Pearl Bailey. Is she an outstanding hoofer? Heck, no.
Any of my chorus kids dance better."

What, then, makes Gertie Lawrence? What kind of
light and heat does this star give out that makes her a
bigger draw at the box office than all the other girls
I've mentioned put together?

Well, that's a question more easily faced than fath-
omed. Ask any five producers why one person is a wow
and another a walk-on, and you're a cinch to get five
different answers. Ask me and I'll mumble about some
mysterious quality I call "X"—the ability to turn it on
when you need it.

Remember that World Series game in Chicago when
Babe Ruth turned to the booing fans, pointed to a spot
in the bleachers and smacked the next pitch right where
he had pointed? That was "X." Remember that day at
Forest Hills when a fairish tennis player named Jones
banged four successive aces past Fred Perry? The fab-
ulous Fred was never noted for his serve, but he saluted
Jones and then aced him right back with four of the

fastest serves of his life. Another example of X-appeal.

Let me tell you, L. B., about one of the times Gertie Lawrence turned it on. In *Lady in the Dark,* she played the boss lady of a slick fashion magazine. The plot of this musical concerned itself with her neuroses which were sprouting neuroses. Moss Hart fashioned the libretto with the English star in mind, and the sainted Sam Harris, who produced the show, had to guarantee Gertie $5,000 a week against a double helping of the gross. Like Cornell and Hayes, she *was* the show, and was in a position to call all the shots. And from what I heard around Broadway, Gertie frequently called them at the top of her voice.

During the last week of rehearsals, Moss got worried. Gertie had some cute ditties, but no slam-bang comic song had been written for her. On the other hand, a kid out of the Borscht Circuit named Danny Kaye had been handed a clever lyric called "Tschaikowsky."

The script called for Danny to sing this song in Act Two while Gertie relaxed in a swing upstage. Well, Moss knew his show business well enough to know that the star wasn't going to sit by happily while a newcomer took the theatre over. "Tschaikowsky" was a cinch to be yanked after the opening performance out of town.

The worried Moss cornered composer Kurt Weill and lyricist Ira Gershwin, locked them in a room, and stood guard. At 6:30 next morning, the boys emerged with a little number called "Jennie." Hart didn't think much of it, and neither did Gertie. The star pointed out that it was only moderately funny and not her style. It might do for a shouting songstress like Sophie Tucker, but after all, Gertie was a lady.

"Look, my pet," Moss pleaded, "we're going to Boston to try things out. Learn the song and see how it goes.

If it doesn't click, Kurt and Ira will write another for you."

"Okay," agreed the star, "but it's a waste of time."

Miss Lawrence memorized the lyric, but during the dress rehearsal in Boston made no secret of her belief that "Jennie" would be jettisoned before the New York première.

And then came opening night at the Colonial Theatre. In Act One, Danny Kaye gave a good account of himself, but Gertie was the star and the audience was given no chance to forget it. But down in Act Two, Danny stepped to the footlights and let go with "Tschaikowsky." As Moss Hart tells it, Danny was scared—scared he was going to stop the show with this murderously good piece of lyric writing. And then have it cut out by order of the star.

But the lyrics of "Tschaikowsky" were too hot to be cooled down, and Kaye had too much of what it takes not to give. When he finished the funny tongue-twister, the crowd applauded for two solid minutes—practically a lifetime in the theatre. The distressed Danny tried to shush the audience, but this was mistaken by the customers for modesty and they clapped all the louder.

In the back of the house, Hart, Weill, and Gershwin gave each other the old "that-does-it" look. Moss was already speculating on what he could substitute for Danny's show-stopping specialty. And then "X" took over.

When the applause finally tapered off, Miss Lawrence slipped off the swing, saluted Danny with a deft gesture, took stage center and went into "Jennie."

Now remember, L. B., she was singing a song that wasn't her style and which she didn't especially like. But the crowd had cheered somebody else—some smart Alec had whipped four service aces past the champ.

Suddenly Gertie stopped being Miss Lawrence and

became Sophie Tucker, Fanny Brice and Gypsy Rose Lee. As she reached the end of the first couplet of "Jennie," Gertie let go with a Beale Street bump. During stanzas two and three, she did things with her aristocratic *Sitzfleisch* that had the audience in a wall-eyed trance. And down near the end of the song, the star went into the most magnificent mock strip-tease ever seen inside a theatre or out.

When Gertie finished, they had to do everything but turn on the sprinkler system to quiet the crowd. And "Jennie," the song nobody liked, went skyrocketing into theatrical history.

Miss Lawrence cashes a pretty big check on payday, but as far as I'm concerned, she doesn't have to blush when she hands it to the bank teller. If I were the teller, L. B., she wouldn't even have to sign her name. Her "X" would be sufficient. . . .

The last picture in our cycle is based on the career of the hottest hunk of woman who ever stepped out of a slip-on—Lola Montez. When I say that a movie about her might outgross *Gone with the Wind,* I'm not kidding.

Lola should be played by Joan Crawford, and, even if the Warner Brothers want Clark Gable in return, I think the swap will pay off. Hecht and MacArthur would be my choices to put this one on paper. As you'll see in a minute, getting Lola ready for Technicolor is not a job for kids.

Hold on to your seat, L. B., here we go! . . .

Lola Montez was born in Ireland in 1818. Her square moniker was Marie Gilbert. When she was two, her father took her to India, and I guess the curry powder got in her blood. When she was seventeen, her mother arranged for her to marry a rich man. But Lola decided to do her own arranging, and eloped with a subal-

tern named James. I don't know what happened to
James, but a year later she turned up in England with a
six-footer named Lennox.

In London, she bought a mantilla and a pair of cas-
tanets in a pawnshop and changed her name to Lola
Montez. Then she sweet-talked the manager of His
Majesty's Theatre into giving her a job. Halfway
through her Spanish dance on opening night, a young
nobleman she had cold-shouldered got up and hollered,
"Swindle! She's from Ireland!" The British audience
hooted the hockshop señorita out of the theatre.

Lola went to Brussels and sang in the streets for pennies. A young student sold his books to pay her fare to
Warsaw. There she wangled an engagement at the
Opera House. Prince Paskievich, a sixty-year-old dwarf
who had conquered Poland, saw her dance and offered
her a palace. She told him to go take a flying jump in
the Baltic.

Next night the Prince sent a claque to hiss her off the
stage. Lola stopped the music, stepped to the footlights
and told the audience the story. The Poles pitched the
hecklers into the alley and carried her on their shoulders
through the streets, singing songs of independence.

Paskievich ordered her arrest. Lola barricaded her
door and threatened to shoot the first soldier who entered. They were about to burn down her house when
the French Consul came along, claimed her as a French
subject, and whisked her out of Warsaw.

We next meet up with her in St. Petersburg. The fellow who kept her in caviar that season was the Czar
of All the Russias.

In Dresden, Franz Liszt walked out on his wife and
children for Lola. In Paris, she bewitched Alexandre
Dumas. Then for the first time, Lola fell in love. Her
boy friend was a radical journalist named Dujaurier.

Her story might have ended here, but the young radical talked out of turn and was killed in a duel.

Henry, Prince of Reuss, offered to make her a Princess, but she patted him on the cheek and kept moving.

Lola was twenty-seven when she turned up in Munich. They told her she wasn't important enough to dance at King Ludwig's favorite theatre. She scratched her way past the palace guards to the King's room and—get this, L. B.—without music, went into her dance. Ludwig of Bavaria was enchanted. She took over his heart and, with it, his kingdom.

Under her influence, Ludwig liberalized schools, canceled censorship, and kicked out his reactionary cabinet. When his sister, the Empress of Austria, tried to bribe Lola to leave him, she showed Ludwig the letter and tossed it in the fire. He made her a Baroness.

An organized mob appeared under her window, jeered and threw stones. Lola stepped out on the balcony and poured champagne on their heads. Finally, the generals told Ludwig to choose between Lola and his kingdom. The old King reluctantly ordered her arrest.

When a mob came to get her, she put on her jewels and walked proudly through her enemies to a waiting barouche. No one could bring himself to molest her. When she had driven off, the hooligans made a shambles of her boudoir. Ludwig, watching, was knocked over and trampled.

In Switzerland, she married an Army officer and was arrested for bigamy. She jumped bail and came to America. Here she danced and married her way right across the continent. During the Gold Rush, Lola was the Texas Guinan of the Barbary Coast. On a sidetrip to Australia, she horsewhipped an editor and clawed a prima donna who had snubbed her.

In 1861, she returned to New York, got religion, and

died. She did all this living in forty-three years. And unless I'm daft, hers was the wildest ride on the romantic merry-go-round in the history of this planet Earth.

That's the package, L. B. And if your hirelings use the sense that God gave geese, they can't go wrong when they make these pictures. It's my hunch that there's nothing but gold in these Iron Butterflies, and that their shenanigans on celluloid should have the movie houses using ice packs on their cash registers.

Of course I know I'm offering you a lot for one little Rembrandt. But if this cycle grosses more than two hundred million, I know you'll do the decent thing and throw in a frame.

Cordially,
Billy Rose

Move Over, De Maupassant

HERE'S WHERE I lead with my chin.

In the chapter coming up there are seven short stories with trick endings. At the end of each story, I'm going to try to bat you over the head with the last line.

I know my chances of getting away with this are none too good. To begin with, it's a cinch you're familiar with the plots of O. Henry, Runyon, Hecht, Gallico, and the other short-short sluggers. You've seen a hundred whodunits in the movies and heard a thousand on the radio. Besides, you figure to be a pretty smart cookie or you couldn't afford the two bits for this book.

Why, then, do I extend my lily-white neck? Why do

I mess with the toughest of the tale-telling techniques?

For two reasons. First, I'm a ham—boned, hickory-smoked, and sugar-cured. Put me on a merry-go-round, and I'll break a finger trying to get the gold ring.

Second, my ragtag life has been one trick ending after another. For twenty-five years, I've been living in a world where the unusual was the usual thing. Consequently, when I grab a plot by the tail, it seems only natural to give the tale a twist. Of course, sometimes the twist comes out like a pretzel.

Occasionally some big brain tells me the trick ending is trite and the blackout untrue to life. I can't buy this. Every day a fellow who uses the pen-name of the Law of Averages pulls finishes out of his hat which make O. Henry read like the *Congressional Record*.

Consider the case of four old friends of mine—the Caesar boys and the Diamond boys. We all went to school together on the East Side. The Caesar kids were toughies, the Diamonds were well-mannered. One day there was a debate in class on the subject, "Resolved: The Pen Is Mightier Than the Sword." The brothers Caesar spoke for the sword while the Diamonds were the partisans of the pen.

Well, the boys who upheld the sword got to be pretty well known for their work with the pen. Arthur Caesar won an Academy Award in Hollywood for writing *Manhattan Melodrama*. Irving Caesar has his name on *Tea for Two*, a dozen hit shows, and a music publishing firm.

Morris and Joe Diamond, who defended the pen, also got to be pretty well known. Some years back, they were electrocuted for murdering two men while robbing a bank.

In the stories I'm serving up, you may grouse about the syntax and grumble about the grammar, but I'd take it kindly if you'd refrain from calling the technique pat and corny. Like kissing, the short-short is here to stay.

Mr. D., move over.

THE LONGEST WAY 'ROUND

It was one of those days. What with the phones going, a show rehearsing, and people popping in and out, my office was like backstage at an Olsen and Johnson musical.

One of my appointments was with an ex-soldier back from the Pacific. Like a thousand other kids, he was anxious to get into show business. I told him I'd get in touch with him if anything turned up, and asked him to excuse the short interview because I was rushed. He smiled and walked toward the door.

"What are you grinning about?" I asked.

"Oh, nothing," he said. "I just happened to think of another fellow who was in a hurry."

The way he said it made me curious. "Tell me about the other fellow," I said.

"He was nobody important," said the ex-GI. "He and his father farmed a small piece of land. But except for their name and the patch of ground, they had little in common. The old man believed in taking it easy. The son was the go-getter type.

"One morning they loaded their cart with vegetables, hitched up the ox and set out for the city. The young fellow figured that if they kept going all day and night, they'd arrive next morning. So he kept prodding the ox with a stick.

" 'Take it easy,' said the old man. 'You'll last longer.'

" 'If we get to market ahead of the others,' said his son, 'we have a better chance of getting good prices.'

"The old man pulled his hat down over his eyes and went to sleep on the seat. Four miles and four hours down the road, they came to a small house. 'Here's your uncle's place,' said the father, waking up. 'Let's stop in and say hello.'

"The young man fidgeted while the two old gentlemen gossiped away an hour.

"On the move again, the father took his turn leading the ox. When they came to a fork in the road, the old man directed the ox to the right. 'The left is the shorter way,' said the boy.

- " 'I know it,' said the old man, 'but this way is prettier.'

" 'Have you no respect for time?' the son asked.

" 'I respect it very much,' said the old fellow. 'That's why I like to use it looking at flowers.'

"Twilight found them in what looked like one big garden. 'Let's sleep here,' said the old man.

" 'This is the last trip I take with you,' said his son. 'You're more interested in flowers than in making money.'

"Before sunrise the young man shook his father awake and they went on. A mile away, they came on a farmer trying to pull his cart from a ditch. 'Let's give a hand,' said the father.

" 'And lose more time?' asked the son.

" 'Relax,' said the old man. 'Some day, you may be in a ditch yourself.'

"By the time the other cart was back on the road, it was eight o'clock. Suddenly a great flash of lightning split the sky. Then there was thunder. Beyond the hills, the heavens grew dark.

" 'Looks like a big rain in the city,' said the old man.

" 'If we'd been on time, we'd be sold out by now,' grumbled the son.

" 'Take it easy,' said the old man. 'You'll last longer.'

"It wasn't until afternoon that they got to the top of the hill overlooking the town. They looked down at it for a long time. Finally the young man who had been in such a hurry said, 'I see what you mean, Father.'

"They turned their cart around and drove away from what had once been the city of Hiroshima."

MOTHER OF THE YEAR

Fourteen years ago, Eva and Joe Twiller moved to Maplehurst and made a down payment on a house. At first, Maplehurst didn't pay much attention to the Twillers. Then one afternoon a neighbor asked Mrs. Twiller if she'd mind taking care of her youngsters for a day or so. Her mother was ill in New York and she had to catch a train.

"We'd love to have them," Eva Twiller said.

By the time the neighbor returned, her kids had adopted the Twillers. For days they talked of how nice Mrs. Twiller was, the goodies in her kitchen, and the bedtime stories she had told them.

"It's none of my business," said the neighbor one day, "but you ought to have some children yourself. You have a way with them."

A year later, Eva followed this advice and gave birth to a girl. And the year after that, a boy.

By this time the Twillers were part of Maplehurst. Joe's contracting business was doing nicely. The men at the Rotary Club liked him and the Mayor had asked him to serve on the town-planning committee. And without anyone specially noticing it, Mrs. Twiller had become active in most of the female goings-on in the community. When there was a church social, her mocha cake was generally the hit of the evening. When the Civic League wanted a job done, the first name that came to mind was Eva Twiller.

As they grew up, the Twiller kids became just as popular as their parents. They were quiet, well-mannered, and nice to look at. The girl had a flair for the piano, and the boy gave a good account of himself on his class basketball team.

Maplehurst often commented on how well the Twillers got along. The girls in Joe's office used to hear him call Eva in the middle of a busy day just to tell her he was stuck on her. And once a year, Joe would take Eva to New York to see the new shows.

A few months ago, Eva didn't appear at the monthly meeting of the Civic League. She phoned to explain that her boy had a bad cold.

Before the League went into session, someone mentioned seeing an item about the Perfect Wife and Mother Contest which the State Chamber of Commerce was going to run.

"If you should ask me," said the chairman, "the person who ought to get that award is Eva Twiller."

It began as a joke, but half an hour later a committee was appointed to draft a letter to the Chamber of Commerce and place Eva Twiller in nomination. The forty-two women present agreed to sign it. As one of them put it, "I hardly know what to write first. There are so many nice things to say about Eva. Why, there isn't a family in this town she hasn't done something for."

A week after the letter was sent to the capital, the secretary of the Chamber arrived in Maplehurst and did some quiet checking. He seemed to like what he heard. Soon, the Civic League got the letter it had hoped for. Eva had been selected as the perfect mate and mom of the year, and the Governor himself was coming to Maplehurst to present her with the silver loving cup.

The following month, the Governor and a committee of Eva's friends rang the Twiller doorbell. With them were reporters and photographers. Eva came to the door wearing an old house dress and an apron. There was a smudge of flour on her cheek.

"This is the Governor," said the committee chairman. "And don't look so frightened, Eva, it's all in your honor."

"Will somebody please tell me what this is all about?" said Eva.

"Mrs. Twiller," said the Governor, "you've been selected as the perfect wife and mother of the year. And judging from what these ladies have been telling me, the choice is an excellent one."

Eva sat down slowly. "I'd rather no one took any pictures," she said.

"Oh, come now," said the Governor. "Don't be so modest. This lovely house, your children, and the high regard the town has for you indicate that the judges' selection is a wise one."

A committee member took a large silver loving cup from its chamois case and handed it to the Governor. The photographers got their cameras ready.

Eva sat there playing with the pleats in her apron. And then she stood up—more like a soldier facing a firing squad than a woman facing old friends who had come to honor her.

"I'm sorry," she said, "but I can't accept. For the past fifteen years, Mrs. Twiller has been in an insane asylum. I am Mr. Twiller's former secretary."

CASE HISTORY

Some months ago, a medical student was found dead in his room at an Eastern university. On the table by his bed were four letters and a bottle of poison. When the case history of the suicide was finally pieced together, it was as follows:

Otto Engel was born in Hamburg. Even as a child,

he wanted to be a doctor. As a member of the Hitler Youth, his knowledge of first-aid brought him to the favorable attention of his leaders.

A month before he was due to enter the University of Heidelberg, his country went to war against Poland. Otto grumbled when he was called up. He grumbled even more when he was assigned to the Wehrmacht instead of the Medical Corps.

The third year of the war he stopped complaining. He was transferred to guard duty at the Oranienburg concentration camp. There he was able to observe the interesting medical experiments on Jewish prisoners. After a while, he was even permitted to assist.

When Germany surrendered, Otto was taken prisoner. But according to the records, he had never been an important Nazi, and so a few months later he was released. He promptly applied for re-admission to the University. Otto was broken-hearted when the American occupation authorities rejected his application because of his Oranienburg background.

During his months as an American prisoner, Otto had learned English, and it wasn't too difficult for him to get a job as waiter at one of the non-com officers' clubs in Frankfort. It wasn't what he had his heart set on, but the work was easy and there were cigarettes and chocolate bars for tips.

Around the club, Otto heard a good deal of talk about something called the GI Bill of Rights. It seemed that anybody in the conquerors' army could go to any school and study any subject he liked.

One day something happened which gave Otto an idea. As he was going to work in his cast-off GI clothes, an American soldier called out, "Hiya, Jonesy!" When Otto waved back and returned the "Hiya," nothing happened.

Otto began to study the men at the club very carefully. Especially a tech sergeant named William Stern. Stern was about the same size and build as Otto. His hair was brown and his eyes were blue. Otto's hair was brown and his eyes were blue.

Tray by tray, the would-be doctor pieced together the story of William Stern. The sergeant had emigrated to America from Vienna a few years before the war. His parents had disappeared in the smoke of the Auschwitz chimneys. Stern had no relatives or friends in the States and didn't seem anxious to get back.

One afternoon the sergeant came into the club with a Headquarters order. "They're sending me home," he announced to the men at the table where Otto was serving.

On the day Stern was scheduled to leave, the club found itself short a waiter. And when the troopship pulled out for New York, the dog tags around Otto Engel's neck read "William Stern" and his uniform was regulation GI.

It had not been too difficult for Otto to dispose of Stern's body in the rubble, and to alter the features so that identification would be unlikely even if the corpse were found.

When the troopship got to New York, Otto was amazed at the size of the back-pay and bonus checks they handed him. And he couldn't help smiling when a major helped him fill out his application for the pre-medical college he had selected.

Otto completed his three-year course in two. One June morning, dressed in black robes and a stiff square hat, he marched to a platform and was handed a sheepskin. He seemed very happy, but two weeks later his body was found in his book-lined room at the university.

The four letters addressed to William Stern were from four important medical schools. They were polite enough, but between the lines they all said the same thing: "Sorry, but our quota for Jewish students is already filled."

BRASS HAT WITH BRAINS

Brigadier General Edward F. Stacy paid off the taxi driver in front of a red brick house in Washington, D. C. As he held his thumb against the doorbell, he noticed the forsythia had grown a lot thicker.

His wife opened the door. Stacy stood there, stretching the second he had been anticipating for four years. Then he reached out. Rose permitted herself to be kissed and carried into the living room. Then she said, "There's a pitcher of Martinis on the table, darling. I know you like a drink before dinner." There was something pat about the way she said it.

Rose was charming during dinner and the hours that followed.

"Perhaps a little too charming," mused the General as he sat in his bathrobe and puffed a 4 A.M. cigarette. "Or maybe it's my fault. When you dream of one evening for 1,500 days, it's apt to be an anti-climax. Besides, Rose was the daughter of a college president and never one for dancing in the streets."

Rummaging through his wife's desk for a stamp next day, he came across one of those cards a man sends with flowers. It read, "The dearest things I know are what you are. Larry." More rummaging uncovered a bit of paper with the full name—Larry Benham.

The General did what only a smart fellow does when he wants to find somebody. He looked in the telephone directory.

By 5 next afternoon, Stacy knew almost as much about Benham as Benham's mother did. Larry was a playwright who had come to Washington shortly after the war started. He had written radio scripts for the

OWI and made recordings for overseas broadcasts to
the troops.

The General flashed his star around a bit and managed to get some of the Benham recordings out of the
Pentagon files. He listened to them. They were pretty
good. Larry's voice had a casual man-to-man quality.

Stacy's impulse was to charge over to Benham's apartment and start throwing punches. But instead, he went
home and took the cover off his portable. He could
always think better when the pros and cons of a problem were in cold type before him. He started typing:

"I love Rose. Rose loves me—maybe. Rose has been
having a thing with Larry Benham. Is she worth holding on to? Well, let's see. People do crazy things during a war. Four years is a lot of nights. A girl wants
something besides a mirror to tell her she's pretty.
Haven't exactly been a monk myself. That girl in New
Caledonia. The lady druggist in Melbourne. What's the
use of kidding myself? Important thing is to hold on to
Rose. So, what now? What now? What nowisthetime-
forallgoodmentocometotheaidof . . ."

A few days later the General faced his wife in the
living room. "Rose," he said, "I know about you and
Larry Benham. Wait—don't say it. Let's see if we can't
talk this out. First, let me say I'm still stuck on you.
Second, if you want a divorce, I won't make a fuss. But
before you walk out, I'd like you to know what kind of
guy you're leaving me for. Larry Benham's not much of
a man. No man is who kisses and tells."

Rose lit a cigarette. "I don't believe it," she said.

"I didn't think you would," said the General. "That's
why I pulled a cheap trick—like something out of a bum
novel. It happens I know an officer who's chummy with
Benham. He told me Benham had been shooting off his
mouth about you. I asked my friend to invite your playwright up to his room for a drink. I planted a dicta-

phone in the room. Would you like to hear what Benham said when my friend brought your name up?"

The General took a wax disc from his briefcase. "Say 'No,' and I'll break it," he said.

"Play it," said his wife.

Stacy walked to the phonograph and put the record on.

"Let me tell you something about Rose," said the voice which was unmistakably Larry Benham's. "She's a pretty smart operator. Wants you to think she's on the up and up. But don't let that pretty voice of hers fool you. She's a lot of fun, if you don't take her seriously. She has a husband somewhere, but I never heard that it bothered her any. . . ."

The General lifted the tone arm. The college president's daughter stubbed out her half-smoked cigarette and lit another.

"Suppose we forget the whole thing," said Stacy. "I'll go out and mix some drinks."

And then Rose broke, and wept for a long time on the shoulder with the silver star.

Depending on your code of ethics, the General was a hero—or a heel. Anyhow, he never told his wife that the label on the record read:

"OWI 369G: for rebroadcast to Pacific troops; subject—Tokyo Rose."

WHITE CHRISTMAS

There was a crowd around the store window watching the electric trains. Down the block the loudspeaker on a sound truck was blaring "Good King Wenceslas." Across the street on the *Argus-Leader* building, an electric sign kept flashing, "Peace on Earth."

"I'll be glad when Christmas is over," the cop on

the corner told Morrissey, the bus starter. "Look at them crowds!"

"*You'll* be glad!" said Morrissey. "*I* got to load them crowds into buses. And each passenger with a dozen bundles."

The cop slapped his sides to keep himself warm. "Anyway," he said, "the kids get a kick out of it."

He smiled as he saw a little man in a Santa Claus suit waiting on the curb. The rabbit fur on the velveteen jacket had yellowed a bit. On the go-signal, the little Santa started across the street, the brass bells on his cap jingling cheerfully. "Probably on his way to play Santa Claus at some church affair," mused the cop.

In front of the *Argus-Leader* building a couple of kids stopped the shabby St. Nick. A small girl hooked her arm around his neck and whispered something in his ear. A smaller boy kept tugging at her dress to let her know he was waiting his turn.

"Nice-looking kids," thought the cop. "Wonder what they're asking for. Dolls? Sleds? Red wagons? . . ."

In the news room of the *Argus-Leader,* one of the editors cranked a sheet of paper into his Underwood and began typing. " 'Peace on Earth, good will toward men.' Once again these words are on the lips of troubled people the world over. Once again we welcome the all-too-brief season when hate and bigotry are forgotten and all men become brothers. . . ."

The phone rang. The editor picked it up. "Who? Oh, Cassidy. The story about the kid with leukemia? Okay, I'll get someone to take it—I have a Christmas editorial to finish."

The editor glanced at the rewrite desks. They were empty. He turned back to the mouthpiece. "I'll take it, Cass. . . . What's that? The doctors give the kid another ten days to live? He figures to die right after the New Year? Some neighbors on the block chipped in fifty dollars and took him to a department store and let him buy all the toys he wanted?

"Good story! The Chief has been yelling for a Christmas feature. We'll run it under a two-column head on page one. Did Foster get any pictures? Good! We can use the one with the kid talking to Santa Claus at the department store.

"What's that? The hell you say! Why didn't you say so in the first place? You know the policy of the paper. The guy in the front office would tear the joint apart if we ran a picture of a colored kid. Kill it and come on in. . . ."

The cop on the corner looked again at the kids and the little Santa Claus. By this time, there were a dozen youngsters clustered around him. St. Nick was bending over, taking their Christmas orders and writing them down in a penny notebook.

"Look at those kids," the cop said to the bus starter. "All they care about is the red suit and the white whiskers."

Morrissey grinned. "It's a hot one, ain't it?" he said. "You'd think them kids'd wise up, wouldn't ya?"

"I don't know," said the cop slowly. "Maybe the kids are smarter than we are."

"Anyway," said the bus starter, "it's a hot one all right —a colored Santa Claus."

HOW CAN I EVER THANK YOU?

The little soldier walked out on the bridge. The wind sliced through his dirty uniform. He looked down into the river. The water was red, as red as the sun going down behind the Bavarian hills.

"Why not?" he mumbled. "Germany is dying. Why not die with her?"

A car rumbled over the boards. He pressed against

the guard rail as it went by. There were French soldiers in it.

He started walking again. Then he stopped. Where was he going? To Munich? What was in Munich? More gray faces. More beaten people. The Oberleutnant had said, "Go home." No papers. No train ticket. Just "Go home."

Thousands like him on the roads. Feet wrapped in rags. Hungry. Sleeping anywhere. Stealing.

The little soldier turned and looked back. He was alone on the bridge. On the far bank the sun caught a bit of metal. Someone was fishing. Someone in a long coat.

The man on the bridge closed his eyes and knuckled them. He tongued his lips. They tasted sour. He rested his hands on the rail. It was cold. Then he jumped.

As he hit the water, there was a great roaring in his head. A roar like a crowd shouting his name. He felt his boots carrying him down. And down. He felt warmer. Then he saw lights—lights like torches in a parade. And crowds. And in the crowd his mother. She came running toward him. She put her arms around him. He closed his eyes and held on.

When he opened his eyes a strange face was looking down at him. A cup of something hot was at his lips. A voice said, "Easy."

He was in a kitchen. The strange face smiled. "Get this inside you," it said. "You'll feel better."

The soldier took the cup in both hands. He saw an oven and by the oven his uniform drying on a chair.

"Lucky I was on the bank when you went under," chuckled the stranger. "You're the only thing I caught today."

The soldier pulled the blanket up around him.

"Got to be too much for you, eh?" the fisherman went on. "A lot of our men feel that way. But it's no good.

There's too much work to be done. You look weak. Why don't you stay here tonight?"

The soldier got up and started putting on his clothes.

"If you're going to Munich," said the man in the kitchen, "maybe I can help you. I have a friend there. I'll give you a letter to him. What's your name?"

The soldier handed him a damp identification card and went on dressing.

Out on the road, he looked at the letter. Under the date, December 21, 1918, it read:

Dear Benjamin,

As a favor to me, would you please give food and lodging to this young man until he can find work? His name is Corporal Adolf Hitler.

Your friend,
Israel Cohen.

BEYOND ALL DOUBT

Most of the village of Villeroi was squeezed into the courtroom. The accused man sat down in the prisoner's box and rested his fat little hands on the rail. Then the judge spoke:

"The prosecution rested its case last night. The attorney for the defense may now proceed."

As Philippe Durand got to his feet, every eye fixed itself on the man who had come down from the Belgian capital to defend Henri Volpin. So this was the legendary criminal lawyer who had cheated the gallows seventy-one times in seventy-three murder trials—this baldish, paunchy little man, whose suit needed pressing!

"Gentlemen of the jury," Durand began quietly, "Henri Volpin is accused of the murder of twelve women. For a week, I have listened as the prosecutor tightened the noose around my client's neck.

"Now I ask you to remember that no eyewitness to any of the murders has been produced. No one has found so much as a fingernail of the missing girls. Your prosecutor has built his case on circumstantial evidence— some half-remembered words, a button here, a few high-heeled shoes.

"At this moment, if you were polled, I know what your verdict would be. Some of you might even be glad to lend a hand with the rope."

"With pleasure," muttered the clerk.

Durand smiled in his direction. "It is clear Henri Volpin's time is running out," the lawyer went on. "Since this is so, perhaps we might use a few minutes of that time to review his life.

"I know something about such a life. Except for the name, the village I was born in is this village. I remember a bookkeeper in my village who was a great deal like Henri Volpin. He was a quiet man—no one ever gave him a second look.

"From the evidence I've heard this week, I gather that in the forty-one years Volpin has lived in Villeroi, scarcely anyone has given *him* a second look. And in a village, that is not the usual thing. An extra glass of cognac, a walk with a girl is enough to get a man talked about.

"According to the testimony, here is what happened to this obscure bookkeeper. One evening a car drove up to your only hotel. An expensively dressed man and a girl without stockings demanded the best room. The hotelkeeper's wife testified she heard loud talk in their room next morning. She told you the man drove away and left the girl behind. That afternoon, the strange girl walked into the café where Henri was reading the Liége paper over a beer. She sat down with him.

"The waiter has told you Henri bought a bottle of cognac, and the pair discussed going to the bookkeeper's house. The strange girl was never seen again. The learned prosecutor has produced no one who actually saw them enter Volpin's house, but he introduced as evidence a high-heeled shoe found in Volpin's bedroom. The hotelkeeper's wife recognized it as the strange girl's.

"A week later, the cinema attendant saw Volpin sit down next to the Molreaux girl with the painted lips. The widow Prejean, Volpin's neighbor, says she heard a woman laughing in Henri's house that night. She swears it was the laughter of the Molreaux girl. The Molreaux girl has not been seen since, and the prosecution lays great stress on a green suède pump found in my client's bureau drawer.

"Next, you heard the testimony about Louise Rhon, the schoolmistress from Saint Vith. The head of the school told you Mlle. Rhon resigned her position to come to Villeroi and marry a bookkeeper named Volpin. The cartman swore he deposited the lady and her baggage at the defendant's door. The prosecutor showed you a brown walking shoe discovered in M. Volpin's cellar, and Mlle. Rhon's sister has positively identified it.

"You have heard detailed testimony regarding the disappearance of eight other girls under more or less similar circumstances. When Moya, the fifteen-year-old daughter of Dr. Bénois, vanished, the police arrested Henri Volpin. The bookkeeper had been seen buying her a bottle of perfume. A later search of Volpin's lodgings uncovered the assortment of high-heeled shoes.

"This is the case against Henri Volpin. Remember that it is not a capital offense to collect shoes. Under the laws of Belgium, you must not send Henri Volpin to his death unless you are convinced—beyond a reasonable doubt—that he committed murder!"

The father of fifteen-year-old Moya jumped up. "There is no doubt!"

"Gentlemen of the jury," Durand went on, "if there is a doubt in your minds, you must acquit." He paused, looking at each juror in turn. "I say you *do* doubt," he whispered, "even though you don't know it yourselves!"

"There is no doubt!" shouted the sister of the missing schoolteacher.

The judge quieted the court, and the paunchy lawyer continued. "If one of the girls you are so sure is dead were to walk into this courtroom, what would you say? Would you then be so positive the other eleven are dead?"

Slowly he raised his arm and pointed to the green-curtained door at the back of the court. "Gentlemen of the jury," he commanded, "*I ask you to direct your eyes to that door!*"

There was a sharp intake of breath as heads throughout the courtroom turned. The stenographer stopped writing. A small boy in front stood up. Almost everyone in the village was related to one of the missing girls.

After what seemed like forever, the attorney spoke:

"Forgive me for building up your hopes. Forgive me for this shabby trick. No one is going to walk through that door. *But I was the only one in this courtroom who was certain of that!* In every other mind there was a doubt. And, gentlemen of the jury, if there was doubt in your minds a minute ago, how can you send this man to his death?"

Philippe Durand sat down.

"Volpin will walk out a free man," the Paris reporter whispered to a colleague.

But the verdict was guilty. The sentence was death by hanging.

One of the jurors had noticed that the bookkeeper had never once looked toward the door.

Some of My Best Friends Are News

I'VE ALWAYS BEEN a psucker for psychos.

All my life, I've been intrigued by the daffydans who were almost, but not quite, ready for the long white shirt with the starch. *You* can pal around with the normal guy who takes the 5:15 to East Orange. *I'll* take the Nutsy Fagen who eats chocolate sundaes for breakfast and bets the room rent on 50-to-1 shots.

Why do I prefer screwballs to solid citizens? Well, I guess it's because screwballs are more fun. Why waste my life on a rich buttonhole maker when I can be listening to the man who sells life-giving elixir—or your money cheerfully refunded?

My favorite psycho was the late Ted Healy. Ted came into my life when I was doing *Crazy Quilt*. I remember when he first exploded into my office. He was wearing a beat-up Skippy hat, carpet slippers, and a camel-hair coat big enough for a camel. He was accompanied by a chimpanzee.

In a voice like a rusty bugle, the comedian sang "Ol' Man River" while the chimp acted it out. Naturally, I had to have such a team in my show.

A few months after *Crazy Quilt* opened, Healy and I were having a beer together. Suddenly he got up and said, "I think I can trust you. Come with me."

He emptied the pretzel bowl into his pocket and led me back to the darkened 44th Street Theatre, where our show was playing. Lighting matches to see our way, we climbed to the floor above the electrician's booth. Finally we got to the door of a low-ceilinged prop room. Healy opened it, and I saw a pair of shining eyes at the far end of the room.

"What is it?" I asked. "A pussycat?"

"Nope," said Ted proudly, "a Zip."

He lit another match. Sitting on some old canvas was one of those pygmies with a head like an inverted ice-cream cone.

"I've had him up here for a month," said Ted as he fed the pinhead the stolen pretzels. "Bought him from a sideshow at Coney. It's good luck to have a Zip."

When we hit the street again, I told Ted the Messrs, Shubert wouldn't like it if they found out what he was boarding in their theatre. I suggested he get rid of the freak.

"Can't," said Healy simply. "He's muh pal."

Some months later when the show was playing Missoula, Montana, I dropped into Ted's hotel room. The chimp was sitting on Healy's bed, sucking a popsicle.

"How can you live in the same room with that aromatic ape?" I asked.

Ted gave what for him was the complete explanation. "He's muh pal."

But my favorite Healy story has to do with his love life. One night the lady of his heart told him she didn't care for him any more. Healy bowed and said, "I'm not a man to be dismissed lightly." He walked out the door, went down into the cellar, and set fire to the house.

Another standout in my cuckoo cavalcade was English Bob, the nose-biter. Bob walked into my office one day, wearing a cocoa-colored suit and an Edward the Seventh derby. He talked like a man with a monocle in his throat.

"Could I interest you in a miniature which once belonged to Madame Pompadour?" he said. "Ten dollars."

"Into the street with you, laddie buck," I said.

My press agent, a sure-footed oldtimer, dragged me into the hall.

"Listen, Thunderhead," he said softly. "I think you ought to buy that miniature."

"Buy it yourself!" I said.

"Don't you know who that is?" said my drummer boy. "You have just met English Bob, the nose-biter. When thwarted, he goes berserk, grabs you by the lapels and bites off the tip of your nose!"

"Let him nibble on Jimmy Durante if he's hungry," I said.

"Don't make any two-bit jokes about this gentleman," said the press agent. "A few years ago Judge McQuade gave him thirty days for vagrancy. In open court, English Bob pointed his finger at His Honor's schnoz and announced, 'I'm going to bite off the tip when I get out.'

"Thirty-one days later he grabbed the Judge on the courthouse steps and snapped off the end of his smeller. He just got out of stir. That schnoz-bob earned him three years at Ossining U."

"On second thought," I said, "that miniature would look very good on my mantel."

Shortly after the Aquacade closed, I hired a scenic designer named Rudolf Richter to do a show for me. Rudy was a talented gent but a bit of a wack, and it was a standard gag along Shubert Alley that when a producer hired him, he had to hire another fellow. The other fellow's job was to follow Rudy and fish him out whenever he dropped into an open manhole.

Although there were several beautiful girls in the show Richter designed for me, he never paid any attention to them. As far as he was concerned, a girl was something that got in the way of his pretty scenery.

And then one day he fell in love with Jane Morgan, the top looker in our show. Naturally, none of the mob backstage thought the daffy designer had a chance with this doll, but they were wrong. The girl started going steady with Rudy, and for a simple reason—he had asked her to marry him. (I've always contended that any Joe Blow could walk up to Greta Garbo and say, "I'd like to marry you," and get a respectful hearing—that this is the one proposition every girl has time to listen to. My wife, of course, disagrees with this theory.)

A month after Rudy proposed, Jane married him. And the day after the wedding, he told me they had rented a six-room apartment on Park Avenue, and invited me to drop around as soon as they were settled.

A few weeks later I did. I was anxious to see how Richter had decorated his apartment, and, figuring she'd get a kick out of it, I took Eleanor along.

Rudy and Jane were at the door to meet us, and when we walked into the apartment, I looked around, and so did Eleanor. And then we looked at each other.

There were no drapes, no carpets and no pictures. In the living room there was a phone on the floor—and nothing else. There was nothing in the master bedroom but a bed, and the only stick of furniture in the dining room was a plain deal table on which Rudy kept his crayons and paints.

I could see that Jane was embarrassed in front of Eleanor, and so, after a bit of small talk, we left. Out on the street, Eleanor said, "I'll be darned if I can understand it."

"I think I do," I said. "Rudy is a special sort of fellow and he lives in the batty world under his hat. We see his place as an empty apartment. But with Jane sharing it with him, Rudy probably sees it as a cross between Solomon's palace and Marie Antoinette's boudoir."

"I don't care what he sees," said Eleanor. "I'm betting the marriage won't last." And how right she was.

A couple of weeks later, I ran into Rudy on Broadway. "How's Jane?" I asked.

"I wish I knew," said the designer. "She left me last week for another guy."

"I'm sorry to hear it," I said. "Who is he?"

"I don't know," said Rudy, "but I think he's in the furniture business."

Another charter member of the Screwball Social and Athletic Club was the late Myron Selznick. Myron was Hollywood's most successful agent, and for years his take-home money was something like $20,000 a week. In 1932, he got me $5,000 for a song that wasn't worth five. And for the wackiest of reasons.

For years I had been hearing stories about Selznick and how handy he was with his fists; that he loved to scrap and that if there wasn't a brawl handy he'd go out looking for one; that when John Barrymore had talked out of turn one night at a party, Myron had dumped him on his distinguished derrière, and it had taken a dozen men to dissuade the little agent from remodeling the world's most famous profile, etc.

In the summer of 1931, I spent several week-ends at Ben Hecht's house in Nyack, New York. One afternoon while Ben and I were fooling around in the gym he had rigged up in his cellar, a West Coast agent I'll call Bill Meyer dropped in. He made some snide crack about the way I was punching the light bag and then asked me to feel his muscle. I reached up and felt him behind the ears.

Meyer got mad and started bragging about how many guys he had licked. Just to be ornery, I offered to bet him Myron Selznick could belt his brains out. We put up twenty bucks and Hecht held the stakes.

The following year I found myself fresh out of folding money and decided to go to Hollywood, figuring I might sell a song or two to some tone-deaf producer. I had hardly been in my Hollywood hotel room ten minutes when Myron's secretary phoned. "Mr. Selznick wants you to come right over," she said.

I knew Selznick didn't send for people unless the deal involved big numbers, and so I put on a clean shirt and panted over to his office. The girl at the reception desk ushered me in with everything but trumpets.

"I've been wanting to meet you," said Selznick. "How long are you going to be in town?"

I told him it depended on how I made out.

"I've instructed the office to put a car at your disposal," said Myron. "How about having dinner at my house tonight?"

During dinner, I kept wondering when Myron would start talking business. At 9 o'clock he tested his knuckles against his palm and said, "Let's go find Bill Meyer."

"Bill who?" I asked.

"Bill Meyer," he repeated. "Ben Hecht told me about the wager. I'm going to knock Meyer through a wall tonight and win your bet for you."

During the next six hours, we cruised around Hollywood looking for the agent. At 3 A.M., Selznick got Meyer's mother out of bed. When she told him her son had flown to New York that morning, Myron took it pretty hard.

"The double-crosser!" he kept muttering.

By this time I knew that the big deal Hollywood's

number-one agent had for me was to hold his coat while he took Meyer apart.

"So long, Billy," he said at the hotel. "Sorry I let you down. Is there anything I can do to make it up to you?"

"Well, just by coincidence," I said, "I happen to have a great ditty in my inside pocket——"

Next day the little game chicken got me $5,000 for a song that wasn't worth five.

Of course no psycho saga would be complete without Nick the Greek. One summer evening some years back, I was standing outside Lindy's Restaurant when Nick strolled up.

"If you have nothing better to do," said the legendary gambler, "walk down to 34th Street with me. They're playing tonight across the street from Macy's."

We walked south on Broadway, and as we picked our way through the after-theatre crowds, Nick told me about some poems he had been reading by Swinburne. I had heard that Nick was a patron of the arts as well as of the freckled cubes, but had never believed it. By the time we got to 34th Street, I did.

At the doorway of an old loft building, a gent with a toothpick in his face gave us the up-and-down. On the third floor, a second toothpick-in-the-face opened a metal firedoor, and we walked into the biggest dice game in the world.

This was the floating crap game of O. K. Coakley—the bootlegger's Bradley. In the center of a low-ceilinged room big as a skating rink stood a billiard table. Around it, four deep, clustered the players. They made room for Nick as fishermen might for Izaak Walton. I recognized Arnold Rothstein, Big Frenchy, and a couple of bootleggers who are now respected partners in big whiskey companies.

As usual, Nick bet against the dice. A few minutes after we came in, a well-known comedian began to roll them. Nick faded him and covered all side bets. The comic made eleven straight passes.

"See you again, gentlemen," said Nick as he turned away from the table.

He had lost $240,000.

On the way back to Nick's hotel, I kept waiting for him to curse, kick a garbage can, do anything. Instead, he told me about a painting he had seen at the Metropolitan Museum—"Old Lady Cutting Her Fingernails" by Rembrandt.

"There's some doubt about its authenticity," he said. "It's been ascribed to Nicolaas Maes, but it's a great picture no matter who painted it."

At the hotel he invited me up for a nightcap. I kept waiting for the gesture which would indicate he was unhappy about losing almost a quarter of a million in a quarter of an hour.

Nick's room was high up and cool. On the night table by his bed was a plate with an orange on it. He poured me a drink, and as I sipped it, I saw his brows pull together in a frown.

"Here it comes," I said to myself.

He reached for the phone. "I want the manager," he said, the softness out of his voice.

"McKelway," said Nick, "when I checked into this hotel, I asked that an orange and a banana be sent to my room each night. The orange is here, but the banana is missing."

Nick listened for a second and hung up. Then the man who had lost enough that night to buy half the bananas in South America smiled.

"Everything's okay," he said. "They're sending the banana right up."

But Nick and the other psychos were Normal Nellies compared to a couple of gents I used to bump into occasionally at an East Side coffeehouse known as the Caledonia Social Club. One was a somewhat reformed pickpocket known as Once Over Lightly, and the other was an unreformed dentist we had nicknamed Dr. Slowly.

For years, Lightly and Slowly played cards for high stakes, but never with each other. However, after each card session they would adjourn to a corner table to play chess, and the psychiatric overtones of their vituperations and name-calling were worthy of Krafft-Ebing's attention.

Lightly, who had a bitter and mordant wit, did most of the insulting. "Hurry up an' play, awreddy," he would screech at Slowly. "Ya fodda steals from da blind an' ya mudda eats dog food, so it's no wonder ya toined out ta be a rat."

"What's the rush?" Dr. Slowly would answer. "Your date with the electric chair isn't until *next* week."

Though they played for only 50 cents a game, this half-buck meant more to them than the hundreds they wagered at the card tables. Lightly played fiercely and angrily, banging his pieces down, while the dentist, lifting his hands in mock surprise, would murmur, "Slowly, slowly . . ." and make each move with the calculated and irritating languor which had earned him his nickname.

A strange dentist, you must be thinking, yet each profession has its low-lifes. Dr. Slowly's office was in a poor neighborhood, and for years he exploited the unfortunates who placed themselves in his hands. Many a cavity was created where none existed, and the dentist, far from being ashamed, would boast of his chicaneries.

"A man rang my bell last night," I once heard him say. "His jaw was the size of a grapefruit. I told him my price for night jobs was $25. He said he didn't have the money. But he was wearing a watch." Dr. Slowly took a wrist watch from his pocket and dangled it proudly. "It's a beauty, isn't it? An Elgin—must be worth $60."

"Before I metcha," Lightly commented, "I useta believe in God."

But despite this hatred, whenever Slowly missed an evening at the coffeehouse, Lightly would walk around like a man minus a dimension. It seemed he lived only to insult the dentist.

One morning a tooth began doing nip-ups in Lightly's head.

"Look, rat," he said when he arrived at the dentist's office, "I gotta hole in my toot'. Fill it up an' ya make two bucks."

Dr. Slowly inspected the cavity. "This is going to hurt," he said happily. "I'd better give you gas."

"Ya must think I'm nuts," said Lightly. "I should letcha gimme gas wid a wallet in my pocket? Start drillin', rat, and rememba I got my eyes on ya."

Dr. Slowly went to it. Remembering Lightly's insults, he pressed the drill deeper and deeper. By the time it was over, the pickpocket's gums looked like raw hamburger. But he didn't crack once—he wouldn't give Slowly the satisfaction. Before leaving, he took out four half-dollars, spat bloodily on each, and threw them on the floor. Next evening the two men resumed their chess game, heaving abominations at each other as if nothing had happened.

Two weeks later, a hood called Dogface Amroff came to the coffeehouse to play pinochle. Dogface had come by his name honestly—he had two enormous buck teeth. While playing with Lightly, he complained that constant exposure to the air had affected one of his tusks.

"Lemme look at it," said Lightly, moving Dogface

over to the window. As he tilted the hoodlum's face back with his left hand, the ex-dip lifted his friend's wallet with his right.

"It sure looks bad," he said. "Betta go see Doc Slowly. And have him give ya gas or it'll hoit."

When Dogface had gone, Lightly handed the hoodlum's wallet to the proprietor. "Amroff dropped dis. It's got $1,100. Hold onta it fer 'im."

Next morning the papers reported the murder of Dr. Slowly. He had been slugged with a blunt instrument and given an overdose of his own gas. The police were puzzled. Though the office had been ransacked, the murderer hadn't touched the dead man's wallet or a number of watches on his person. He had evidently been looking for something else.

The coffeehouse set figured it this way: When Dogface came out of the ether, Slowly demanded payment. When it wasn't forthcoming, he suspected a stall. Dogface, in turn, suspected the doctor and took appropriate action.

This theory seemed even more logical when Dogface walked into the club that night with a puffy mouth. The hoodlum was startled when the proprietor gave him his wallet. When told that Lightly had turned it in, he handed the pickpocket a C-note.

"Tanks, pal," he said. "I had it figured different."

The only man who mourned the passing of the dentist was Lightly. For hours on end, he would sit gazing at the corner table where he and Slowly always had played. Now and then he would insult some old friend, but his heart wasn't in it. Within a year, he passed away.

I don't know how the student of psychiatry would explain Lightly's death, but I have my own theory. I think he died of a broken heart.

A few doors away from the Caledonia Social Club is Harry's 10th Street Bar and Chop House (pronounced cha-fowse by the select). Harry is an old friend of mine and a former sports writer, and it was he who introduced me to Yonkel the Jink, the standing, sitting, running, jumping, all-time champ in the psycho sweepstakes.

I was watching the preliminaries to the first Louis-Walcott fight when a gent with a balloon head and ears to match walked into the room.

"Who's that?" I asked Harry.

"That's Yonkel the Jink," said the proprietor.

"What's a jink?"

"A jink," explained Harry, "is a fellow who used to be a jinx and graduated. And Yonkel is the hardest luck guy on the East Side—a carrier of misfortune, far, wide, and nearby. By being on hand or underfoot, the Jink can take all the aces out of a pinochle deck and cause horses to run backwards."

"Who are the two individuals with Yonkel?" I asked.

"One is Willie the Zeppelin," said the proprietor. "The little guy—Worm Donovan—is almost as hard lucky as Yonkel. Sort of a junior jink."

"Surely you don't believe any of this nonsense," said a white-haired gent standing next to me at the bar.

"For a long time I didn't," said Harry. "But Yonkel has me convinced. There was, for instance, the day at Hialeah when Alsab broke the world's record for the mile in his morning workout. He went to post that afternoon a one-to-ten favorite. Yonkel bet his roll, $186, on the horse—to *show*! Well, you know what happened. Alsab came fifth."

"Proving nothing," I said.

"Proving everything," said Harry. "Who bet on Army to beat Columbia? Yonkel! Who backed Graziano to lick Zale? Yonkel! Who had his rent money on Count Fleet the only time the horse ever lost? Yonkel the Jink!"

"Is the Jink unhappy about losing all the time?" I asked.

"The reverse," said the proprietor. "It's made him one of the most important fellows on the East Side. Dozens of people make a living by checking his selections and betting the opposite. Actually, Yonkel is proud of being the number-one squitch, and brags about his ability to disrupt the affairs of men, horses, and the little ivory cubes with the momentous markings on them. And when he discusses past achievements, it's always 'The day I beat Army,' or 'The night I knocked out Graziano.'"

"How is the Jink betting on tonight's fight?" I asked.

"Yonkel has five dollars on Walcott to last four rounds," said my host. "Poor Walcott! He'll be having an early dinner tonight."

Just then the preliminaries ended and I watched the champ and contender climb into the ring. When Walcott dropped Louis in round one, I heard the Jink say, "It don' mean nuttin'."

At the end of the fourth, Walcott seemed to be winning and Yonkel looked unhappy. "It wuz ony fer a feevsy," he alibied to the Worm. "Now, if I hadda bet real dough—"

"If ya ast me," said Willie the Zeppelin, "dis jink stuff isa bunk."

"Lissen to da guy," protested Yonkel. "Evrabudy an' his mudda knows there ain't no bigga jink anna Yonk. Tellya what I do. I betcha Louis winsa fight. Bet enybudy inna jernt. Wassamatta, ya yella? Lay eight ta fife. Ya scairt? Two ta one. Take alla mazoo ya wanna bet."

"How much do you want to wager?" the white- haired gent said quietly.

Yonkel glowered at the heckler. "Wadeveya say, chum," he said.

The man laid a hundred-dollar bill on the mahogany.

The Jink dug wildly through his pockets and came up with $48. "All I got on me," he apologized.

"You may hold the stakes," said the old gent, shoving the money down the bar to the Jink.

Yonkel pushed it back. "Watcha tryin' to pull?" he jeered. "Hol' it chaself an' safe botha us trouble."

For the next eleven rounds, it looked pretty bad for Louis. At the final gong, Yonkel was grinning. "Well, I jus' beat da champ," he boasted.

"They haven't announced the decision yet," the white-haired gent pointed out.

"Ain'tcha got eyes?" said Yonkel. "Puda money inya pocket."

A few seconds later, Louis was declared the winner. The Jink was bewildered. "I wuz framed," he kept mumbling.

The stranger paid for his drinks with the hundred, handed Yonkel $96, bid us good night, and walked out.

"Some jink!" sneered Willie the Zeppelin. "Two winnas in one night!"

"Don't brood about it, Yonkel," said the proprietor. "The gentleman you were up against is a pretty good jink himself."

"Waza guy's name?" asked Yonkel.

"Whitehead," said Harry. "Timothy Whitehead. In '29 he lost five million in the crash. A few years ago he promoted a fresh roll and formed an insurance company which specialized in air-travel policies. Well, you know what happened. Planes started cracking up all over the country."

Yonkel smiled like a man with a reprieve from the Governor. "Tha's diffrunt," he said. "Winnin' from dat kinda fella don't mean I'm all washed up azza jink. I wuz outclassed, dat's all. . . ."

Ted Healy, English Bob, Doc Slowly, and Yonkel

are only a few of the inspired loonies I've known in my thousand weeks on Grifter's Gulch. Looking at the world through their eyes has been like looking at it through the wrong end of a whiskey bottle.

Without question, they were all candidates for an analyst's couch.

Of course, *I'm* all right.

Man Bites Pencil

LAST YEAR four lumberjacks, all named Sven, chopped down a tree in Saskatchewan.

In succession, the following things happened: A river carried the tree to a sawmill, a circular blade sliced it into boards, a crane loaded the boards on flatcars, and a locomotive lugged the cars to Brooklyn.

There, one of the boards was fed into a mechanical monster, and when it emerged it was in many pieces. A cutting arm sliced one of the pieces lengthwise, a sliver of graphite was placed in the middle, the halves were glued together, and the words "Eberhard Faber" stamped on them. My secretary paid a nickel for it at a Sixth Avenue stationery shop.

Which all adds up to this: If you don't like this chapter, you can go to Saskatchewan and sue four lumberjacks named Sven.

HEINZLEMAN OF VIENNA

Why can't I ever win an argument from my wife? I've been around more, I've read more, and I once got a medal for debating in P. S. 44. But as we approach our tenth anniversary, the score is, Eleanor, 1,132; Billy, a big fat goose egg.

And it isn't that I'm an amateur at arguing. I grew up in a neighborhood where you had to win arguments to remain vertical, and not being big enough to win with uppercuts, I studied how to win with words. But at an early age I learned a basic fact which has won me hundreds of arguments and lost me dozens of friends—you can't win with Reason. Like a fine tennis player, you've got to put the ball where your opponent can't reach it with radar.

For instance: I recently crossed words with a fellow who insisted that smoking before breakfast gives you gallstones, and who had a hatful of statistics to prove it. Well, I like to smoke before breakfast—let the stones fall where they may. So, like a vaselined seal, I slipped away from his facts.

"Have you read Heinzleman of the University of Vienna?" I asked.

"Who?" he said, reeling back.

"Bah!" I sneered. "When you've read Heinzleman on gallstones, come back and argue with me!"

He slunk from the room and for all I know, he's still looking for Heinzleman. It's an interesting name and it's quite possible that someone at the University of Vienna has it. Dirty trick, you say? Maybe so—but it's better than not smoking before breakfast.

Another bone-crusher is the "Don't you see the connection?" gambit. This is especially effective in company. Let's say you're arguing about inflation, and your opponent has just delivered a masterly analysis of what the Marshall Plan will do to the purchasing power of the dollar. Just as the spectators figure you're on the ropes, you let fly with a completely irrelevant line, "Do you admit that an ounce of silver costs less to refine than an ounce of gold?"

Your opponent bites, and says, "Sure I admit it, but I don't see the connection."

You turn to the gallery and patronizingly announce, *"He doesn't see the connection."* Do the spectators admit they don't see it either? Not a chance—they don't want to look dumb. You smile and exit.

I could go on for pages on "How to Win Arguments and Irritate People," but none of my tested tricks do me any good when I'm arguing with my frau.

"Look at this picture of James Forrestal in the paper," she said one day at breakfast. "He looks like Jimmy Cagney. Don't you think he'd make a good President?"

"You're not being logical, darling," I said. "What has looking like Jimmy Cagney got to do with being a good President?"

"Look who's talking about logic!" said my wife. "Is it logical to come into the house with wet rubbers and track up my clean floor?"

"What has wet rubbers got to do with it?" I asked.

"I'll bet Jim Forrestal's wife doesn't have to follow him around with a mop," Eleanor concluded. "I think he'd make a wonderful President."

Of course there's no answer to that kind of logic, and maybe it's just as well. A long time ago I learned that only a chump insists on the last word with the girl he's crazy about.

I know one or two fellows who consistently win arguments from their wives. But here of late I've been seeing their wives out with other fellows.

IT'S NOT MUCH FUN SINGLE-O

For twenty years, it has seldom occurred to me that

anybody might have trouble meeting a girl. In show business, most fellows have more phone numbers than they have nickels, and so naturally, I've assumed that every guy could dig up something in curls to laugh at his jokes and split a bowl of chop suey with him.

But recently, a lonely man walked into my office and taught me a lot about the boy-girl situation.

This fellow didn't figure to be a Lonesome Luke. He's worth five million bucks, has most of his hair, and there's nothing wrong with his figure that two weeks on Ry-Krisp wouldn't fix.

He wanted me to handle the midway for an industrial exposition he was planning in Florida, and when I told him I needed a forty-hour day to handle what I was already doing, he looked a little disappointed.

"There's a lot of money in this for both of us," he said.

"What do you want more money for?" I asked. "Instead of batting your brains out on an exposition, why don't you take it easy and enjoy the money you've got?"

"I don't get much enjoyment out of enjoying myself," said the millionaire. "It's not much fun single-o."

"Why aren't you married, then?"

"I used to be," he said, "but I guess I didn't give my wife enough time. She walked out ten years ago."

"Why didn't you get yourself another wife?"

"I don't know," he said. "Maybe it's because I've been too busy, or maybe it's because I'm too proud to settle for a girl who's only stuck on my dough."

It was getting late and I knew Eleanor was waiting for me at the house. My visitor was stopping at the Plaza, so I offered to drop him off. On the corner I watched him spend five cents of his five million for a morning paper, and as he walked into the hotel, I got a picture of him with the two hotel pillows propped behind his head, reading the comic strips before he turned out the light.

As my taxi headed toward the East River, I was suddenly conscious of how many men were walking alone. And I knew that for every lonely guy there was at least one lonely gal—eating alone, listening to the radio alone, going to the movies alone.

If a man wants to be President, I said to myself, he ought to figure out some way for lonely people to get together. Even Two Chickens in Every Pot couldn't stand up against the campaign promise that Boy Will Meet Girl.

HIGH FUNANCE

As a night-club proprietor, I meet a lot of gents in the investment business—fellows who regard the money they spend on a girl as an investment.

For years, I've watched these investors make their entrances. On the left arm, like a badge of honor, they usually wear one of the better-publicized cuties of the season. And when they order her a drink and a bite of supper, it's like Diamond Jim Brady giving away a bucket of rubies. Everything about them screams, "You lucky girl! Coal Oil Johnny is spending a ton of money to give you a big evening!"

Well, for twenty-five years I've been catering to this Big Eastern Spender and I think I know to the dime what a night out costs him. And here's a piece of news which may open his motel eyes: The girl usually spends more on the evening than he does!

Let's oil up the adding machine and see if this investor rates the quick dividend he's generally after. He has sent her an orchid from Goldfarb's—$5. Dinner at Armando's—$12. Two tickets to a show—another $12. And then, ringside at El Morocco.

Here, unless he goes for imported champagne—and as a rule he doesn't—his tab will be fifteen bucks or less.

Another five or six will cover taxis and tips. Add another quarter for the pro in the men's room and you're up around $50.

Pretty big score? Well, the investor thinks so. In fact, if he loses the brief but intense struggle at her door and winds up with the morning paper, he is likely to call his darling a bad thing.

Now let's look at the girl's outlay for the evening. First, clothes. Heavy-breathing Harry wore his tuxedo, good for five years if he watches his waistline. The girl was wearing a little number ransomed from Hattie Carnegie for 300 plunks—and she mustn't be seen around in it too often, so each wearing sets her back about $30.

The hair-do and facial at Elizabeth Arden's annihilated a $20 bill, and the scented man-killer she dabs behind the earlobes comes out of a jug that starts at $30 for the small, no-economy size. And as for that mad, mad hat from John Frederics—at least $40.

Bag and gloves from Lederer's, shoes from Delman's, jewelry and furs from wherever she can get them—whether the girl knows it or not, it has cost her $20 an hour to hear Harry's autobiography.

It's my hunch that any certified public accountant will testify that she has a right to say, "Good night, Mister, I'm a little tired."

AND A LITTLE DOG SHALL LEAD THEM

The other morning I got up on the wrong side of the percentage. My slippers weren't there when I felt for them, and in the medicine chest was a new kind of toothpaste that tasted like turnips. Worst of all, the morning paper was mussed.

"Darling," I said to my wife, "when are you going to stop using my paper as a dustcloth?"

"Steady, Ivan," said the big L of my life.

As I left the house I slammed the door, but I didn't slam it fast enough to keep our pooch from dashing after me. I chased Mike back into the house, but as I walked to the office I got to thinking about him.

The trees and grass were extra green the summer we bought him and took him up to Mt. Kisco, and judging by the way he acted, Roseholm must have looked to him like one big dog biscuit. He barked at butterflies, nibbled leaks in our garden hose, and gave the Westchester squirrels a good workout.

Indian Summer that year was like the Chicago fire in Technicolor. And then, one November morning, an early snowfall covered the fields, and Mike was face to face with a world he had never seen before.

He looked at it for a few seconds and then began to bark at it, and when it didn't bark back, he pawed at it a little. Suddenly he made up his mind, took off like a tipsy rocket, and disappeared into a snow-drift.

When Mike emerged a minute later, he and the snow were buddies, and for the rest of the day he rolled, frisked, and carried on as if he were quintuplets. It had taken him only a sniff and a jump to decide that this new white world was wonderful.

Well, by the time I got to my office, I was feeling pretty silly. If the pooch could get along with a world which had pulled such a colossal switch on him overnight, why was I taking it so big because my wife had mussed up my newspaper?

ME AND MY BIG MOUTH

An actor once bragged that his name on a marquee meant real money at the box office. Instead of yessing him, I was mean enough to bet him ten dollars that the first hundred people we met on the street wouldn't recognize him. Well, I won the bet, but it was like giving him a hundred kicks in the breadbasket.

I used to write fast shorthand, and at parties I'd sometimes take down verbatim the conversation of some of New York's self-declared wits, and then read it back to show them how unfunny they were.

I used to tell girls who didn't belong in the theatre that they didn't belong in the theatre, and once, Heaven forgive me, I even offered a character part to a fifty-year-old juvenile.

But, thanks to a few extra years and some tough talk from Eleanor, I've stopped jabbing lighted cigarettes into people's toy balloons. Or perhaps I should say I've almost stopped.

The other night I was at my cabaret when Arthur Freed of M-G-M came in with his wife. I invited the pair to join me at my table, and over the second highball, Arthur told me he had taken up painting and had sold one of his oils to Buddy de Sylva for a thousand dollars.

This sounded fishy to me. Buddy is a discriminating art buyer who recently presented a fine collection of moderns to the Los Angeles Museum, and though he does a little painting himself, he's too hep to have any illusions about his skill with the brush.

Instead of letting Arthur get away with his little fib, I decided to play Mr. District Attorney. Casually I asked him if he had added any important paintings to his collection during the year. Sure enough, he had acquired an original de Sylva for a thousand dollars.

"You're a faker," I said. "All you California Rembrandts did was to exchange checks."

"Why do you say that?" pouted Freed. "Buddy liked one of my paintings, bought it, and gave me a check for a thousand dollars. A few days later I admired one of his and gave him my check for a thousand dollars."

"Let's take it from the top," I said. "You took up painting as a hobby, figuring it was more cultural than gin rummy. One day, who should come to your house but Buddy de Sylva, who also puts squiggles on canvas. You showed him your paintings. De Sylva said they were interesting and well painted—always safe comments—and then, with a straight face, he offered you a thousand dollars for one painting—more than Van Gogh earned in a lifetime.

"When you delivered the painting to Buddy's house, he showed you some of his handiwork. Well, you're a big boy and you know when it's your turn to buy the drinks, and so you picked out one of his paintings and gave him *your* check for a thousand dollars. Look me in the eye, Arthur, and tell me if that isn't the way it happened?"

"I guess you're right," said Arthur as he collected his wife, and stumbled out into the night.

I sat there hating myself. Why didn't I keep my big mouth shut?

STEALING FROM THE BOSS

The other day I nearly stole a clock. I was poking around an antique shop, and took a fancy to an old enameled timepiece, worth perhaps thirty dollars.

No one was watching and I was about to walk off with it when I realized what I was doing. "Wait a minute, Itchy Fingers," I said to myself. "Why are you stealing the man's clock? You've got thirty dollars. If you want it—buy it."

I put the clock back and walked out of the shop. I didn't like it well enough to buy it—I only liked it well enough to steal it.

"Aha!" I can hear you saying. "I always knew that Rose guy was a thief." Well, maybe I am, but don't be so quick to point a finger at me. Maybe you're a thief yourself.

If you'll step up to the witness stand, I'd like to ask some questions. To begin with, did you ever finger the coin-return slot of a pay telephone after you hung up? If you found a nickel there, did you or did you not mail it back to the company? That's not your nickel, you know. If you kept it, you stole it.

Another question: Did you ever borrow a book and conveniently forget to return it? Remember, you're under oath, you bookkeeper. And where did you get that towel with the hotel name on it? Oh, you embroidered it yourself? Very interesting!

Perhaps we'd better get the children out of the courtroom before I ask the next question. Did you ever steal anything from the boss? I thought so! But don't worry, I'm not going to press charges, and with the Court's permission I'd like to tell you why.

Stealing from the boss is almost as popular as baseball and kissing. It's the old tug-of-war between the have-lots and the have-littles, and folks who never miss a Sunday in church think nothing of mailing a letter with the boss's stamp, or making personal calls on his telephone and time. But there's not much the boss can do about it—it's pretty hard to cancel out 5,000 years of human nature.

I once knew a soda jerk who worked for a drugstore chain that protected its registers with everything but electric eyes. One day someone told the jerk that he looked like Adolphe Menjou, so he went out and bought himself a fancy suit on the installment plan. He told me that in five months he paid for five suits out of the register, and when he quit, he had a wardrobe to match the splendid reference they gave him.

At Monte Carlo they sew up the croupiers' pockets, but they have never figured out how to sew up the pockets of the croupiers' confederates. And the Kimberley diamond mines admit they are oontzed out of a bushel of stones each year, even though they inspect the native workmen in the oddest places before checking them out.

Take my own nightclub, the Diamond Horseshoe. I had a system there to prevent pilfering which was almost maniacal in its exactness. At any instant I could tell you the percentage cost of a pat of butter on each dollar's sales.

For years I slept easy, figuring nobody could get away with so much as a radish. But last year one of my bookkeepers came to see me. "I've been thinking about your food-control system," he said, "and it would be easy for a smart fellow to rob you blind."

Then he proceeded to tear down my system like Willie West and McGinty tear down a house. "But don't worry," he said when he had finished. "I've also figured out a way to plug up the holes."

When he had finished explaining the new system, I shook his hand and gave him a raise. But I've been worried ever since. If this bookkeeper can figure out a way to break my system, it's a cinch he can figure out a way to break his own—and me with it. And if I fire him, I'm in worse trouble. He might get mad and give his successor a few pointers. Interesting problem, isn't it?

THEY'RE NEVER HELPLESS

No gambling house ever won a dollar of my money, and no gambling house ever will. Is it because I'm a bum sport, or is it because I know too much about gambling house percentages? Well, let's see.

To get the little white ball rolling, I offer a quote from *The Theory of Games and Economic Behavior* by

Professors John von Neumann and Oskar Morgenstern of Princeton University: "In roulette, the mathematical expectation of the players is clearly negative. Their motive for participating in the game cannot be understood if one identifies the monetary return with utility."

In cap-and-gown words, the professors are saying, "The sucker hasn't got a chance."

I used to know a gambler named Honest John Shaughnessy, and I once asked him if gambling houses were crooked. "Let me put it this way," said Shaughnessy. "They're never helpless."

I once had an off-the-record chat with a director of the Monte Carlo Casino. He told me that the odds against my breaking the bank were 48,000,000,000,000,-000,000,000,000-to-1. Then he smiled and asked me what I was waiting for.

The only player who ever had the Monte Carlo operators winging was a Yorkshireman named Jaggers. A mechanic by trade, he knew it was impossible to maintain a delicate machine in perfect condition, and that every roulette wheel was a little off true. And so he hired six assistants to sit at six different tables and mark down the winning numbers as they came up all day, and then correlate the figures into an analysis of the weaknesses of each wheel.

At the end of a month, his statistics showed that certain numbers came up at certain tables more frequently than they figured to by the law of averages. He started to play, and at the end of a week, he had won $600,000.

The Monte Carlo directors put their well-barbered heads together and decided that the way to beat Jaggers' system was to keep switching wheels from table to table. Jaggers lost $200,000 before he got wise and stopped playing. And then one day he noticed that each wheel had some identifying nick or scratch in the shiny metal. He started playing again and won back the $200,000.

One of the bright boys at Monte Carlo then suggested sending for the manufacturer of the wheels. The manufacturer pointed out that Jaggers' numbers were coming up oftener than they should because the partitions into which the ball fell were slightly irregular. He suggested that these fixed partitions be made movable. The wheels would still be untrue, but by shifting the partitions the irregularities would never be the same on any table two days in succession.

Against this, Jaggers could do nothing. Within a couple of days he realized what was going on, and went back to Blighty about a half million out in front.

Well, if a smart fellow like Jaggers had to quit playing roulette, I see no point in my starting. And it's a lucky thing for the gambling fraternity that more people don't know the old Abe Martin line—"The best way to double your money is to fold it once and put it back in your pocket."

OLD SILVERTOP ON GOLD

Some time ago, I read a magazine piece about gold by a fellow who usually knows what he is talking about. He opined it was silly for the United States to trade tractors and wheat for little bars of yellow metal which we bury in the ground.

The articles scared me a little, and so I took my fears to my old boss, who was sunning himself on a bench in Central Park.

"Mr. Baruch," I said, "tell me about gold. Why are we filling that cavity at Fort Knox with it? Do you agree with the economists who say it's only good to plug leaks in old rowboats?"

The old boy, for whom Presidents holler when their noses are in the nutcracker, gave me a little lecture.

"The thing that makes an ounce of gold worth $35," he said, "is that it costs almost that much to locate it, dig it out of the ground and refine it. Of course, there's an occasional Klondike where they get it out for less, but by and large, $35 is a fair world average. And so, because it represents hard work, for centuries people have been willing to trade the labor that goes into goods and services for the labor that goes into digging gold."

"But why gold?" I asked. "Why not tin or coal?"

"They're too bulky," said Old Silvertop. "We have twenty billion dollars' worth of gold in one cellar in Kentucky. Coal worth that much would darn near blanket the Blue Grass State."

"Why not diamonds?" I said.

"There aren't enough to go around in a world with almost two billion humans. Besides, you can mold gold and stamp it, it's rare and attractive, and no alchemist or scientist has come up with a process whereby a man-day of work would give you a ton of it. And until that happens, the gold in Fort Knox will be valuable because it represents the labor necessary to duplicate it.

"Backed up by this gold, our currency has muscles. True, it had bigger muscles when we had a dollar's worth of gold for every dollar's worth of paper issued against it. But even with only twenty billion backing up several times that much in paper, we're not in bad shape.

"Like Aesop's fox who lost his tail, nations without gold have in recent years been trying to convince the world that it's much prettier not to have a tail. Every now and then, they send us an economist in striped trousers who tells us our gold is only good for charm bracelets, and unfortunately, some of our own economists have fallen for this monetary mumbo-jumbo.

"Some time back, these economists had the ear of a

very important gentleman in our setup, and they tried to persuade him to stop buying gold—said we didn't need it to back up our dollars. When this important gentleman honored me by asking for my opinion, I gave him my answer in the form of a little story.

"Once an archeologist unearthed an ancient chest which dated back to Alexander the Great. It contained gold coins and paper fiat money. The folding money was very pretty and could be used to paper a wall, but the coins—minted two thousand years back—were, as the saying goes, good as gold. In any city of the world, you could use them to buy a meal, hire a room, or get your pants pressed."

"That's a good story," I said. "Was the important gentleman impressed?"

"He didn't say," said Mr. Baruch, "but I do know the United States continued buying gold."

"This important gentleman didn't happen to have a wife with the same first name as mine?" I asked.

The man on the park bench stretched his long legs and smiled.

OLD MONEY AND NEW MONEY

At Mr. Baruch's house one night, the butler announced an unexpected guest.

"I'm sorry to barge in like this," said a man I'll call Joe Smith, "but I got a phone call from Washington and I need some advice."

Mr. B. introduced the visitor and I recognized him as the gent who had mated a grocery store with imagination and wound up with one of the largest chains of super-markets in the East.

"Here's my problem," he said. "The government wants me to go to Europe and help out on its food distribution plan."

"When do you leave?" asked my old boss.

"That's what I want to talk to you about," said Smith. "The job pays six thousand a year and I don't see how I can afford to take it."

The man who used to out-trade the House of Morgan polished his specs. "How much does it cost you to live a year?" he asked.

The businessman shrugged. "About a hundred thousand," he said.

"How much have you got saved up?"

Smith looked at me as if I were a Communist spy, and hesitated.

"You don't have to answer," said my old boss. "*Fortune* magazine recently estimated your wealth at over three million. In other words, at a hundred thousand a year, you have enough eating money for the next thirty years."

"What are you driving at?" asked Smith.

"Just this," said Mr. Baruch. "You're in your fifties and the insurance companies give you a life expectancy of another twenty years. Your old money will last until 1979, and you can't get around to using any new money until 1980."

"I don't follow," said Smith.

"Let me see if I can't ease it up," said my old boss. "Have you ever noticed how a penny gum machine works? It holds fifty pieces of gum, one on top of the other, and when you put a penny in, the bottom slice pops out. The only way you can get to the top slice is to use up the forty-nine ahead of it.

"Well, it's the same when you have a lot of money. Before you can use the new money, you first have to use up the old money that's ahead of it."

"How about my wife and kids?"

"There's plenty for your wife," said Mr. B., "and probably too much for your kids. You know, you can handicap a child by making it too easy for him. Let me ask you one more question. Are you having any fun running your grocery stores?"

"It used to be fun," said Smith, "but it's routine now."

"That's what I thought," said the park bench philosopher. "And I think you've reached the age where you ought to start thinking about a little fun."

"That job in Europe doesn't exactly sound like a good time," said the groceryman.

"I don't agree," said Mr. Baruch. "I think you'll get a bigger kick out of it than anything else you've ever done. For one thing, you'll be helping your country, and for another, you'll be helping millions of hungry people."

"I knew I shouldn't have come to see you," said Smith as he reached for his hat. "Wait till I tell the wife what you said about old and new money."

"When do you sail?" asked Mr. Baruch.

"I'll probably fly," said the businessman.

THE COUNTRY IS BASICALLY SOUND

There's a legend around Broadway that I get inside information about the stock market, and I'll be darned if I know how the story started.

What I know about Wall Street you can find in Gypsy Mary's Dream Book, but my friends refuse to believe it. When I refuse to predict the future of stocks like du Pont or U. S. Rubber, they denounce me for holding out on them and whisper, "If that Rose would ever open up we could all retire."

One morning I got a phone call from California. It was the head of one of the big Hollywood studios, and a man worth many millions. I shall call him Maxwell B. Maxwell.

"Billy," he said, "thank God I found you in! The way

the market has been acting lately, I don't know whether
to buy or sell. This morning I said to myself, 'What's
the use of guessing when I can talk to the man who
knows?' Tell me, pal, what do you think of the oils?"

"I don't know anything about oil stocks," I said.

"Don't give me that," said the Hollywood producer.
"*You* know."

"I don't know a thing," I said, "except, perhaps, that
the country is basically sound."

"That's good enough for me," said the big shot. "I'm
going to buy myself a bundle as soon as I hang up."

I knew that by a bundle Max meant several hundred
thousand dollars. "Hold on," I said. "Before you buy
anything, let me discuss this with a man who really
knows."

"Who do you mean?" he asked.

"I can't mention his name on the phone," I said. "I'll
call you back."

I hung up and phoned a friend of mine in Washington
I shall call Horace B. Horace. He is so influential in government that he never goes to a movie without leaving
his name at the box office, so the President can get him
if he needs him.

"Horace," I said, "just between us, what do you think
of the oil stocks?"

"Why ask me?" said Horace. "I never owned a share
of stock in my life."

"Please, Horace," I said, "don't give me any double-
talk. A lot of money is riding on your answer."

"Well, Billy," he said, "I think conditions are funda-
mentally okay, but if it means that much to you, I'll get
you the opinion of a man who really knows."

Fifteen minutes later Horace phoned me. "You can
rest easy," he said. "I just talked to the one man in
America who knows, and he assured me that the country is basically sound."

"Horace," I said, "I know I'm out of line asking, but I wonder if you'd mind telling me whom you talked to."

"Ssh," said Horace, "the wires may be tapped."

"We'll have to chance it," I said. "On my honor, I won't ever tell a soul."

There was a pause, and then Horace said, "All right, if it's that important, I'll tell you. It was Maxwell B. Maxwell of Hollywood."

THE THREE E'S

The other night I had a nightmare and woke up screaming. I dreamt I was a schoolteacher.

A group of us teachers had gone to the state capital to tell the Governor we couldn't pay today's prices on 1933 salaries. As we walked up the Capitol steps, we were met by a politician wearing a gold derby and three waistlines. He led us to an abandoned icehouse near the railroad tracks. There was a sign on it—"Subnormal School."

"Fellow Amurricans," he boomed, "there's a lot of subversive talk going around that $30 a week is not a living wage. After giving it a lot of thought, the best brains here at the capital decided that the way to stand off this Communist ·plot was to set up this Subnormal School and teach you how to get along on what you make. This way to the classrooms!"

The first course was Dietetics. "You've got to stop thinking about the Three R's," the politician told us. "The important thing is to learn how to get along without the Three E's—Eatin' Breakfast, Eatin' Dinner and Eatin' Supper."

"What'll we live on, then?" asked a skinny chemistry instructor.

"Apples," said the politico. "If you lady teachers will make yourselves up real pretty, the kids will bring you big red apples. What you can't eat, you can pass on to the men, and what they can't eat, they can sell on street corners."

Then he rolled down a chart and gave us a little lecture on the caloric content of dandelion greens, potato peelings, and stale bread. And then a demonstration on how to make soup from an old baseball glove. After that, there was a recess and we were all served tall glasses of ice water.

Then came a quiz on Economics. There were many interesting questions:

(1) Roy Rogers' horse makes $1,000 a week. Give three reasons why you are glad you were born a human.

(2) The big bad wolf wanted to eat Little Red Riding Hood. What school did *he* teach at?

(3) How can a lady teacher dress on 50 cents a month so as to look plain to mothers and attractive to fathers at the same time?

(4) Describe a steak.

None of us could answer question No. 4.

Then we were marched to the assembly hall, where the Governor appeared and did a softshoe dance while balancing the budget on his nose. For a finish, he asked us to join him in singing, "America, the Beautiful."

Halfway through the chorus, a teacher in the back began to scream. Then a couple down front started, and soon every teacher in the place was screaming. But I screamed the loudest, and kept on screaming until I woke up.

LIVERWURST AND HELICOPTER PARTS

Wherever you are, Mr. Perkins, I forgive you.

For thirty-six years, I've hated you, and this hate started the day I answered the "Boy Wanted" sign in your window. You looked me over as if I were a sore throat and offered me $2 a week to help out around your drugstore after school.

For months I washed bottles, ran errands and aired Mrs. Perkins' pooch. But more than anything else, I swept the sidewalk. No matter how hot or cold it was, at least twenty times a day, you would hand me the broom and tell me to sweep up outside.

Yes, I've always hated you, Mr. Perkins, but recently something happened which gave me a different slant on you and the drugstore business.

I was up in Washington Heights and wanted to call my office, so I stepped into a drugstore and asked the man behind the counter to let me have two nickels for a dime. When I finished the call, I remembered a couple of letters Eleanor had given me to mail, and not having a penny to go with the unused nickel, I handed the druggist a ten-dollar bill and said, "May I have two three-cent stamps?"

After I licked the stamps, my mouth felt gluey and so I asked him for a glass of water.

As the proprietor walked behind the soda counter, I could tell from his shuffle that he had misery in the feet. But instead of complaining, he smiled and said, "At least you haven't got a baby. Some customers want me to mind their brats while they shop at the cut-rate down the street."

This druggist reminded me a lot of you, Mr. Perkins. Same patchy hair, same watery eyes, same steel-rimmed specs. And maybe that's why my tone wasn't so friendly when I said, "What's biting you, Mister? You make a pretty good living, don't you?"

"I suppose so," said the pharmacist, "if you call it living to work sixteen hours a day and sleep over a store. Last night a fellow rang my bell at 2 A.M., and when I came downstairs, he said that all he wanted was a dime's worth of bicarbonate for his indigestion. I told him he had a heck of a nerve waking me up when a glass of hot water would have straightened him out.

" 'Thank you,' he said, putting the dime back in his pocket. 'Then I won't disturb you.' "

"A wise guy," I said.

"The wise guys are only part of it," said the druggist. "In the old days I used to sell drugs, but today I have to stock up on everything from liverwurst to helicopter parts. And when a customer asks for a tablet, it's up to me to guess whether he has a headache or wants to write a letter.

"And now, on top of everything else, a lot of my lady customers have stopped buying medicine. A good-looking psychiatrist recently opened an office in this neighborhood, and now the girls are convinced that their sicknesses are all mental."

At that moment a skinny kid came in, walked back of the counter, and started fixing himself a marshmallow sundae.

"Keep away from the ice cream," said the druggist. "Get the broom and sweep the sidewalk!"

"I swept it an hour ago," said the kid.

"Sweep it again!" yelled the druggist.

Well, I had heard enough. I bought a pocket comb I didn't need and left. And as I was saying, Mr. Perkins, wherever you are, I forgive you.

RIDDLE ME THIS

I'll give you three guesses—what's the biggest box-office attraction in the world?

Love? Wrong. It sells a lot of tickets but there is something that sells more.

Comedy? Close, but still wrong. Fred Allen, Donald Duck, Jimmy Durante—they're great, but there's something that outdraws them.

Music? Go to the foot of the class.

The biggest box-office attraction is death. Death, or the promise of death, has always been and I'm afraid always will be mankind's most popular form of entertainment.

In Cleveland some years ago, I saw more than half a million people at one performance of·a show. They overflowed grandstands, streets, and fields to see the National Air Races. Why? Because they were aviation enthusiasts? My eye! They were there to see daredevils like Jimmy Doolittle coquetting with death at five miles a minute.

Maybe they didn't know it, but they were waiting for a wing to tear away, for those flames which stream out of a plane and turn it into a comet. They sat through hours of what I thought was only a fair show, waiting for those seconds of terror and ecstasy between the loss of control and the sickening, satisfying crash on the ground.

And what do you think draws over a hundred thousand people to the Indianapolis Speedway every year? Is it the race, or are they waiting for a wheel to fly off, for a car to lift suddenly from the track and float through the air until it explodes into scrap iron and fire against a wall?

Well, you know the answer. There's a man inside that car—mortal stuff, bones that can snap like pencils, flesh that can be sliced like bacon, fifty cents' worth of chemicals held together by a spark. And any time a guy is willing to thumb his nose at the Great Man-Eater, people by the hundred thousand will be there, on the chance that he won't get away with it.

What performer got as much as $40,000 for a single appearance? A bullfighter named Manolete, who was gored to death not long ago. I watched him perform in 1945 in Mexico City and the friend who took me paid a

speculator $100 apiece for our tickets. When Manolete
strutted around the ring after killing his bull, I saw
women throw mink coats and jewelry into the ring—
yes, even their underpants.

I'll let you put any four movie stars you name on any
four corners of midtown Manhattan, and I'll bet you a
shiny lollipop they won't cause as much commotion as a
poor fool named John Ward, who once crawled out on
an eleventh-story ledge and pondered his suicide all
afternoon. By the time he jumped to his death, his audience was greater than the population of Cincinnati.

I wish it weren't so, but as a showman I know that
people will always buy destruction. Twice in my life,
I've seen the world spend hundreds of billions on a
show where the star performer was wearing the skull
and crossbones. And now they're talking about bringing
him back for another engagement.

Take it away, Sigmund Freud.

A TEN-MILLION-DOLLAR IDEA

Right after the Aquacade closed in 1940, I spent a
year planning a spectacle which could gross a million
dollars a week. The star of this show was to be the
gent with the skull and crossbones I discussed in the
previous piece. But I never got to stage this extravaganza because around that time a couple of impresarios
named Adolf and Benito rang up the curtain on a death
spectacle of their own.

However, I still have the blueprints around my office
and I'd like to pass them along to any firecracker kid
who thinks he has it in him to be the P. T. Barnum
of tomorrow. Here, in easy inspirations, is the notion
which, properly staged and exploited, will make him
his first billion pennies. . . .

The new glamour guy of the globe is the air pilot,

and the new poetry is the roar of the propeller. I'm
suggesting that the P. T. Barnum of tomorrow cash in on
this and stage a musical comedy in the sky.

The chorus of this show would consist of one hundred Beautiful Planes—count 'em, one hundred. And
its comedians would be those priceless maniacs who
lock wings in the clouds, miss the top of the grandstand by inches, hang by their toes thousands of feet
up, and perform other shenanigans you've got to see to
believe.

I have two tentative titles for this spectacle—Aircade
or Sky Show.

Where could P. T., Jr., present an attraction that big?
Well, when I was working on it eight years ago, I was
going to use the Roosevelt Raceway on Long Island,
which seats fifty thousand, covers almost two hundred
acres, and is near several airfields. And on tour, I intended to book the racetracks and speedways which are
idle most of the year.

Let me tell P. T., Jr., how I saw the show, and I wish
he wouldn't brood about its not being practical. Every
detail has been checked with aviation engineers.

I was going to moor a Zeppelin at each end of the
raceway and replace the cabins with suspended plat-
forms. I figured on putting Paul Whiteman and his orchestra on one platform, Fred Waring and his glee club
on the other, and amplifying the music and words with
giant loudspeakers.

The Aircade would start with a single plane on the
field. A pilot who could sing—and there are such—
would climb into the plane with the heroine of the
piece, and as the plane took off, he would start singing the opening song into a mike. Probably something
about love and pink clouds.

As our hero was making smoke hearts in the sky, the

chorus would come into view, flying in formations of fours, eights and twelves, and for the first time in entertainment history, words, music and sky choreography would be blended. Then, as our planes exited, we would trot out our first specialty—parachute jumpers trying to land within large white circles on the field.

Another number was to be a nostalgic nifty built around old-fashioned biplanes, triplanes and single-seaters of the Orville Wright period. And, of course, the show would have the usual bust-in-the-head finale —boy gets girl somewhere between Orion and the Big Dipper, while the planes, outlined in neon, form a giant American flag.

What would it cost to operate this show? My guess is $50,000 a week. What could it gross daily at the ticket window? Well, it all depends on how rich you want to get, and how fast. . . .

There it is, P. T., Jr. Put this one over and Darryl Zanuck will be asking for *your* autograph—and all I want for the notion is a credit line in the program down where it says, "Deodorant by courtesy of Hiram Glotz."

If the show is that good, I suppose you're wondering why I'm offering to give it away. Wouldn't I like to wear the Barnum mantle myself? You're darn tootin' I would, Junior. The trouble is I'm an old kid and I no longer feel like investing the hours and headaches this project calls for. But lawsy, lawsy, if I were only thirty again.

NEXT TIME THEY GIVE A WAR

Not long ago the Pittsburgh papers printed a story of great human courage. Oddly enough, it depressed me. But before I tell you why, let me give you the story.

Two kids were playing on a street in suburban Pittsburgh. One of them, Jimmy Boustead, age eight, started poking around a large storm sewer. He slipped, fell through the grating into the black water, and the current swept him underground toward the flood-swollen Allegheny River, a few hundred feet away.

His chum, Lawrence Wildi, age ten, heard his scream. He knew Jimmy couldn't swim, so he sprinted to the next sewer opening, shoved aside the safety bars, and dropped into the evil-smelling stream below. And this despite the fact that (a) he couldn't swim either, and (b) he didn't know whether the water was three or thirty feet deep.

Fortunately it was only up to his waist. He braced himself against the torrent and waited, and in a few seconds Jimmy came tumbling out of the darkness, struggling weakly.

Larry grabbed him, held on and hollered until a couple of grownups came along and pulled the two sprouts back into the sunlight.

How's that for nerve! . . .

And now, let me tell you why the story depressed me, and why practically all stories of heroism depress me.

If Larry Wildi and the millions of kids like him weren't so all-fired brave, I doubt whether they could be sold on the Big Blood Bath every couple of decades. If they had less sand in the craw and more yellow in the belly, you couldn't strike up the band and get them to go singing onto a battlefield where the new grass barely covers the old scars.

I'll be darned if I know where man gets all his moxie. On the evolutionary calendar he came only a day after Charlie the Chimp. But while the chimp slinks from flame, Larry Wildi joins volunteer fire companies; while the chimp shrinks from pain, Larry's brothers have been known to offer their bare arms to mosquitoes full of yellow fever. And don't tell me it's because Larry has brains and the chimp hasn't. Deeds of heroism usually have little to do with the think-tank.

I read recently where a youngster got into a rocket plane and flew faster than sound. The boy knew he and his plane might disintegrate at 750 miles an hour, but he was willing to try it anyhow. I applaud his courage, but I can't help wishing more people were more afraid of the things there are to be afraid of.

That way, what a little girl once said might come true—"Some day they'll give a war—and nobody will come."

ME AND MY PEA-SHOOTER

As daffy as it seems, I may have had something to do with Hitler's decision to commit suicide. Before you say "Ridiculous," let me present a curious set of facts:

On June 27, 1941, I wrote the following letter:

Lord Halifax
British Embassy
Washington, D. C.
Dear Lord Halifax:

I see by the papers that Rudolf Hess is in an English prison. May I suggest that your Government let me put him on exhibit—all receipts to go to British War charities?

Your Majesty's Government may rest assured that its distinguished prisoner will receive the consideration he deserves. He will be housed in an air-conditioned cage similar to the one in which the Ringling Brothers display Gargantua, and this cage will be fumigated every hour on the hour.

The price of admission would depend on the distance from the cage—25 cents for the seats down front, $25 for those in the rear.

The coast-to-coast tour of Mr. Hess would take at least two years, and by that time, Mr. Hitler himself might be available as a follow-up attraction.

Respectfully,
Billy Rose

On July 2, 1941, I received the following answer from His Lordship:

Dear Mr. Rose:

Thanks for your amusing letter. Your idea concerning Herr Hess is not without merit.

The cage you mention should be quite satisfactory, since Gargantua and Herr Hess have the same kind of eyes and probably other qualities in common.

We are currently doing our utmost to secure Mr. Hitler for you.

Yours sincerely,
Halifax

On July 5, I released these two kidding letters to the press, and the story hit most of the front pages around the country.

In October of that year, the *Völkisher Beobachter*, Hitler's own paper in Berlin, ran an unflattering cartoon of me on page one. An accompanying editorial denounced the loud-mouthed American showman, of a certain frowned-upon ancestry, who had the audacity to talk about putting Der Fuehrer on exhibition like an ordinary monkey.

We now come to a book called *The Last Days of Hitler* by H. R. Trevor-Roper, the celebrated crime-detection scholar who was called from Oxford by British Intelligence to make a thorough investigation of how and why Hitler committed suicide.

In his book, Trevor-Roper reconstructs the last scene in the underground bunker in Berlin and says that on April 29, immediately following his marriage to Eva Braun, Hitler sent for his secretary, Frau Junge, and dictated two documents for posterity. Each document contained the same line:

"I have, therefore, decided to remain in Berlin, and there to choose death voluntarily. . . . I will not fall into the hands of an enemy who requires a new spectacle, exhibited by the Jews, to divert his hysterical masses."

This statement by Hitler on page 177 of the Trevor-Roper book, and again on page 197, prompts me to ask this $64 question.

When Hitler said he'd rather die than be used as a spectacle to divert the masses, was he thinking of the story which had appeared in *his own newspaper* about the American showman of a certain frowned-upon ancestry who was eager to exhibit him in a cage like an ordinary monkey?

I don't know, but I certainly hope so.

Through Rose-Colored Glasses

IF ANY freak-show proprietor is looking for a two-headed man, I know where he can hire one cheap.

This believe-it-or-noddity has an interesting case history. When he was born almost fifty years ago, he had only one head. But day and date with his first paycheck, he began to sprout another. Today, he's a badly confused man—his two brains seldom agree on anything. As a result, he doesn't know whose corner he's in, what team he's rooting for, which cheering section he belongs to.

Let me give you a for-instance. He owns ten shares of Standard Oil of New Jersey. Therefore, Head No. 1 wants the price of gasoline to go up. But he also owns a car. Ergo, Head No. 2 wants the price of gas to go down.

Consider his tax problem: This fellow fancies himself a liberal. He's in favor of more social security, more TVA's, socialized medicine, old-age pensions and so on. This, of course, involves a high tax rate. Head No. 1 says it doesn't mind. Head No. 2 says it'll be darned if it's going to work all year and have a tax collector wind up with the dough on March 15.

What are the political beliefs of this curio? Is he a Communist? Yes and No. Is he a Republican? No and Yes. After talking the matter over with him, it's my hunch that he's a Communist-Republican. He thinks the left-of-center lads have some fine ideas, but he wants a middle-of-the-roader to carry them out.

The personal problems of this two-headed bozo are even more pathetic. In his teens, he used to press his nose against Sulka's window on Fifth Avenue and dream of the day when he could afford a hand-painted cravat. Now that he has enough scratch to fill several drawers with them, his new head tells him that hand-painted cravats are corny and not in keeping with the dignity of his station.

At mealtimes, the plight of this freak would break your heart. When he was a kid, he could eat potatoes all day long and still have a figure like an ironing board. But at the time, he was lucky to have mustard to put on his hot dog. Today, when he can buy the goodies he used to long for, he's got a built-in cantaloupe under his vest, and his wife warns him that the hot rolls he loves are crawling with calories.

Head No. 1 tells him that everybody loves a fat man. Head No. 2 spouts insurance statistics about fat men dying young. The result is he dines on Ry-Krisp and buttermilk, and has a box of candy stashed away under the bed.

Consider his love-life. He's married to a pretty girl and wants her to knock everybody's eyes out. But his wife's idea of being well-dressed is to wear a hat that looks like a lopsided bird cage—price tag, $49. Consequently, when he gets the bills at the end of the month, his two heads give him a bad time.

Head No. 1 says it's silly to let her spend 49 fish for some twisted wire and a few tassels. Head No. 2 says, "Stop beefing, cheapskate. Wives are a lot happier with $49 bird cages than they are with the ones that cost $3.95 in a bargain basement."

Unless his cardiogram is lying, our two-headed friend figures to live another twenty years. Head No. 1 says, "Let's relax and live the good life. We've got a house, a great girl to share it with, a television set and a few bob in the bank." But Head No. 2 says, "Don't talk crazy. You know we can't relax that long. Twenty years is 1,040 weeks, 7,304 days, 174,296 hours."

Head No. 1 says, "Let's be sensible, chum. We've used up almost seventy percent of our three-score-and-ten chasing a hot buck. Now that we have the buck, why not be smart and use the remaining thirty percent having fun? Remember how hard we were hit by that piece in *Reader's Digest*—the one about the plaque in an old Chinese garden, which read, "Enjoy yourself—it's later than you think"?

"Stuff and stuff," says Head No. 2. "You and I came up the hard way and we'll go out the way we came. Let's not kid ourselves. We may talk about quitting—perhaps even quit—but one of these days a stranger will walk in with a dream in his briefcase, and we'll be back in the fireworks business again. And I'll let you in on a secret, pal—we're only happy when the skyrockets are going off. . . ."

Side-show entrepreneurs who are interested in the services of this two-headed galoot can address their inquiries to the Ziegfeld Theatre, Sixth Avenue and 54th Street, New York 19, N. Y.

FINIS—FOR NOW

If you have enjoyed reading *Wine, Women and Words* you will probably want a more permanent edition for your own library, or as a gift for a friend. It can be obtained easily from any bookseller, or by writing direct to the publisher: Simon and Schuster, Inc., New York.

BEST SELLERS

GENUINE **POCKET** BOOK EDITIONS

Are there any you have missed?
Of the more than 650 POCKET BOOK *titles that have been published to date, these are some outstanding favorites:*

Erle Stanley Gardner

Pocket Books

Printed in U.S.A.

January, 1950